# WHITAKER'S WORLD OF FACTS

# RUSSELL ASH

# WHITAKER'S WORLD OF FACTS

A & C Black • London

This edition published 2007
First published in 2005 by
A&C Black Publishers Ltd
38 Soho Square
London W1D 3HB
www.acblack.com

www.whitakersworld.com

Produced for A&C Black by
White-Thomson Publishing Ltd
210 High Street,
Lewes BN7 2NH

and

Bookwork Ltd,
Unit 17, Piccadilly Mill
Stroud, Gloucestershire, GL5 2HT

**Illustrators** Alan Baker (Illustration),
Julian Baker, KJA-artists

**Heraldry consultant** Henry Bedingfeld,
College of Arms
**Religions consultant** Martin Palmer,
ICOREC
**Sports consultant** Ian Morrison

A CIP catalogue record for this book
is available from the British Library.

ISBN  978-0-7136-8556-5

Printed and bound in China by
C&C Offset Limited

This book is produced using paper that
is made from wood grown in managed,
sustainable forests. It is natural,
renewable and recyclable. The logging
and manufacturing processes conform
to the environmental regulations of the
country of origin.

**CONTENTS**

CONTENTS

This new edition of *Whitaker's World of Facts* has been completely updated from cover to cover and excitingly re-designed. Inside, you will find hundreds of amazing facts and pictures. Keep up-to-date with the most recent world record-breakers, the hottest new technologies from the iPhone to YouTube, the latest and greatest achievements (and failures!). Find out about today's biggest celebrities and the most important events that shape our world.

## Everything you want to know

*Whitaker's World of Facts* is divided into 20 sections – Space, Planet Earth, Human Body, World History, People and Conflict and Crime, to name but a few. It includes information on a huge range of subjects, from the Solar System to the world's biggest and smallest populations, with data from authoritative sources and specialists on every subject under the Sun – and beyond.

## Inside information

Detailed lists and charts show global comparisons. Features and FactDisks provide information on such things as the fastest animals, types of insect, all the US presidents, every astronaut who has been to the Moon, the highest-earning films, child inventors and other young achievers, the latest electric cars, and global warming. Many surprising unique facts are revealed in a range of *One and Only* entries, from the one and only flight of the "Spruce Goose" to the one and only female saint to have grown a beard!

A section on countries gives essential facts and figures including population, capital city and currency for every country in the world, as well as the flag of each one.

Timelines on subjects such as telecommunications, astronomy, weapons and inventions give a see-at-a-glance overview and pinpoint important milestones.

Useful maps, tables and formulae include conversions and scales, from Beaufort (weather) to Richter (earthquakes).

You will also discover a huge range of bests and worsts, oddities from the smelliest flower to the biggest robberies, the strangest museums and the craziest inventions, the deadliest creatures and the longest names.

## Other features

*Web link* boxes suggest useful websites to explore subjects further. *See also* boxes guide you to information on a particular subject elsewhere in the book. There is an extensive index at the back of the book, as well as a list of sources.

## Whitaker's World Website

You can write to me with comments, suggestions and corrections at the publisher's address on page four or via the *Whitaker's World of Facts* website www.whitakersworld.com

*Russell Ash*

# About this book

216
AIR TRANSPORT
Aviation pioneers
John Alcock (UK, 1892–1919) and Arthur Whitten Brown (UK, 1886–1948)
On 14–15 June 1919, they completed the first ever non-stop flight across the Atlantic from Newfoundland to Ireland.
Louis Blériot (France, 1872–1936)
On 25 July 1909 Blériot became the first person to fly across the English Channel.
Samuel F. Cody (USA, c. 1861–1913)
The first person to fly in England, 16 October 1908.
Glenn Curtiss (USA, 1878–1930)
Rival to the Wright Brothers, Curtiss made the first public flight in the USA on 4 July 1908. He set up the first aeroplane manufacturing company in the USA.
Amelia Earhart (USA, 1898–1937)
The first woman to fly the Atlantic. She went on to establish many flying records but disappeared during an attempt to fly round the world.
Amy Johnson (UK, 1903–41)
She made the first solo flight from England to Australia in 1930.
Charles Lindbergh (USA, 1902–74)
The first pilot to fly solo across the Atlantic, from New York to Paris, 20–21 May 1927, in The Spirit of St Louis.
Harriet Quimby (USA, 1875–1912)
America's first female pilot. On 16 April 1912 she was the first woman to fly the English Channel – but on the day the sinking of the Titanic was reported, so her triumph was barely noticed.
Wilbur Wright (USA, 1867–1912) and Orville Wright (USA, 1871–1948)
The Wright brothers, two bicycle mechanics from Dayton, Ohio, made the first ever powered flights on 17 December 1903.
Concorde
AIR FRANCE
Concorde fact file
Concorde, the only passenger aircraft ever to fly faster than the speed of sound, was first named in a speech by General de Gaulle on 13 January 1963. The Anglo-French project began the following year.
The first prototype Concorde was shown at the Toulouse Air Show on 11 December 1967.
The first French flight took place on 2 March 1969.
The first British flight took place on 9 April 1969.
The first landing at London Heathrow was on 13 September 1970.
The first Concorde landing in the USA was at Dallas-Fort Worth on 20 September 1973.
The only Concorde crash was near Paris, 25 July 2000, when 109 passengers and crew and four people on the ground died.
Concorde's last flight took place on 24 October 2004. All surviving BA and Air France Concordes are on public display in museums and airports in the USA, UK, France, Germany and Barbados.
The Wright brothers demonstrate their Wright Model A plane
The Wright brothers
Orville Wright was the first person to fly a powered aircraft. He also became the first to fly a plane for more than one hour, on 9 September 1908 at Fort Meyer, Virginia, USA. His brother Wilbur became the first to fly for more than two hours, on 31 December 1908 at Auvours, France. On 20 May 1909 French pilot Paul Tissandier became the first person other than the Wrights to fly for more than an hour
See also
Steve Fossett: page 153
Amelia Earhart: page 153
217
TRANSPORT AND TRAVEL
Breaking the sound barrier
Charles "Chuck" Yeager became the first person to break the sound barrier on 14 October 1947. His Bell X-1 rocket plane was dropped from a carrier aircraft above Muroc Dry Lake, California. At 12,800 m (42,000 ft) he reached a speed of 1,078 km/h (670 mph). He did not break the air speed record because only aircraft that take off and land under their own power are eligible. The speed of sound is not fixed and varies according to height and air conditions. In dry air at sea level the speed of sound is 1,229 km/h (263.67 mph), but at high altitudes, where air density is less, it is lower.
One and only
The only flight of the Hercules H-4 aircraft, known as the "Spruce Goose", took place on 2 November 1947. It was the largest flying boat ever built. It had the greatest wingspan (97.54 m/320 ft) of any aircraft and eight engines. Millionaire aviator Howard Hughes built and flew it himself, just 20 m (65.6 ft) above the water off Long Beach, California, USA. It travelled only 1.6 km (1 mile). The flight is recreated in the film The Aviator (2004).
www.flyingmachines.org
search
First manned balloon flights
The first balloons worked on the principle that when air is heated, it rises. They were filled with hot air by burning things under them, such as paper, straw and wool – and even old shoes and rotten meat!
The balloons often caught fire and once the air cooled, they quickly came down. Soon after the first hot-air flights, people realized that the gas hydrogen could be used instead. Hydrogen is the lightest of all elements – almost 15 times lighter than air. Gas balloons can also be filled with helium, which is not as light as hydrogen but does not catch fire so easily. Most balloons today use hot air made by burning propane gas.
First hot-air balloon flight
The Montgolfier brothers, Joseph and Etienne, tested their first unmanned hot-air balloon on 5 June 1783. On 21 November 1783, François Laurent, Marquis d'Arlandes and Jean-François Pilâtre de Rozier took off from the Bois de Boulogne, Paris, in a Montgolfier hot-air balloon. They travelled about 9 km (5.6 miles) in 23 minutes.
First hydrogen balloon flight
On 1 December 1783, Jacques Alexandre César Charles and Nicholas-Louis Robert made the first flight in a hydrogen balloon. They took off from the Tuileries, Paris, watched by a crowd of 400,000, and travelled 43 km (27 miles) north to Nesle in about two hours. Charles then took off again alone, so was the first ever solo pilot.
First British flight
On 27 August 1784 James Tytler, a doctor and newspaper editor, took off in a home-made balloon from Comely Gardens, Edinburgh. He reached an altitude of 107 m (350 ft) in a 0.8 km (0.5 miles) hop.
First Channel crossing
On 7 January 1785 Jean-Pierre Blanchard made the first Channel crossing in a balloon with Dr John Jeffries (the first American to fly). They also carried the first airmail letter. As they lost height, they had to reduce weight, so they threw almost everything overboard – including their clothes!
First flight in the USA
On 9 January 1793 in Philadelphia, Blanchard made the first balloon flight in America. He took a small black dog with him as a passenger.
First hot-air balloon flight
The flight was watched by George Washington, who gave Blanchard a passport permitting his flight, which was the first pilot's licence and America's first airmail document.
First non-stop solo flight
US adventurer Steve Fossett made the first non-stop solo and fastest round-the-world balloon flight, 19 June to 3 July 2002.

Coloured bars identify each section of the book

Follow these *web links* for more information

*One and Only* boxes identify unique facts

190
TOYS AND GAMES
Valuable toys
Some wealthy collectors prize rare toys, especially those that are in good condition – in their original box, and never played with. These are just some of the toys that may have cost very little when they were made, but now sell for high prices.
GI Joe prototype was sold by Heritage Galleries & Auctioneers of Dallas, Texas for $200,000 (£126,580) in 2003.
A Kämmer and Reinhardt doll was sold at Sotheby's, London, on 8 February 1994 for £188,500 ($277,981).
Titania's Palace, a doll's house with 2,000 items of furniture, was sold at Christie's, London, in 1978 for £135,000 ($258,728).
Dingley Hall, a doll's house dating from 1877, was sold at Christie's, London, in 2003 for £124,750 ($211,938).
A 1906 train set made by German toymaker Märklin was sold at Christie's, London, in 2001 for £113,750 ($165,290).
A black mohair Steiff teddy bear, made in about 1912, was sold at Christie's, London, in 2000 for £91,750 ($132,157). It was one of only 494 black Steiff bears made as a mark of respect after the sinking of the Titanic. They are known as "mourning teddies".
A tinplate clockwork motorcycle with Mickey Mouse and Minnie from about 1930 was sold at Christie's, London, in 1997 for £51,000 ($83,650).
"Teddy Girl" teddy bear made in 1904
Birth of Barbie
The first Barbie doll appeared in February 1959. It was made by Ruth and Elliot Handler, co-founders of American toy manufacturers Mattel, and they named the doll after their daughter Barbara. The doll was dressed in a black and white striped swimsuit, with sunglasses, high heels and gold hoop earrings. In the first year a total of 351,000 Barbies were sold at $3 (£1) each. The doll went on to become one of the bestselling toys of all time
The first Barbie dolls, in the Barbie Museum, Palo Alto, California
Top Teddy
"Teddy Girl" is a teddy bear made by the German manufacturer Steiff in 1904. It was sold at Christie's, London, on 5 December 1994 for a record £110,000 ($171,600). A Japanese collector named Yoshiro Sekiguchi bought the bear for his teddy bear museum near Tokyo.
Toy-buying countries
Forecast sales of traditional toys (eg construction toys, model vehicles, indoor games, dolls and teddy bears) and video games in 2008 are estimated to average £16.9 ($33) for every person on the planet. There are huge differences between countries: North Americans spend the most and people in African countries the least per child.
USA $42,634,900,000
Toys world total $113,109,000,000
Other $41,591,700,000
UK $8,343,800,000
Japan $8,393,500,000
Germany $5,801,400,000
France $6,343,700,000
Computer games
The first computer games were played on televisions and appeared in the 1970s. They were basic arcade games like PONG (1972), an electronic table-tennis game, and Pac-Man (1980), in which a yellow blob is steered round a maze, gobbling up everything in its path.
As computer technology advanced, games and consoles improved, with better graphics, sound and choice of themes. Second generation 8-bit games had removable cartridges, while the fifth 32-bit and 64-bit generation games could be played in 3D. Sixth and seventh generation games are more realistic than ever before and can be played online with anyone around the world. These are popular consoles of different generations.
First generation Atari PONG (1975)
Second generation Atari 2600 (1977)
Third generation Nintendo Entertainment System (1983), Nintendo Game Boy (1989)
Fourth generation Sega Mega Drive (1988), Super Nintendo (1990)
Fifth generation Nintendo 64 (1986), Sony PlayStation (1994)
Sixth generation Sega Dreamcast (1998), Sony PlayStation 2 (2000), Microsoft Xbox (2001)
Seventh generation Xbox 360 (2005), PlayStation 3 (2006), Nintendo Wii (2006)
Scrabble
Scrabble was invented in the USA during the 1930s by an architect named Alfred Mosher Butts. First he called it Lexiko, then it and Criss-Cross, before hitting on the name Scrabble. Well over 100 million sets have been sold in more than 130 countries. The numbers of letters included vary according to the language. In Dutch, for example, there are 18 Es, 10 Ns and two Js. The Slovak version has 41 different letters – more than any other version.
Monopoly®
Monopoly was invented in 1934 by an unemployed engineer called Charles Darrow, who lived in Philadelphia, USA. In his first version of the game he used street names from Atlantic City in New Jersey because he dreamed of going there, but could not afford the fare. The game was so successful that Darrow became a millionaire and spent the rest of his life travelling and growing rare orchids.
Monopoly was soon adapted for other countries, using street names from their main cities. The British version uses London place names and Mayfair is the most expensive street. There are also versions of Monopoly based on popular TV series, such as The Simpsons. Parkers, the US manufacturers of the game, print more Monopoly money than the US Treasury prints dollars.
Monopoly® around the world
Country / City* / Mayfair becomes
Australia / Canberra + state capitals / Kings Avenue
Canada / Vancouver, etc / Robson Street
China / Hong Kong / Victoria Peak
Egypt / Cairo / Shari Qasr El Nil
France / Paris / Rue de la Paix
Germany / Munich / Schlossallee
Ireland / Dublin / Shrewsbury Road
Netherlands / Amsterdam / Kalverstraat
New Zealand / Auckland / Queen Street
Portugal / Lisbon / Rossio
Russia / Moscow / Arbat
Singapore / Singapore / Queen Astrid Park
South Africa / Johannesburg / Eloff Street/Elofftstraat
Spain / Madrid / Paseo Del Prado
Switzerland / Zurich, etc / Paradeplatz
US / Atlantic City / Boardwalk
* Some feature streets from more than one city
Russian Monopoly board
191
WORK AND HOME

Find cross-references throughout the book in these boxes

*FactDisks* highlight key facts

All new graphics used to illustrate facts and figures

Lists give you the latest facts and figures, dates and top tens for all kinds of subjects

Detailed information and statistics

# Time

### Sunrise at Stonehenge

People first developed a sense of time through observing the Sun and Moon. Stonehenge, UK, may have been an early form of astronomical calendar when it was built more than 3,000 years ago.

# The Universe in a year!

The American astronomer Carl Sagan (1934–96) first suggested a "cosmic calendar" as a way of helping people understand the history of the Universe. He put everything into the scale of a calendar year: the galaxies are formed over nine months and the Earth appears in September.

Human history is crowded into the last five minutes of the year. Recent time is divided into seconds and fractions of a second. So everything that happened in the last 475 years takes place in less than the last second of the last minute of the year.

## The world in a single day

In one day (24 hours or 1,440 minutes or 86,400 seconds) the world turns once on its axis. During that time, on average:
**364,936** people are born
**152,029** people die

## Earth's life in a year

**1 Jan (midnight)** Big Bang – Universe forms
**15 Mar** First stars and galaxies form
**1 May** Milky Way galaxy forms
**8 Sep** Sun forms
**9 Sep** Solar system forms
**12 Sep** Earth forms
**13 Sep** Moon forms
**20 Sep** Earth's atmosphere forms
**1 Oct** Earliest known life on Earth
**7 Oct** Earliest known fossils
**18 Dec** First many-celled life forms
**19 Dec** First fish
**21 Dec** First land plants; first insects
**23 Dec** First reptiles
**24 Dec** First dinosaurs
**26 Dec** First mammals
**27 Dec** First birds
**28 Dec** First flowering plants
**28 Dec** Dinosaurs extinct
**31 Dec** (11:55 pm)
  *Homo sapiens* (modern humans)

## The last day

**11:59.50.487 pm** Great Pyramid is built (2520 BC)
**11:59.55.333 pm** Great Wall of China is built (215 BC)
**11:59.56.785 pm** Roman Empire falls (AD 476)
**11:59.58.026 pm** Battle of Hastings (1066)
**11:59.58.921 pm** Columbus lands in America (1492)
**11.59.59.pm** Shakespeare writes his first plays (1588–90)
**11:59.59.874 pm** World War II ends (1945)
**11:59.59.891 pm** Mount Everest is climbed (1953)
**11:59.59.924 pm** Man lands on the Moon (1969)
**Midnight** Today

Royal Observatory, Greenwich; the "time ball" on the roof falls daily at 1.00 pm

## Timetellers — 1500BC

The following are some landmarks in the history of telling the time.

**1500–1300 BC** Sundials are used in Egypt: as the Earth rotates, the gnomon – the upright part of the sundial – casts a shadow which moves to indicate the time.

**c. 400 BC** Water clocks are used in Greece: as water drains from a container, each level it reaches represents a period of time.

**c. 890** In England people use candles marked with time intervals.

**12th century** The hourglass, familiar to us as an eggtimer, is used by monks to show times of prayer.

**1325** The first clock with a dial is installed in Norwich Cathedral, England.

**1335** The first clock to strike the hours is made in Milan, Italy.

**1350** The oldest known surviving alarm clock is made in Würzburg, Germany.

**1364** Clocks are first used in people's homes.

**1386** The clock is installed in Salisbury Cathedral, England. This is the world's oldest clock in working order.

**1462** The earliest description of a watch is written in Italy.

**1641** The pendulum clock is proposed by Vincenzio Galilei, son of the astronomer Galileo.

**1657** The first pendulum clocks are made in Holland.

# Time zones

The Earth is constantly turning on its axis. If people everywhere set their clocks to the same time, midnight would be in the middle of the night on one side of the globe, but the middle of the day on the opposite side. To avoid this problem the Earth is divided into artificial time zones. These generally follow lines of longitude – imaginary lines running from the North to the South Pole. Some large countries, such as the USA, cover several time zones. Mainland USA is divided into Atlantic, Eastern, Central, Mountain, Pacific and Alaska zones, with Hawaii and other islands falling into further zones.

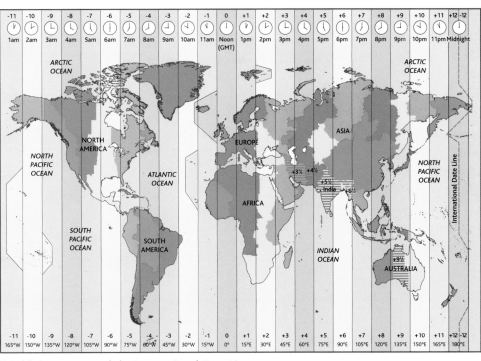

World time zones and the International Date Line

Since the Greenwich Prime Meridian (0°) was established in 1884, there have been 24 time zones, each of 15° longitude and an hour apart. Those to the east are ahead of Greenwich by one hour per zone.

Those to the west are behind by one hour each. Some countries, such as India, have chosen zones halfway between those on either side, so that the whole country can use the same time.

Two sides of the Earth

## The International Date Line

The Earth makes one complete turn in every 24 hours. In that time, each of the 360 degrees of longitude passes the Sun. This means that time progresses eastwards by four minutes for every degree of longitude.

The International Date Line is an imaginary line between the North and South Poles. It marks the end of one day and the start of another. Countries to the east of the Date Line are always a day ahead of those to the west. Travellers who cross the line gain or lose a day, depending on which direction they are going.

Most of the Date Line follows the 180° Meridian (on the opposite side of the globe from 0°, the Greenwich Meridian). The line generally passes through sea, but where it would pass through or near certain land areas, it is adjusted. It zigzags around islands, putting them either into the west or the east, and avoids dividing Siberia in north-east Asia into two time zones.

### See also
Galileo Galilei: page 26

2007

**c. 1665** The first watches with minute and second hands are made.

**1759** John Harrison's marine chronometer is made. Accurate timekeeping at sea is important for calculating position, but previously the rolling of a ship had made it impossible.

**1880** Greenwich Mean Time becomes the standard from which time around the world is set.

**1880** The first practical wristwatches are made for the German navy.

**1928** The first quartz crystal clock is made in the USA.

**1949** The first atomic clock is built in the USA.

**1957** The first battery watches are marketed in the USA.

**1969** Quartz wristwatches are first sold in Japan.

**1970** Digital watches and displays become widely used worldwide and can be made and sold cheaply.

**2007** The British national time signal, used by radio clocks, is transmitted from the National Physical Laboratory, Anthorn, Cumbria.

www.rog.nmm.ac.uk          search

Thor was the Scandinavian god of thunder and war. He is often shown brandishing a hammer. Thursday, or Thor's day, is named after him.

## Names of months

The names of the months in English (as well as in many other languages) come from Latin words.

### January
*Januarius* – this month was dedicated to Janus, the Roman god of doors. Janus had two faces, one looking back at the old year and the other looking forward to the new year.

### February
*Februarius* – Februa was the Roman purification festival, which took place at this time of year.

### March
*Martius* – from Mars, the Roman god of war.

### April
*Aprilis* – from *aperire*, Latin for open, because plants begin to open during this month.

### May
*Maius* – probably comes from Maia, the Roman goddess of growth and increase.

### June
*Junius* – either from a Roman family name Junius, which means young, or perhaps after the goddess Juno.

### July
*Julius* – after Julius Caesar. This month was named in Caesar's honour by Mark Antony in 44 BC. Previously this month was called Quintilis from the word *quintus*, five, as it was the fifth month in the Roman calendar.

### August
*Augustus* – named in 8 BC in honour of Emperor Augustus.

### September
*September* – from *septem*, seven, because it was the seventh month in the Roman calendar.

### October
*October* – from *octo*, eight (as in octopus, which has eight legs), the eighth month in the Roman calendar.

### November
*November* – from *novem*, nine, the ninth month in the Roman calendar.

### December
*December* – from *decem*, ten, the tenth month in the Roman calendar.

### Leap seconds

The rotation of the Earth is slowing down. This means that a solar day (the time it takes Earth to make one complete revolution) and the time shown by atomic clocks would gradually diverge. This problem has been solved by adding "leap seconds". There have been 22 leap seconds since 1972. The last one was added on 31 December 2005, which delayed New Year's Day 2006 by one second!

## Naming the days of the week

The ancient Babylonians, then the Romans, named the days of the week after planets and other bodies they saw in the sky. Some names we know today come from the names of Scandinavian gods.

**Monday**
Moon's day

**Tuesday**
Tiu's day: Mars, the Roman god of war, was adopted in Scandinavian mythology as the warrior Tiu or Tiw.

**Wednesday**
Woden's day: the Roman god Mercury became the Scandinavian god Woden.

**Thursday**
Thor's day: like the Roman god Jupiter, Thor was a thunder god.

**Friday**
Freyja's day: like Venus, Freyja or Frigg was the goddess of love.

**Saturday**
Saturn's day

**Sunday**
Sun's day

# How long does it take?

**One beat of a fly's wing** (1/1,000 second) 0.001 seconds
**Flash of lightning** (1/1,000 second) 0.001 seconds
**One beat of a hummingbird's wing** (80 times a second) 0.0125 seconds
**Mouse heartbeat** (10.8 times a second) 0.09 seconds
**Blink of a human eye** 0.33 seconds
**Human heartbeat** 1.0 seconds
**Land speed record: car *ThrustSSC* travelling 1 km (0.62 miles)** 2.9 seconds
**Record-breaking Jamaican athlete Asafa Powell to run 100 m (328 ft)** 9.77 seconds
**Bullet train to travel 1 km (0.62 miles)** 13.75 seconds
**Space Shuttle to travel 100 km (62 miles)** 15 seconds
**Light reaching Earth from the Sun** 497 seconds

# Watches at sea

At sea, the 24-hour day is traditionally divided into seven watches, during which some of a ship's crew are on duty.

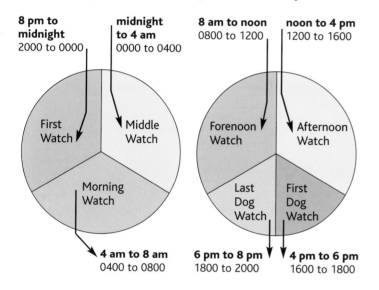

**8 pm to midnight** 2000 to 0000
**midnight to 4 am** 0000 to 0400
**8 am to noon** 0800 to 1200
**noon to 4 pm** 1200 to 1600

First Watch / Middle Watch / Morning Watch
Forenoon Watch / Afternoon Watch / Last Dog Watch / First Dog Watch

**4 am to 8 am** 0400 to 0800
**6 pm to 8 pm** 1800 to 2000
**4 pm to 6 pm** 1600 to 1800

www.physics.nist.gov/Genint/Time **search**

## Just a second

It will take you almost five seconds to read this sentence. During an average-length film more than 5,000 seconds will pass. In a lifetime of 80 years, there are more than 2.5 billion seconds – but you will spend more than 800 million of them asleep!

**1 minute** 60 seconds
**1 hour** 3,600 seconds
**1 day** 86,400 seconds
**1 week** 604,800 seconds
**1 year** 31,536,000 seconds

*ThrustSCC* set the first supersonic land-speed record, at 1,227.986 km/h (763.035 mph).

# Time words

Here are some of the words used for units of time.

**chronon** One-billionth of a trillionth of a second (the time a photon would take to cross the width of one electron at the speed of light)

**femtosecond** 0.000000000000001 of a second

**picosecond** 0.000000000001 (one-trillionth) of a second

**nanosecond** 0.000000001 (one-billionth) of a second

**microsecond** 0.000001 (one-millionth) of a second

**millisecond** 0.001 (one-thousandth) of a second; the blink of an eye takes 50–80 milliseconds

**centisecond** 0.01 (one-hundredth) of a second

**second** 1/60 of a minute

**minute** 60 seconds

**hour** 60 minutes

**day** Sunrise to sunrise, or sunset to sunset, or midnight to midnight; 24 hours

**week** Seven days; in Shakespeare's time, it was also called a sennight, or seven nights

**fortnight** Two weeks (from the Old English for 14 nights)

**month** Full Moon to full Moon; 1/12 of a year; 4 weeks, or 28, 29, 30 or 31 days, depending on month

**bimester** Two months

**trimester** A period of three months

**year** 365¼ days, 52 weeks, or 12 months

**solar day** The time it takes for a place on the Earth directly facing the Sun to make one revolution and return to the same position (about 23 hours 56 minutes)

**solar year** The time it takes for the Earth to make a complete revolution around the Sun, equal to 365.24219 solar days or 365 days, 5 hours 48 minutes, 45.51 seconds; also called a tropical year or astronomical year

**leap year** 366 days

**decade** 10 years; also called a decennium

**century** 100 years

**millennium** 1,000 years; also called a chiliad

**bimillennium** 2,000 years

**era** A period of time measured from some important event

**aeon or eon** A long period of time, usually thousands of years; in geology and astronomy it is one billion years

**epoch** A geological era or very long period of time

**See also** Geological time chart: page 34

# Gregorian calendar

The Gregorian calendar is the one most used nowadays. It is named after Pope Gregory XIII who introduced it in 1582. There is a leap year every four years (or more precisely, 97 leap years every 400 years). This means that the year corresponds closely with the astronomical year (365.24219 days) so that it gets just one day out of sync in every 3,300 years.

## Calendar problems

Some non-Catholic countries such as Britain refused to adopt the Gregorian calendar at first. The Julian calendar previously used in Britain was based on a solar year, the time taken for the Earth to rotate around the Sun. This is 365.25 days, which is fractionally too long (it is actually 365.24219 days), so the calendar steadily fell out of line with the seasons. In 1752 Britain decided to correct this by abandoning the Julian calendar in favour of the Gregorian. By doing so, 3 September instantly became 14 September – and, as a result, nothing whatsoever happened in British history between 3 and 13 September 1752. Many people believed their lives would be shortened. They protested in the streets, demanding, "Give us back our 11 days!"

| | | |
|---|---|---|
| **1 January** 31 days | **5 May** 31 days | **9 September** 30 days |
| **2 February** 28 days* | **6 June** 30 days | **10 October** 31 days |
| **3 March** 31 days | **7 July** 31 days | **11 November** 30 days |
| **4 April** 30 days | **8 August** 31 days | **12 December** 31 days |

\* In a leap year, February has 29 days.

## Time pyramid

The Mayan pyramid at Chichen Itza, Mexico, built around 1050, has four stairways, each with 91 steps and one platform. This makes a total of 365, the number of days in a year. The stairways also divide the nine terraces of each side of the pyramid into 18 segments, representing the 18 months of the Mayan calendar.

# Mayan calendar

The Mayan people lived in the Yucatan area of present-day Mexico and the neighbouring region. They built many amazing pyramids and temples, and had an astonishing knowledge of astronomy.

Mayan culture had declined by the time Spanish invaders occupied their territory in the 16th century, but we know something about it from the remains found. The Haab or civil calendar of the Maya had 18 months made up of 20 days each. Five extra days were added at the year's end, known as Uayeb, giving a year of 365 days.

Chichen Itza, Mexico

# Calendar timeline

Most of the world's countries and cultures use the Gregorian calendar, but some base their calendars on more ancient systems. Other countries have adopted an alternative calendar at some point in their history.

**3761 BC** Jewish calendar starts

**2637 BC** Original Chinese calendar starts

**45 BC** Julian calendar adopted by Roman Empire

**0** Christian calendar starts

**79** Hindu calendar starts

**597** Julian calendar adopted in Britain

**622** Islamic calendar starts

**1582** Gregorian calendar introduced in Catholic countries

**1752** Julian calendar abandoned, Gregorian calendar adopted in Britain and its colonies, including America

**1873** Japan adopts the Gregorian calendar

**1949** China adopts the Gregorian calendar

# Mayan months

| | |
|---|---|
| **1** Pop | **10** Yax |
| **2** Uo | **11** Zac |
| **3** Zip | **12** Ceh |
| **4** Zotz | **13** Mac |
| **5** Tzec | **14** Kankin |
| **6** Xul | **15** Muan |
| **7** Yaxkin | **16** Pax |
| **8** Mol | **17** Kayab |
| **9** Chen | **18** Cumku |

# Chinese calendar

Present-day China uses the Gregorian calendar for most purposes, but traditional festivals, such as Chinese New Year, take place according to the ancient Chinese calendar. Legend has it that this was started during the reign of Emperor Huangdi in 2637 BC, and relates to the positions of the Moon and Sun.

The ancient Chinese calendar follows a 60-year cycle which combines a heavenly stem and earthly branch, represented by a zodiac animal. The first year of the cycle is jia-zi, the second yi-chou, and so on; the 11th year is jia-xu, 12th yi-hai and 13th bing-zi. This continues until the 60th year (gui-hai) and then starts again. Each earthly branch is believed to be linked with certain qualities.

Chinese dragon

## Calendars meet

The Islamic year is about 11 days shorter than a year in the Gregorian calendar. The Islamic calendar started 622 years later than the Gregorian so its date is behind. But because the year is shorter, the Islamic calendar is gradually gaining on the Gregorian. The two will eventually coincide – in the year 20874.

🔍 http://webexhibits.org/calendars    search

# Hebrew and Islamic calendars

The Hebrew (Jewish) and Islamic (Muslim) calendars are based on the lunar (Moon) cycle. Every month starts approximately on the day of a new Moon, or when a crescent moon is first seen.

The visibility of the Moon varies according to the weather so the start date cannot be determined in advance. Printed calendars may vary by a few days. Tishri/Muharram corresponds approximately with September/October in the Gregorian calendar, Heshvan/Safar with October/November, and so on.

| Hebrew | Islamic | Hebrew | Islamic |
|---|---|---|---|
| 1 Tishri | Muharram* (30 days) | 7 Nisan | Rajab* (30 days) |
| 2 Heshvan | Safar (29 days) | 8 Iyar | Sha'ban (29 days) |
| 3 Kislev | Rabi'a I (30 days) | 9 Sivan | Ramadan † (30 days) |
| 4 Tevet | Rabi'a II (29 days) | 10 Tammuz | Shawwal (29 days) |
| 5 Shevat | Jumada I (30 days) | 11 Av | Dhu al-Q'adah* (30 days) |
| 6 Adar | Jumada II (29 days) | 12 Elu | Dhu al-Hijjah (29 days) |

* Holy months   † Month of fasting

# Indian calendar

The Indian calendar is based on the motions of the Sun and Moon and is dated from the so-called Saka Era, equivalent to AD 79. It is used for dating religious and other festivals, but the Gregorian calendar is used for official dates.

| Month | Length | Gregorian calendar |
|---|---|---|
| 1 Caitra | 30 days* | 22 March |
| 2 Vaisakha | 31 days | 21 April |
| 3 Jyaistha | 31 days | 22 May |
| 4 Asadha | 31 days | 22 June |
| 5 Sravana | 31 days | 23 July |
| 6 Bhadra | 31 days | 23 August |
| 7 Asvina | 30 days | 23 September |
| 8 Kartika | 30 days | 23 October |
| 9 Agrahayana | 30 days | 22 November |
| 10 Pausa | 30 days | 22 December |
| 11 Magha | 30 days | 21 January |
| 12 Phalguna | 30 days | 20 February |

* In a leap year, Caitra has 31 days and 1 Caitra = 21 March

# Chinese calendar and Gregorian equivalents

| HEAVENLY STEMS | EARTHLY BRANCHES | | Zodiac animal | Gregorian calendar year beginning | Zodiac animal | Gregorian calendar year beginning |
|---|---|---|---|---|---|---|
| 1 jia | 1 zi (rat) | 11 xu (dog) | Rat | 19 Feb 1996 | Sheep | 1 Feb 2003 |
| 2 yi | 2 chou (ox) | 12 hai (pig or boar) | Ox | 7 Feb 1997 | Monkey | 22 Jan 2004 |
| 3 bing | 3 yin (tiger) | | Tiger | 28 Jan 1998 | Rooster | 9 Feb 2005 |
| 4 ding | 4 mao (hare or rabbit) | | Hare | 16 Feb 1999 | Dog | 29 Jan 2006 |
| 5 wu | 5 chen (dragon) | | Dragon | 5 Feb 2000 | Pig | 18 Feb 2007 |
| 6 ji | 6 si (snake) | | Snake | 24 Jan 2001 | Rat | 7 Feb 2008 |
| 7 geng | 7 wu (horse) | | Horse | 12 Feb 2002 | Ox | 26 Jan 2009 |
| 8 zxin | 8 wei (sheep or ram) | | | | | |
| 9 ren | 9 shen (monkey) | | | | | |
| 10 gui | 10 you (rooster) | | | | | |

# Space

## Former planet

In 2006 Pluto (seen here from its moon Charon) was officially stripped of its status as a planet. Now classified as a "dwarf planet" at just 2,360 km (1,467 miles) across, Pluto is smaller than some moons in the solar system.

# Twinkle twinkle little star...

Stars appear to twinkle because we see them through the layers of the Earth's atmosphere. Light is distorted as it passes through these layers, so that the amount we see changes constantly. Stars nearest the horizon seem to twinkle the most because the light is passing through a greater depth of atmosphere. Stars do not twinkle when viewed from space, so telescopes in space, such as the Hubble, give the best possible view of distant stars and galaxies.

## Star facts

A star is a luminous body of gas, mostly hydrogen and helium. Stars generate light, which makes it possible for us to see them with a telescope or the naked eye.

### ● Brightest
Not counting the Sun, the brightest star as seen from Earth is Sirius, known as the dog star, in the constellation of Canis Major. It has a diameter of 149,598,020 km and is more than 24 times brighter than the Sun. The star LBV 1806–20 in the constellation of Sagittarius may be 40 million times as bright as our Sun, but dust clouds make it almost invisible from Earth.

### ● Largest
The largest star is VY Canis Majoris, which has an estimated diameter of about 1,950 times greater than the Sun. For comparison, if it were a football, the Sun would be no bigger than a pinhead.

### ● Nearest
Proxima Centauri, discovered in 1915, is 4.22 light years (39,953,525,879,212 km) from Earth. A spaceship moving at 40,000 km/h – which is faster than any human has yet travelled in space – would take more than 114,000 years to reach it.

### ● Supernovae
These are vast explosions in which a whole star blows up. They are extremely bright, rivalling for a few days the combined light output of all the stars in the galaxy. Supernovae are rare – the last one in our galaxy was seen in 1604 by the German astronomer Johannes Kepler.

### ● Quasars
These are extremely distant radio galaxies – galaxies giving out large amounts of radio energy – and the brightest objects in the Universe. Their radio emission is typically 1,000,000 to 100,000,000 times greater than that of a normal galaxy.

### ● Black holes
A black hole is a star that has collapsed into itself. It has a surface gravity so powerful that nothing can escape from within it.

Photographs all taken by the Hubble Space Telescope

Supergiant VY Canis Majoris

The Sun

Black Eye Galaxy

Swan Nebula

Monocerotis V838 (a red supergiant star surrounded by dust)

## Travelling at the speed of light

In space, light travels at a speed of 299,792.46 km a second, or 1,079,252,956 km an hour. When we look at even the nearest star, we see light that left it more than four years ago. Here are the times it takes light to reach Earth from various bodies in space.

### ● Light years
A light year measures distance, not time. Distances in space are often described as light years, the distance light travels in a year.

# Galaxy facts

Galaxies are groups of billions of stars held together by the force of gravity. Most are either spiral or elliptical, but some are irregular in shape.

● **The Milky Way**
This is the best-known galaxy. The word galaxy comes from the Greek for milk. Before telescopes were powerful enough to prove that they were made up of individual stars, galaxies looked like milky or cloudy areas in the sky. Our Solar System is only one of 100–200 billion stars in the Milky Way, which is 100,000 light years in diameter. The Sun and all the planets take about 200,000,000 years to complete one orbit around its centre.

● **Brightest**
The Large Magellanic Cloud, which is visible only in the southern hemisphere, is 170,000 light years from Earth and 39,000 light years in diameter.

● **Largest**
The central galaxy of the Abell 2029 galaxy cluster was discovered in 1990. It is 1,070 million light years distant and has a diameter of 5.6 million light years, 80 times the diameter of our own galaxy. It has a total light output equivalent to 2 trillion times that of the Sun.

● **Nearest**
Discovered in 1993, the Canis Major Dwarf galaxy is approximately 25,000 light years from the Solar System.

# Constellations

Groups of stars form patterns in the night sky, which are called constellations. There are 88 known constellations. The Sumerians, a Middle Eastern civilization, probably named them, about 5,000 years ago.

The largest is Hydra, the sea serpent, and the smallest is Crux Australis, the Southern Cross. Centaurus, the Centaur, has the most stars that can be seen with the naked eye (94). Others include Aquila, the Eagle; Canis Major, the Great Dog; and Orion, the Hunter.

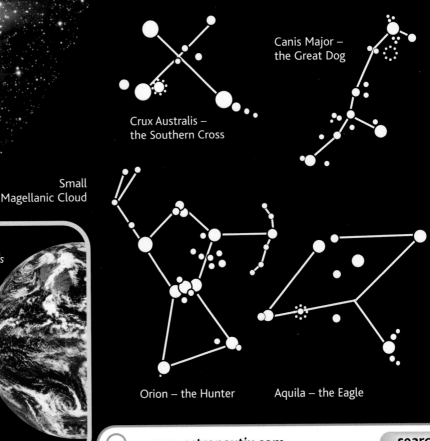

Canis Major – the Great Dog

Crux Australis – the Southern Cross

Small Magellanic Cloud

Orion – the Hunter

Aquila – the Eagle

**Moon** 1.26 seconds
**Sun** 8 minutes 17 seconds
**Furthest planet (Neptune)** 4 hrs 21 mins when the planet is at its maximum distance from Earth
**Nearest star** 4.22 years
**Distance at which the Sun would no longer be visible to the naked eye** 60 years
**Most distant star in our galaxy** 62,700 years
**From nearest body outside our galaxy** 174,000 years
**Furthest visible star** 2,309,000 years
**Most distant known quasar** 14,000,000,000 years

www.astronautix.com    search

# Solar System

The Solar System was formed about 4,560 million years ago. It is made up of the eight planets – Mercury, Venus, Earth, Mars, Jupiter, Saturn, Uranus and Neptune – as well as their moons, comets and other bodies. These all orbit our Sun, to which they are attracted by gravity.

## Mercury

Mercury was named after the speedy messenger of the gods because it seemed to move more quickly than the other known planets. In 2004 NASA launched its MESSENGER probe, which is due to reach Mercury in 2011.

**Diameter:** 4,880 km
**Mass:** 3,302,000,000,000 tonnes
**Average distance from Sun:** 57,909,175 km
**Rotation:** 58.6462 days
**Orbit:** 87.969 days
**Average temperature:** +166.86°C
**Moons:** 0

## Venus

In size, mass, density and volume Venus is the planet most similar to Earth. Venus rotates backwards, from east to west, so the Sun would appear to rise in the east and set in the west. In April 2006 the European Space Agency's *Venus Express* spacecraft reached Venus. Japan's Venus Climate Orbiter *PLANET-C* will be launched in 2010.

**Diameter:** 12,103.6 km
**Mass:** 48,690,000,000,000 tonnes
**Average distance from Sun:** 108,208,930 km
**Rotation:** 243.0187 days
**Orbit:** 224.701 days
**Average temperature:** +456.85°C
**Moons:** 0

> **See also**
> Planets visited by spacecraft: page 29

## Mars

Several space probes have flown past or landed on Mars, providing information on its atmosphere and features, such as the volcano Olympus Mons. This stands 27 km high – more than three times the height of Mount Everest. The latest craft to visit the red planet is *Mars Reconnaissance Orbiter*, which began a four-year orbit in 2006. NASA's *Phoenix* Mars lander is scheduled to land on Mars in 2008 (see p. 27).

**Diameter:** 6,794 km
**Mass:** 6,421,900,000,000 tonnes
**Average distance from Sun:** 227,940,000 km
**Rotation:** 1.025957 days
**Orbit:** 686.98 days
**Average temperature:** -63°C
**Moons:** 2

## Jupiter

Jupiter is the largest planet in the Solar System and is big enough to contain more than a thousand Earths. Four of its many moons were among the first ever astronomical discoveries made with a telescope, by Galileo in 1610. More were identified by later astronomers and in 1979 by the space probe *Voyager 2*. The NASA Juno mission to Jupiter is planned for launch in 2011.

**Diameter:** 142,984 km
**Mass:** 18,986,000,000,000,000 tonnes
**Average distance from Sun:** 778,412,010 km
**Rotation:** 9 hours 50 minutes
**Orbit:** 11 years 314 days
**Average temperature:** +14.85°C to +19.85°C (30,000°C at core)
**Moons:** 63

## Earth

Earth is a watery planet – 70 per cent of its surface appears blue – and the only one that can support life. From space, astronauts have observed cities, forest fires, roads, airports, dams and other large structures, such as the Great Pyramid and the Great Wall of China.

**Diameter:** 12,756.3 km
**Mass:** 59,720,000,000,000 tonnes
**Average distance from Sun:** 149,600,000 km
**Rotation:** 0.99727 days
**Orbit:** 365.256 days
**Average temperature:** +15°C
**Moons:** 1

www.nineplanets.org          search

The Sun, as seen through a telescope

## Sun facts

The Sun is 149,597,893 km from Earth and has a diameter of 1,391,940 km. This is more than 100 times larger than Earth. Its mass is equivalent to 99.98 per cent of the mass of the entire Solar System.

### Elements

The Sun is mostly made up of two light gases, 75 per cent hydrogen and 23 per cent helium, with relatively small quantities of other elements – including metals such as gold. Helium was discovered in the Sun before it was detected on Earth. Its name comes from *helios*, the Greek word for sun.

### Temperature

The Sun has a surface temperature of 5,880 K but it can be 56,000,000 K at its core. (K represents Kelvin, which is an astronomical temperature; it can be converted to Celsius by subtracting 273.16.) At the Sun's centre, nuclear fusion constantly changes hydrogen into helium, and the energy and heat released from this process rise to the surface. The yellow surface we see is called the photosphere.

### The corona

The outermost layer of the Sun extends millions of kilometres into space but is visible only during eclipses. At a height of 75,000 km in the corona, the temperature may reach 2,000,000 K.

### Rotation

The Sun rotates once every 25.4 days, but because it is not solid, the poles spin at a different rate, taking as much as 36 days to complete a single revolution.

### Solar eclipses

When the Moon is between Earth and the Sun, it blocks out the light causing a partial or total eclipse. At this time, astronomers are able to observe the corona in detail.

## Ex-planet

On 24 August 2006, the International Astronomical Union downgraded Pluto from planetary status. It is now regarded as belonging to a new "dwarf planet" category, along with Eris, discovered in 2005, and Ceres, which used to be regarded as the largest asteroid. The spacecraft *New Horizons* is scheduled to reach Pluto in 2015.

## Saturn

Saturn is the least dense planet. Its rings are made of pieces of ice and rock which were probably parts of asteroids and comets. They are being examined by the joint NASA/European Space Agency project *Cassini/Huygens*. Launched in 1997, *Cassini* began a four-year orbit of Saturn in 2004.

**Diameter:** 120,536 km
**Mass:** 5,684,600,000,000,000 tonnes
**Average distance from Sun:** 1,426,725,400 km
**Rotation:** 10 hours 34 minutes
**Orbit:** 29 years 168 days

## Uranus

All the satellites of Uranus are called after characters from either William Shakespeare's plays or Alexander Pope's poem *The Rape of the Lock*. Uranus has rings like those of Saturn, but they are visible only with a powerful telescope.

**Diameter:** 51,118 km
**Mass:** 868,320,000,000,000 tonnes
**Average distance from Sun:** 2,870,972,200 km
**Rotation:** 17 hours 17 minutes
**Orbit:** 84 years 4 days
**Average temperature:** -197.15°C

## Neptune

Neptune is the furthest body from the Sun. Surface winds are the strongest of any planet at up to 2,000 km/h. Neptune's year is so long that it has not completed an orbit round the Sun since its discovery and will not until 2011.

**Diameter:** 49,522 km
**Mass:** 1,024,700,000,000,000 tonnes
**Average distance from Sun:** 4,498,252,900 km
**Rotation:** 16 hours 7 minutes
**Orbit:** 164 years 298 days
**Average temperature:** 200.15°C

The Moon's near side

**Our Moon's far side**
The far side of our Moon always faces away from Earth, so it was unknown until October 1959, when the Soviet *Luna 3* probe sent pictures of it back to Earth.

Buzz Aldrin, walking on the Moon

## Moon facts

Earth's Moon is the most familiar and also the largest satellite in relation to its planet in the Solar System. It is the first body in the Solar System on which vehicles from Earth landed, and the only one to be explored by humans.

**Diameter:** 3,475.6 km
**Distance from Earth:** 406,711 km (furthest, 1912) to 356,375 km (closest, 1984), 384,403 km (average)
**Mass:** 734,556,000,000 tonnes; a person weighing 65 kg on Earth would weigh 10.79 kg on the Moon
**Rotation:** 27 days 7 hours 43 minutes 11.5 seconds
**Surface temperature:** -163°C to +117°C
**Largest crater:** South Pole Aitken (far side) 2,100 km diameter, 12 km deep (largest in the Solar System)

## Asteroid facts

Asteroids are often called minor planets. They are lumps of rock orbiting the Sun, mostly in the asteroid belt between the orbits of Mars and Jupiter.

● Ceres was once considered the largest asteroid but it has been recently reclassified as a dwarf planet. It is 936 km in diameter and was found on New Year's Day, 1801. Since then thousands of asteroids have been found. Twelve of them are more than 250 km wide and 26 are larger than 200 km in diameter. As telescopes have improved, more and more small asteroids have been detected. There are probably about 100,000 asteroids larger than 1 km in diameter. Some experts think there may be as many as 1.2 million.

● Vesta, the fourth asteroid to be found (in 1807), is the only one bright enough to be seen without a telescope.

Part of the Bayeux Tapestry, showing Halley's comet top left

## Halley's comet

### 240BC

### 1450s

British astronomer Edmond Halley (1656–1742) was the first to prove that comets travel in orbits, making it possible to calculate when they will next be seen from Earth. He predicted that the comet he saw in 1682 would return in 1759. It did and was named in his honour. The regular orbit of Halley's comet means that we can find historical accounts of its appearances going back more than 2,000 years. They were often believed to foretell great events.

**25 May 240 BC** Seen in China
**10 October 12 BC** Believed to mark the death of Roman general Agrippa
**28 June AD 451** Believed to mark the defeat of Attila the Hun
**20 March 1066** William (later William the Conqueror)

believed the comet foretold victory over King Harold at the Battle of Hastings. The comet and battle are later depicted in the Bayeux Tapestry.
**9 June 1456** The defeat of the Turkish army by Papal forces was thought to be linked to the comet.

● Astronomers believe that, on average, one asteroid larger than 0.4 km strikes Earth every 50,000 years. Some 65 million years ago a 10 km diameter asteroid crashing to Earth may have been responsible for wiping out the dinosaurs. It would have caused a catastrophic explosion, affecting the climate and chemical composition of the atmosphere and destroying the plants and animals on which the dinosaurs fed. As recently as 1991 a small asteroid came within 170,600 km of Earth, the closest recorded near miss. On 30 Jan 2052 an asteroid is predicted to pass as close as 119,678 km.

● Toutatis (asteroid 4,179) was discovered in 1989. It is named after the Celtic god Toutatis, whose name is used as an oath by the comic strip character Astérix the Gaul. Toutatis measures 4.6 by 2.4 by 1.9 km. It passes Earth every four years and is one of the largest space objects to come so close to us. On 29 September 2004 Toutatis came within 1,555,818 km of Earth. Its next visit will be on 9 November 2008, when it will come within 7,524,773 km.

## Titanic moon

Titan is the largest of Saturn's 34 moons. It is 5,150 km in diameter – larger than the planet Mercury. Dutch astronomer Christiaan Huygens discovered Titan in 1655. We still have no idea what its surface looks like because Titan has a dense atmosphere containing nitrogen, ethane and other gases which shroud its surface – not unlike that of Earth four billion years ago.

Information sent back by the space probe *Voyager 1* during 1980 and recent radio telescope observations suggest that Titan may have ethane "oceans" and "continents" of ice or other solid matter. *Cassini*, a space probe launched by NASA and the European Space Agency, arrived in Saturn's orbit on 1 July 2004. On 14 January 2005 it launched the *Huygens* probe on to the surface of Titan and sent back scientific data.

### Neptune's moon

Triton, discovered in 1846, is the only known large moon in the Solar System with a retrograde orbit. It revolves around its planet (Neptune) in the opposite direction to the planet's rotation.

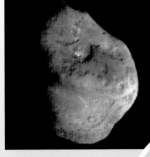

Comet Temple 1 as photographed by NASA's *Deep Impact* probe in 2005

Comet Hale-Bopp as seen from Earth in 1997

Titan, the largest moon of Saturn

### Returning comets

More than 20 comets return more often than Halley. The most frequent visitor is Encke's comet, named after the German astronomer Johann Franz Encke (1791–1865). In 1818 he calculated the 3.3-year period of its orbit.

2000s

**15 September 1682** Observed by Edmond Halley, who predicted its return

**13 March 1759** The comet's first return, as predicted by Halley, proving his calculations correct

**16 November 1835** The American author Mark Twain is born. He always believed that

his fate was linked to that of the comet, and soon after it reappeared in 1910, he died.

**10 April 1910** There was panic as many believed the world would come to an end.

**9 February 1986** The Japanese *Suisei* probe, Soviet *Vega 1* and *Vega 2* and the European Space

Agency's *Giotto* passed close to Halley's comet. Astronomers concluded that the comet is made of dust held together by water and carbon dioxide ice.

**28 July 2061** Next due to appear. The orbit of Halley's comet is not exactly 76 years. Astronomers have to take into account the gravitational pull from planets when calculating its return.

www.spacetoday.org            search

# Famous astronomers

**John Couch Adams** (Britain, 1819–92) studied the Leonid meteor shower and predicted the existence of Neptune, which was discovered in 1846.

**Edward Emerson Barnard** (USA, 1857–1923) discovered Barnard's Star and Amalthea, a moon of Jupiter.

**Nicolaus Copernicus** (Poland, 1473–1543) showed that the Sun was at the centre of the Solar System.

**Galileo Galilei** (Italy, 1564–1642) made important discoveries concerning gravity and motion. He built some of the first telescopes used in astronomy and used them to discover many previously unknown space objects.

**George Ellery Hale** (USA, 1868–1938) pioneered the astronomical study of the Sun and founded observatories, one with a major telescope named after him.

**Edmond Halley** (Britain, 1656–1742) predicted the orbits of comets, including the one that bears his name.

**William Herschel** (Germany/Britain, 1738–1822) built huge telescopes, compiled catalogues of stars and discovered moons of Saturn and Uranus.

**Edwin Hubble** (USA, 1889–1953) made important discoveries about galaxies. The Hubble Space Telescope was named in his honour.

**Christiaan Huygens** (Holland, 1629–95) discovered Saturn's rings and devised the wave theory of light.

**Percival Lowell** (USA, 1855–1916) was founder of the Lowell Observatory, Arizona. He predicted that a planet would be found in the region where Pluto was later discovered.

**Charles Messier** (France, 1730–1817) studied comets and eclipses, but he is best known for his catalogue of stars first published in 1774.

Yerkes Observatory, Wisconsin, USA

**Isaac Newton (Britain, 1643–1727)** is considered one of the greatest of all astronomers. His theories of gravity and the motions of planets revolutionized the subject.

# Telescopes and observatories

The following are some of the world's most famous telescopes and observatories.

## Royal Observatory, Greenwich, London
Founded by King Charles II in 1675, but atmospheric and light pollution in London reduced its efficiency. In 1884 the Prime or Greenwich Meridian, 0°, which passes through the Observatory, was adopted as the basis for all mapping and measurements. Longitude measurements refer to west or east of the meridian.

## Herschel's "Forty-foot" reflector, Slough
A giant telescope built in 1788 with a 1.2 m (3.9 ft) mirror.

## Birr Castle, Co. Offaly, Ireland
The Earl of Rosse's 1.8 m (5.9 ft) reflecting telescope, built in 1845, was used to discover the spiral form of galaxies. It was the world's largest until the opening of Mount Wilson.

## Yerkes Observatory, Williams Bay, Wisconsin, USA
This 1 m (3.25 ft) telescope is the biggest refracting instrument made up to this time. It was completed in 1897.

## Mount Wilson Observatory, California, USA
The telescope was installed in 1917 with a mirror size of 2.5 m (8.2 ft). It was the world's largest until the Hale.

## Hale Telescope, Palomar Observatory, California, USA
The Hale's 5 m (16.4 ft) telescope was first used in 1949.

## Jodrell Bank, Cheshire
Britain's first, and once the world's largest radio telescope, with a 76 m (249.3 ft) dish, began operating in 1957.

## Arecibo Observatory, Puerto Rico
Completed in 1963, this is the world's most powerful radio telescope. Its uses include searching for pulsars and quasars and the search for alien life forms under the SETI (Search for Extra-Terrestrial Intelligence) programme. Its giant 305 m (1,000.65 ft) dish features in the final scenes of the James Bond film *Golden Eye* (1995).

# Astronomy milestones

Astronomy is the scientific study of the Universe and the bodies it contains (excluding Earth). Astronomers are the scientists who study astronomy.

**585 BC** First prediction of eclipse of the Sun

**130 BC** Hipparchus calculates distance and size of Moon

**AD 1543** Copernicus shows that the Sun is at the centre of the Solar System

**1609** Johannes Kepler describes laws of planetary motion

**1610** Galileo Galilei discovers moons of Jupiter

**1655** Christiaan Huygens discovers Titan, moon of Saturn

## 1600s

**1668** Isaac Newton builds first reflecting telescope

**1687** Isaac Newton publishes theories of motions of planets, etc

**1705** Edmond Halley predicts return of comet

**1671–84** Giovanni Cassini discovers four moons of Saturn

**1774** Charles Messier compiles star catalogue

**1781** William Herschel discovers 7th planet, Uranus

## 1800s

**1801** First asteroid, Ceres, discovered by Giuseppe Piazzi

**1846** Johann Galle and Urbain Le Verrier discover 8th planet Neptune

**1787–89** Herschel finds two moons of Uranus and two of Saturn

**1839–40** First photographs of the Moon

**1894** Flagstaff Observatory, Arizona, founded

**1905** Einstein's Special Theory of Relativity first proposed

## Hubble Space Telescope

The HST was launched in 1990 and orbits 600 km (372.8 miles) above Earth's atmosphere. It can photograph distant objects with ten times the detail possible with ground-based telescopes.

## Keck I & II Telescopes, Mauna Kea Observatory, Hawaii, USA

The two Keck telescopes were opened in 1992–96. They are situated 4,000 m (13,123 ft) up a Hawaiian mountain, so above 40 per cent of the Earth's atmosphere. They are the world's most powerful ground-based instruments, with a 10.82 m (35.5 ft) total aperture made up of 36 hexagonal mirrors.

## Hobby-Eberly Telescope, McDonald Observatory, Texas, USA

This telescope is designed to collect light for spectrum analysis rather than for visual exploration. It has been in operation since 1999, and has an overall diameter of 11 m (36.1 ft), making it one of the largest ever optical telescopes.

## Large Binocular Telescope, Arizona, USA

The Large Binocular Telescope, completed in 2007, is the largest and most advanced optical telescope ever built. Sited at the Mount Graham International Observatory, it has two 8.4 m (27.5 ft) mirrors, giving a total area equal to one giant 11.4 m (37.4 ft) diameter mirror. It is expected to produce images as much as 10 times the resolution of those produced by the much smaller Hubble Space Telescope.

## First telescopes

The first telescopes were made in 1608 by Dutchman Hans Lippershey. Galileo built his own soon after and used it to discover Jupiter's moons. The earliest type of telescope, known as a refracting telescope, produced a slight distortion of images (called aberration). Since about 1670, astronomers have used reflecting telescopes, which use mirrors that compensate for the distortion.

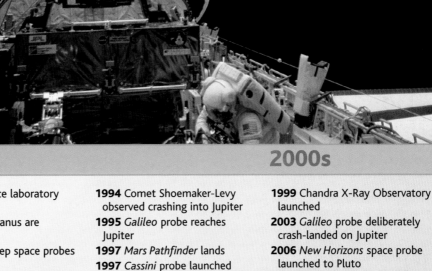

Hubble Space Telescope

## 1900s

**1908** Giant and dwarf stars described

**1923** Galaxies beyond the Milky Way proved

**1927** Big Bang theory proposed

**1930** Pluto discovered by Clyde Tombaugh

**1959** First photographs of the far side of the Moon by Soviet satellite *Luna 3*

**1961** First quasars discovered

**1967** First pulsars identified

**1971** Black hole first detected

**1973** *Skylab* space laboratory launched

**1976** Rings of Uranus are discovered

**1977** *Voyager* deep space probes are launched

**1971** *Mariner 9* spacecraft maps Mars

**1980** *Voyager 1* explores Saturn

**1978** Space probes *Pioneer 1* and *2* reach Venus

**1985–89** *Voyager 2* discovers moons of Uranus and Neptune

## 2000s

**1994** Comet Shoemaker-Levy observed crashing into Jupiter

**1995** *Galileo* probe reaches Jupiter

**1997** *Mars Pathfinder* lands

**1997** *Cassini* probe launched to Saturn

**1998** *International Space Station* construction starts

**1999** Chandra X-Ray Observatory launched

**2003** *Galileo* probe deliberately crash-landed on Jupiter

**2006** *New Horizons* space probe launched to Pluto

**2007** *Phoenix* mission to Mars launched; scheduled to land on the planet in 2008

www.absoluteastronomy.com          search

# Animal space pioneers

Before humans went into space animals were used to test equipment. The first animal to be sent up in a rocket – but not into space – was Albert 1, a male rhesus monkey, in 1948. He and his successor, Albert 2, died during the tests.

However, on 20 September 1951, a monkey and 11 mice were recovered after a launch in a US *Aerobee* rocket. Many further animal experiments were carried out before the first manned space flight.

## Space dogs, and a cat

Laika, a female Samoyed husky, became the first animal in orbit after being launched by the USSR in *Sputnik 2* in November 1957. There was no way to bring her down and she died after ten days in space. Two female huskies, Belka and Strelka, orbited successfully in August 1960. Strelka later gave birth to puppies, one of which was given to US President John F. Kennedy. In October 1963, a French *Veronique AGI* rocket put a cat called Félix into space and returned him safely to Earth by parachute.

## Monkey business

Able, a female rhesus monkey, and Baker, a female squirrel monkey, were launched by the USA in May 1959. They did not orbit and successfully returned to Earth. In November 1961 Enos, a male chimpanzee, completed two orbits and survived. The USSR's first space primates were monkeys Abrek and Bion, who orbited in December 1983 in one of a series of Bion satellite experiments.

## Flying frogs

In November 1970, the USA's Orbiting Frog Otolith satellite (OFO-A) launched two bullfrogs into orbit for a week. In December 1990, Toyohiro Akiyama, a Japanese journalist, took six green tree frogs to the Soviet *Mir* space station to conduct weightlessness experiments.

## Worldwide web

Arabella, a garden spider, went to the US *Skylab-3* in July 1973. She spent almost 60 days in orbit in an experiment to test the effect of weightlessness on her web-weaving skills.

## A space menagerie

The *STS-90* mission of space shuttle *Columbia* (April/May 1998) contained the *Neurolab* – a space menagerie with 170 baby rats, 18 mice, 229 swordtail fish, 135 snails, four oyster toad fish and 1,514 cricket eggs and larvae.

In January 2006, an *Atlas V* rocket launched NASA's *New Horizons* probe on its 9-year journey to Pluto.

### Can of worms

On 1 February 2003, space shuttle *Columbia STS-107* broke up on re-entry and its crew were killed. On-board animal experiments involving silkworms, spiders, carpenter bees, harvester ants and Japanese killfish were destroyed, but, amazingly, canisters of worms were found alive.

http://kids.msfc.nasa.gov    search

*Long Duration Exposure Facility* satellite (USA) orbited the Earth 34,422 times between 1984–90. Space Shuttle *Columbia* eventually brought it back to Earth.

# Space junk

When satellites reach the end of their useful life, they may be deliberately directed back in such a way that they burn up as they re-enter the Earth's atmosphere or come down in the oceans or away from places where they could cause damage. So far, no one has been killed or seriously injured by space debris.

## ● Returned to Earth
The 69-tonne *Skylab* re-entered in 1979, scattering large chunks in the Australian desert, and Russia's *Mir* space station, which weighed 120 tonnes, came down in the Pacific.

## ● Orbiting junk
About 100–200 objects, each larger than a football, re-enter every year, but there are still many pieces of space junk in orbit. A survey carried out in June 2000 calculated that there are 90 space probes and 2,671 satellites still in space. There are as many as 100,000 objects between 1 and 10 cm in diameter and about 11,000 objects larger than 10 cm including parts of rockets: an *Ariane* rocket booster exploded in 1986, scattering 400 fragments large enough to be tracked. In 1991 space shuttle *Discovery STS-48* narrowly avoided a discarded Soviet rocket.

# Artificial satellites

The USSR's *Sputnik 1* was the first artificial satellite to enter Earth's orbit. This 83.6 kg (184 lb) metal sphere transmitted signals back to Earth for three weeks before its batteries failed.

In 1958 the USA began to launch its own satellites. Five went into orbit. All of the earliest satellites have since crashed back to Earth, except *Vanguard 1* (USA, 1958) which is still in space – and likely to remain so for another 200 years.

Over the past 50 years, many more artificial satellites have been launched, with a greater range of uses.

## Astronomy
The Hubble Space Telescope has been taking photographs of distant galaxies since 1990. In 2008 the Herschel Space Observatory is scheduled for launch. This new telescope will have the biggest mirror ever in space (3.5 m across).

## Communications
Over 5,000 satellites have been launched to transmit telephone, radio and television signals around the world. Fewer than half are still orbiting, and many have stopped working.

## Earth observation satellites
These transmit images of the weather and the Earth's environment. They helped to show the depletion of the ozone layer.

## Military satellites
Governments use these "spies in the sky" for surveillance but their precise functions are secret.

## Global Positioning System
This is a system of 24 linked satellites that allows people to pinpoint their exact position anywhere on Earth. The system is operated by the US Department of Defense and is used by aircraft and ships. GPS systems are now common in cars, too.

## Space rockets

Thrust is the force required to lift a vehicle such as an aircraft or rocket off the ground. Rockets often have several stages. Each one provides a proportion of the thrust required to carry a satellite, space shuttle or other vehicle into orbit or into space, dropping away as their propellant has been used so that their weight no longer needs to be carried.

# Planets visited by spacecraft

No human has yet set foot on any space body other than Earth and the Moon. But unmanned spacecraft have taken photographs, made scientific readings and gathered data from all the planets in the Solar System, either by flying past or landing.

**Venus** *Mariner 2* (USA) flyby 1962; *Venera 4* (USSR) landed 1967; MESSENGER (USA) flybys 2006, 2007

**Mars** *Mariner 4* (USA) flyby 1965; *Mars Pathfinder* (USA) landed 1997; *Mars Reconnaissance Orbiter* (USA) in orbit 2006– ; *Phoenix Mars* (USA) scheduled to land in 2008

**Jupiter** *Pioneer 10* (USA) flyby 1973; *Galileo* (USA) landed* 2003; *New Horizons* (USA) flyby 2007

**Mercury** *Mariner 10* (USA) flyby 1974; MESSENGER (USA) flybys 2008, 2009 and scheduled to orbit 2011

**Saturn** *Pioneer 11* (USA) flyby 1979; *Cassini/Huygens* (USA/ESA) orbiter/ lander 2004/2005

**Uranus** *Voyager 2* (USA) flyby 1986

**Neptune** *Voyager 2* (USA) flyby 1989

* Deliberately destroyed entering Jupiter's atmosphere, rather than risk contaminating moon Europa with bacteria from Earth.

# Manned space missions

During the 1950s, there was a "space race" between the USA and USSR to be the first country to send a human into space. NASA's *Mercury* missions were originally unmanned, or carried only animals. The USSR launched the first man into orbit in 1961.

Each country's subsequent space missions had different aims. The USA focused on Moon landings with their *Apollo* programme and later the re-usable space shuttle. The Soviets and later Russia concentrated on long-duration missions, with the *Mir* space station. The latest manned mission is the *International Space Station*, which is four times larger than *Mir*.

| Mission | Country | Years |
|---|---|---|
| *Mercury* | USA | 1959–63 |
| *Vostok* | USSR | 1961–63 |
| *Voskhod* | USSR | 1964–65 |
| *Gemini* | USA | 1965–66 |
| *Apollo* | USA | 1967–72 |
| *Soyuz* | USSR | 1967–76 |
| *Salyut* | USSR | 1971–82 |
| *Skylab* | USA | 1973 |
| *Apollo Soyuz* | USA/USSR | 1975 |
| Space shuttle | USA | 1981 |
| *Mir* space station | USSR/Russia | 1986–2001 |
| *International Space Station* | USA, Canada, Japan, European Space Agency, Russia, Brazil | 1998– |
| *Shenzhou* | China | 2003– |

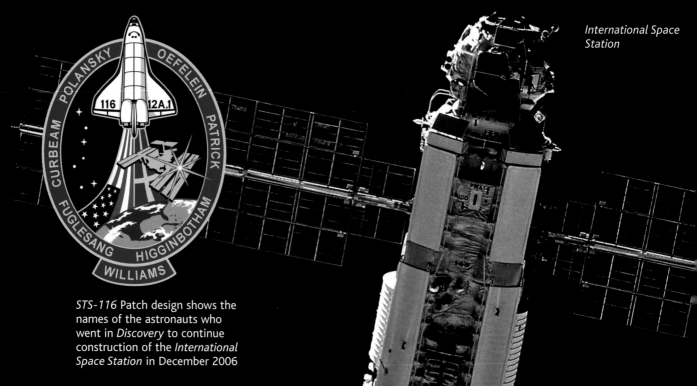

*International Space Station*

*STS-116* Patch design shows the names of the astronauts who went in *Discovery* to continue construction of the *International Space Station* in December 2006

## Astronauts and cosmonauts

The word "astronaut" was first used in 1880 by the British writer Percy Greg. It was the name he gave to a spaceship in his novel *Across the Zodiac*. By the 1950s it was the word used for a space voyager. The Russian word is cosmonaut.

**12 April 1961 First person in space** Soviet cosmonaut Yuri Gagarin made a single orbit of Earth in *Vostok 1*, a flight that lasted 1 hour 48 minutes.

**5 May 1961 First US astronaut** America's first astronaut Alan B. Shepard Jr, entered space aboard *Mercury 3* but did not orbit during his 15 minute 22 second mission.

**6 August 1961 First flight of over 24 hours** Gherman S. Titov (USSR) in *Vostok 2* made the first flight of more than 24 hours. He was also the youngest ever astronaut at 25 years 10 months 25 days.

**20 February 1962 First US orbit** John H. Glenn Jr in the *Friendship 7* capsule made the first US orbit, completing three orbits in 4 hours 55 mins.

**16 June 1963 First woman in space** Valentina V. Tereshkova (USSR) in *Vostok 6* was the first woman in space. She spent 2 days 22 hours 50 minutes 8 seconds in space. She remains the youngest (26 years 3 months 10 days) woman in space.

**18 March 1965 First space walk** Aleskei Leonov (USSR) made the first space walk, from *Voskhod 2*. It took 24 minutes and it almost ended in disaster when his spacesuit ballooned. He was unable to return through the airlock until he reduced the pressure in his suit to a dangerously low level.

**23 March 1965 First two-man US mission** John Young and Virgil "Gus" Grissom made the first two-man US mission in *Gemini 3*.

**3 June 1965 First US spacewalk** Edward H. White II made a 36 minute spacewalk from *Gemini 4*.

**24 April 1967 First space death** After 18 orbits in *Soyuz 1*, Vladimir M. Komarov (USSR) died when his parachute got tangled and his capsule crash-landed.

**24 December 1968 First manned spacecraft to orbit the Moon** *Apollo 8* (followed in 1969 by *Apollo* missions 9 and 10) orbited the Moon but did not land.

# All the men on the Moon

The human exploration of the Moon lasted just over three years and involved a total of six missions. In each, a pair of US astronauts went down to the surface in a LEM (lunar excursion module) while a third orbited in a CSM (command service module). The missions provided scientists with a huge amount of information about the Moon.

| Astronaut | Spacecraft | Total EVA* hr:min | Mission dates |
|---|---|---|---|
| 1 Neil A. Armstrong | Apollo 11 | 2:32 | 16–24 Jul 1969 |
| 2 Edwin E. "Buzz" Aldrin | Apollo 11 | 2:15 | 16–24 Jul 1969 |
| 3 Charles Conrad Jr | Apollo 12 | 7:45 | 14–24 Nov 1969 |
| 4 Alan L. Bean | Apollo 12 | 7:45 | 14–24 Nov 1969 |
| 5 Alan B. Shepard | Apollo 14 | 9:23 | 31 Jan–9 Feb1971 |
| 6 Edgar D. Mitchell | Apollo 14 | 9:23 | 31 Jan–9 Feb 1971 |
| 7 David R. Scott | Apollo 15 | 19:08 | 26 Jul–7 Aug 1971 |
| 8 James B. Irwin | Apollo 15 | 18:35 | 26 Jul–7 Aug 1971 |
| 9 John W. Young | Apollo 16 | 20:14 | 16–27 Apr 1972 |
| 10 Charles M. Duke Jr | Apollo 16 | 20:14 | 16–27 Apr 1972 |
| 11 Eugene A. Cernan | Apollo 17 | 22:04 | 7–19 Dec 1972 |
| 12 Harrison H. Schmitt | Apollo 17 | 22:04 | 7–19 Dec 1972 |

* Extra vehicular activity: time spent out of the lunar module on the Moon. The six US *Apollo* missions above resulted in successful Moon landings. *Apollo 13*, 11–17 April 1970, was aborted and returned to Earth after an oxygen tank exploded.

## Longest space walk

The record for the longest-ever spacewalk was broken from 10–11 March 2001, when mission specialists James Voss and Susan Helms stepped outside space shuttle *Discovery STS-102* to do construction work on the space station. Their EVA (extra vehicular activity) lasted 8 hours 56 minutes.

Astronaut Christer Fuglesang resumes construction work on the *International Space Station*, December 2006

## Naming the space shuttles

Unlike space rockets, NASA's space shuttles, or orbiter vehicles, were designed to be re-used. Each has a name, but every mission on which it goes is given a unique number.

The acronym *STS* (Space Transportation System) has been used throughout the shuttle programme. The first nine flights were simply numbered *STS-1* to *STS-9*. A more complicated system was then used, but the original system of *STS* + number has been revived. They do not always follow numerical order, as a mission may be delayed and a later-numbered mission may take its place before it can be rescheduled.

### The shuttles
Five space shuttles were built; *Discovery* (first launch 1984), *Atlantis* (1985) and *Endeavour* (1992) remain in service. *Challenger* was destroyed during its 10th mission on 28 January 1986 and *Columbia* was lost on re-entry from its 28th mission on 1 February 2003.

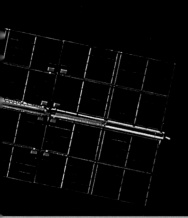

**20 July 1969 First Moon landing** Neil Armstrong and Edwin E. "Buzz" Aldrin became the first men on the Moon.

**18 June 1983 First US woman in space** Sally Ride was launched in the space shuttle *Challenger STS-7*, which was the first reusable space vehicle.

**18 May 1991 First British astronaut** Helen Sharman travelled to the *Mir* space station and spent a week in space.

**29 June 1995 First space shuttle/space station docking** Space shuttle *Atlantis STS-71* docked with the Soviet space station *Mir*.

**26 September 1996 US endurance record** On her 5th mission, US astronaut Shannon Lucid completed 188 days aboard the Russian *Mir* station, setting a world record for women. Lucid was born in China. She flew more missions than any woman and at 53 was the oldest female in space.

**4 December 1998 International Space Station** First stage of the *International Space Station* was established.

**2 November 2000 First crew on ISS** An American and Russian crew began living aboard the *International Space Station*.

**28 April–6 May 2001 First space tourist** US millionaire Dennis Tito became the first space tourist, paying $20 million for his Russian *Soyuz TM-32* flight to the *International Space Station*.

**15–16 October 2003 First astronaut launched by China** Chinese astronaut Lang Liwei made eight orbits of Earth in a *Shenzhou 5* spacecraft. China made its second flight, *Shenzhou 6*, with two astronauts on 12–16 October 2005.

**21 June 2004 First private spaceflight** Mike Melvill, aged 63, became the second oldest astronaut when he entered space aboard his privately funded *SpaceShipOne*.

**2010 Last Space shuttle retires** *Atlantis*, *Discovery* and *Endeavour* are to be progressively taken out of service and replaced by NASA's *Orion* spacecraft in a programme that will take astronauts back to the Moon and to Mars.

http://amazingspace.stsci.edu    search

WHITAKER'S WORLD OF FACTS

# Planet Earth

## Melting ice

Global warming is causing the Ilulissat Glacier, Greenland, to shrink by several kilometres a year. 15,000 tourists visited the melting ice sheet in 2006 and twice as many visitors are expected in 2007, following the introduction of commercial flights direct from the US.

# Layers of the Earth

The Earth is made up of a number of layers. At the top is the crust – the thinnest layer. Next is the mantle, then the outer and inner cores. The outer core is probably liquid and the inner core solid.

**Ocean** 3 km (1.9 miles)

**Crust** 21 km (13 miles)

**Mantle** 21–2,865 km (13–1,780 miles)

**Outer core** 2,865–5,125 km (1,780–3,185 miles)

**Inner core** 5,125–6,371 km (3,185–3,959 miles)

Inside the Earth showing the average depth of its layers

# The largest meteorite craters

About 500 meteorites reach Earth every year. Many collision sites have been altered by weather over millions of years, and scientists are unsure whether some craters are actually the craters of extinct volcanoes. Those below are all agreed to be meteorite craters.

**1 Vredefort, South Africa** 300 km (186 miles) in diameter
**2 Sudbury, Ontario, Canada** 250 km (155 miles) in diameter
**3 Chicxulub, Yucatan, Mexico** 170 km (106 miles) in diameter
**4 Manicougan, Canada** 100 km (62 miles) in diameter
**5 Popigai, Russia** 100 km (62 miles) in diameter

# The 10 degrees of hardness

The Mohs scale, named after German mineralogist Friedrich Mohs (1773–1839), is used for comparing the relative hardness of minerals. Each mineral on the scale can be scratched by the harder ones below it.

Meteor Crater, Arizona

| Mohs scale No. | Substance | Mohs scale No. | Substance |
|---|---|---|---|
| 1 | Talc | 6 | Orthoclase |
| 2 | Gypsum | 7 | Quartz |
| 3 | Calcite | 8 | Topaz |
| 4 | Fluorite | 9 | Corundum |
| 5 | Apatite | 10 | Diamond |

# Geological time 2007

**CENOZOIC ERA**
**Quaternary period**
Recent/Holocene epoch: 11,000 years ago (y.a.) to present day – modern humans
Pleistocene epoch: 1,800,000 to 11,000 y.a. – humans

**Tertiary period**
Pliocene epoch: 5,000,000 to 1,800,000 y.a. – ape-like human ancestors
Miocene epoch: 23,000,000 to 5,000,000 y.a. – apes and whales

Oligocene epoch: 38,000,000 to 23,000,000 y.a. – cats and dogs
Eocene epoch: 54,000,000 to 37,000,000 y.a. – grasslands
Palaeocene epoch: 65,000,000 to 54,000,000 y.a. – large mammals

**MESOZOIC ERA**
**Cretaceous period**: 146,000,000 to 65,000,000 y.a. – flowering plants; dinosaurs became extinct
**Jurassic period**: 208,000,000 to 146,000,000 y.a. – birds and mammals
**Triassic period**: 245,000,000 to 208,000,000 y.a. – dinosaurs and flying reptiles

## Uluru

The rock formerly known as Ayers Rock in Northern Territory, Australia, is believed to be the world's largest free-standing rock. It is made of sandstone and is 335 m (1,100 ft) high, 3.6 km (2.2 miles) long and 2 km (1.5 miles) wide. It was originally called after South Australian premier Sir Henry Ayers, but it is now known by the name given to it by local Aborigines, to whom it is sacred.

## Rocks

There are three categories of rock – igneous, sedimentary and metamorphic.

● Igneous rocks originate deep in the Earth. They erupt from volcanoes as magma and cool or solidify as they rise to the upper layers. Basalt is an igneous rock and so is granite, a very hard rock often used in building. Pumice stone is a soft igneous rock that is ejected from volcanoes. As it cools, it often fills with so many air bubbles that it floats in water.

● Sedimentary rocks can be formed by deposits in water and occasionally by wind. Sandstone is a common example. Organic sedimentary rocks are formed by living plants and animals – coal comes from plant matter and limestone from the calcium from billions of plants and animals. Chemical sedimentary rocks occur when chemical processes take place and minerals are deposited.

● Metamorphic rocks are igneous or sedimentary rocks that have changed as a result of high temperatures or pressures. Slate used on roofs is a familiar example.

www.webmineral.com     **search**

## Giant meteorites

Many meteorites land in the sea and in unpopulated areas so they are never seen. The Hoba meteorite, the largest in the world, was found in Namibia in 1920. It measures 2.73 x 2.43 m (9 x 8 ft) and is 82 per cent iron and 16 per cent nickel. It weighs more than 60 tonnes. Second largest is the Tent, found in Greenland in 1894 and now known by its original Eskimo name, Ahnighito. This meteorite weighs about 57.3 tonnes and is on display in the New York Museum of Natural History.

### Minerals

Minerals are naturally occurring substances with a definite chemical composition. Most mineral names end in "ite". Many have a practical use or contain a chemical compound or element that can be extracted and used commercially. Bauxite, for instance, is the main source of aluminium. Gems are minerals that are highly prized for their rarity or appearance, eg diamonds, sapphires, emeralds and rubies.

## 4,500,000,000 years ago

**PALAEOZOIC ERA**
**Permian period**: 286,000,000 to 245,000,000 y.a. – deciduous plants
**Carboniferous Pennsylvanian period**: 325,000,000 to 286,000,000 y.a. – reptiles
**Carboniferous Mississippian period**: 360,000,000 to 325,000,000 y.a. – winged insects

**Devonian period**: 410,000,000 to 360,000,000 y.a. – amphibians
**Silurian period**: 440,000,000 to 410,000,000 y.a. – land plants and insects
**Ordovician period**: 500,000,000 to 440,000,000 y.a. – corals and molluscs

**Cambrian period**: 544,000,000 to 500,000,000 y.a. – fish and shelled creatures

**PRECAMBRIAN ERA**
**Proterozoic period**: 2,500,000,000 to 544,000,000 y.a. – earliest fossils; jellyfish

**Archaic period**: 3,800,000,000 to 2,500,000,000 y.a. – living cells
**Hadean period**: 4,500,000,000 to 3,800,000,000 y.a. – environment unable to support life; from 4,500,000,000 or earlier – the Earth was formed

# Largest deserts

Deserts cover about a third of the world's land area. They range from extremely arid and barren sandy deserts (about four per cent of the total land surface of the globe), through arid (15 per cent) to semi-arid (just under 15 per cent).

Most deserts have features of all these, with one zone merging into the next, so the start and finish of any desert is not exact. Many of the world's largest deserts are broken down by geographers into smaller desert regions – the Australian Desert includes the Gibson, Great Sandy, Great Victoria and Simpson, for example.

**1 Sahara, Northern Africa** – 9,100,000 sq km (3,514,000 sq miles)

**2 Australian, Australia** (Includes Gibson, Great Sandy, Great Victoria and Simpson) – 3,400,000 sq km (1,313,000 sq miles)

**3 Arabian Peninsula, Southwest Asia** (Includes an-Nafud and Rub al Khali) – 2,600,000 sq km (1,004,000 sq miles)

**4 Turkestan, Central Asia** (Includes Kara-Kum and Kyzylkum) – 1,900,000 sq km (734,000 sq miles)

**5 Gobi, Central Asia** – 1,300,000 sq km (502,000 sq miles)

**6 North American Desert, US/Mexico** (Includes Great Basin, Mojave, Sonorah and Chihuahuan) – 1,300,000 sq km (502,000 sq miles)

The Devil's Marbles in the Australian desert

## The highest mountain?

The height of mountains is usually measured from sea level. Mauna Kea in Hawaii is only 4,245 m (13,957 ft) above sea level, but it rises a total of 10,203 m (33,474 ft) from the floor of the Pacific Ocean, making its real height 1,353 m (4,439 ft) greater than Mount Everest!

Mount Everest, the world's highest mountain

# Highest mountains

People used to think that Kangchenjunga in Nepal/India was the highest mountain. Then the Great Trigonometrical Survey of India measured all the country's land features. The survey was completed in 1852 and showed that Everest (then called Peak XV) was the world's highest mountain.

Everest's height was then reckoned to be 8,840 m (29,002 ft). This has since been adjusted as improved measuring methods have been used. The mountain's name was suggested in 1865 as a tribute to Sir George Everest, the Surveyor General of India, who had led the survey.

Everest (base moved to sea floor)

Mauna Kea

sea level

sea floor

**Highest mountains**
**1 Everest, Nepal/China** – 8,850 m (29,035 ft)
**2 K2 (Chogori), Pakistan/China** – 8,607m (28,238 ft)
**3 Kangchenjunga, Nepal/India** – 8,598 m (28,208 ft)
**4 Lhotse, Nepal/China** – 8,511 m (27,923 ft)
**5 Makalu I, Nepal/China** – 8,481 m (27,824 ft)

# Largest island

An island is a piece of land surrounded by water. Australia is so large it is a continent, not an island; otherwise it would rank first. The smallest island with country status is Pitcairn, at 4.53 sq km (1.75 sq miles).

**1 Greenland (Kalaatdlit Nunaat)** – 2,175,600 sq km (840,070 sq miles)
**2 New Guinea** – 789,900 sq km (312,190 sq miles)
**3 Borneo** – 751,000 sq km (289,961 sq miles)
**4 Madagascar (Malagasy Republic)** – 587,041 sq km (226,674 sq miles)
**5 Baffin Island, Canada** – 507,451 sq km (195,926 sq miles)
**6 Sumatra, Indonesia** – 422,200 sq km (163,011 sq miles)
**7 Honshu, Japan** – 230,092 sq km (88,839 sq miles)
**8 Great Britain** – 218,041 sq km (84,185 sq miles)
**9 Victoria Island, Canada** – 217,290 sq km (83,896 sq miles)
**10 Ellesmere Island, Canada** –196,236 sq km (75,767 sq miles)
**11 Celebes, Indonesia** – 179,000 sq km (69,100 sq miles)
**12 South Island, New Zealand** – 151,971 sq km (58,676 sq miles)
**13 Java, Indonesia** – 126,900 sq km (49,000 sq miles)
**14 North Island, New Zealand** – 114,489 sq km (44,204 sq miles)
**15 Newfoundland, Canada** – 108,860 sq km (42,031 sq miles)
**16 Cuba** – 104,945 sq km (40,519 sq miles)
**17 Luzon, Philippines** – 104,688 sq km (40,420 sq miles)
**18 Iceland** – 102,819 sq km (39,699 sq miles)
**19 Mindanao, Philippines** – 94,630 sq km (36,537 sq miles)
**20 Ireland** 84,406 sq km (32,589 sq miles)
(Area excludes offshore islands)

# Lowest places on land

Sea level is the average height of the sea at a point midway between high and low tides. The shore of the Dead Sea is the lowest exposed ground below sea level. Some land in Antarctica is 2,538 m (8,327 ft) below sea level, but is covered by a 2,100 m (6,890 ft)-deep ice cap.

**1 Dead Sea, Israel/Jordan** – 400 m (1,312 ft) below sea level
**2 Lake Assa, Djibouti** – 156 m (511 ft) below sea level
**3 Turfan Depression, China** – 154 m (505 ft) below sea level
**4 Qattâra Depression, Egypt** – 133 m (436 ft) below sea level
**5 Mangyshlak Peninsula, Kazakhstan** – 132 m (433 ft) below sea level

## Geysers

Geysers are jets of boiling water and steam that erupt from beneath the ground where water is heated by volcanic activity. The name geyser comes from a hot spring called Geysir at Haukadalur, Iceland. Yellowstone National Park, Wyoming, USA has more geysers than anywhere else. There are 500 active ones including Steamboat, which erupts to a height of 120 m (374 ft), and Old Faithful, which erupts about every 91 minutes.

Geyser erupting in Yellowstone National Park

# The seven continents

The Americas are named after the explorer Amerigo Vespucci (1451–1512). Africa was perhaps originally a Berber tribal name. This was adopted by the Romans as the name of their province and later spread to the whole continent.

The name of Europe may simply mean mainland. Asia is probably from the Assyrian, *asu*, meaning sunrise or east. Australis is Latin for southern; Australia, with New Zealand and other islands, is also considered as part of Oceania, a name invented by the geographer Conrad Malte-Brun (1775–1826). Antarctica is Greek for opposite the Arctic. Arctic comes from the Greek for bear, because the region lies under the stars of the Great Bear constellation.

**North America** Land area: 24,349,000 sq km (9,401,000 sq miles) % of world total: 16.4

**Europe** Land area: 10,498,000 sq km (4,053,000 sq miles) % of world total: 7.1

**Asia** Land area: 43,608,000 sq km (16,837,000 sq miles) % of world total: 29.3

**Africa** Land area: 30,335,000 sq km (11,712,000 sq miles) % of world total: 20.4

**South America** Land area: 17,611,000 sq km (6,800,000 sq miles) % of world total: 11.8

**Australasia** Land area: 8,923,000 sq km (3,445,000 sq miles) % of world total: 6.0

**Antarctica** Land area: 13,340,000 sq km (5,151,000 sq miles) % of world total: 9.0

Niagara Falls

## Longest river

The source of the Nile was discovered by Europeans in 1858 when British explorer John Hanning Speke reached Lake Victoria Nyanza, in what is now Burundi. About one hundred years later, in 1953, the source of the Amazon was identified as a stream called Huarco flowing from the Misuie glacier in the Peruvian Andes mountains.

By following the Amazon from its source and up the Rio Pará, it is possible to sail for 6,750 km (4,195 miles), which is slightly more than the length of the Nile. But geographers do not consider the entire route to be part of the Amazon basin, so the Nile is considered the world's longest river.

1 **Nile**\* flows through Burundi, Dem. Rep. of Congo, Egypt, Eritrea, Ethiopia, Kenya, Rwanda, Sudan, Tanzania, Uganda – 6,695 km (4,158 miles)
2 **Amazon** flows through Peru and Brazil – 6,448 km (4,007 miles)
3 **Chang Jiang (Yangtze)** flows through China – 6,378 km (3,964 miles)
4 **Huang He (Yellow)** flows through China – 5,464 km (3,395 miles)
5 **Amur** flows through China and Russia – 4,415 km (2,744 miles)
\* In 2006 the British and New Zealand Ascend the Nile team sailed from the mouth to the source of the river. Using Global Positioning, they measured their journey and came up with a total length 107 km (66.5 miles) longer than the official figure.

## Greatest waterfalls

The flow of many waterfalls varies according to the season, and some have been reduced by building dams to harness their power for hydro-electric plants.

The flow of the Boyoma waterfall is equivalent to 17m. litres (36m. gall) a second – enough to fill more than 140,000 baths per second, or enough for every person on Earth to have two baths a day!

1 **Boyoma (Stanley), Democratic Republic of Congo** – 17,000 m$^3$/sec (22,235 yd$^3$/sec)
2 **Khône, Laos** † – 11,330 m$^3$/sec (14,819 yd$^3$/sec)
3 **Niagara (Horseshoe), Canada** – 5,830 m$^3$/sec (7,625 yd$^3$/sec)
4 **Grande, Uruguay** – 4,500 m$^3$/sec (5,886 yd$^3$/sec)
5 **Paulo Afonso, Brazil** – 2,800 m$^3$/sec (3,662 yd$^3$/sec)
(Based on volume of water)
† Also the widest waterfall at 10.8 km (6.7 miles)

The Nile flowing through Cairo, Egypt

# Highest waterfalls

Waterfalls form when a river or stream goes over a drop, often where softer rocks are eroded faster than harder ones. The drop is the distance from top to bottom of the waterfall.

**1 Angel Falls, Carrao river, Venezuela** – 979 m (3,212 ft)*
**2 Tugela Falls, Tugela river, South Africa** – 948 m (3,110 ft)
**3 Ramnefjellsfossen, Jostedal Glacier, Nesdale, Norway** – 800 m (2,625 ft)
**4 Mongefossen Falls, Monge river, Mongebekk, Norway** – 774 m (2,540 ft)
**5 Gocta Cataracta, Cocahuayco river, Peru** – 771 m (2,531 ft)
**6 Mutarazi Falls, Mutarazi river, Zimbabwe** – 762 m (2,499 ft)
**7 Yosemite Falls, Yosemite Creek, California, USA** – 739 m (2,425 ft)
**8 Østre Mardøla Foss, Mardals river, Eikisdal, Norway** – 656 m (2,152 ft)
**9 Tyssestrengane Falls, Tysso river, Hardanger, Norway** – 646 m (2,120 ft)
**10 Cuquenán Falls, Arabopo river, Venezuela** – 610 m (2,000 ft)
* Longest single drop 807 m (2,648 ft)

## The Great Lakes

The Great Lakes are a group of five freshwater lakes in North America on the border between the USA and Canada. Superior is so called because it is higher upstream that the others. Huron takes its name from the name French settlers gave to a local Indian tribe (from *hure*, a boar's head). No one knows where the name Michigan comes from, but Erie and Ontario are both from the Iroquois language. Erie means cat, the animal the tribe used as its symbol. Ontario simply means beautiful lake.

**1 Superior, Canada/USA** – 82,414 sq km (31,820 sq miles)
**2 Huron, Canada/USA** – 59,596 sq km (23,010 sq miles)
**3 Michigan, USA** – 58,016 sq km (22,400 sq miles)
**4 Erie, Canada/USA** – 25,719 sq km (9,930 sq miles)
**5 Ontario, Canada/USA** – 19,477 sq km (7,520 sq miles)

# Longest glaciers

During the last Ice Age, more than 30 per cent of the Earth's surface was covered by glaciers – frozen rivers of ice that move very slowly. Today, as much as 10 per cent is covered with glaciers.

The Lambert-Fisher Glacier is the longest in the world and was discovered (from the air) in 1956. The longest glacier in North America is the Hubbard Glacier, Alaska, which measures 146 km (91 miles). The longest in Europe is the Aletsch Glacier, Switzerland, at 35 km (22 miles).

**1 Lambert-Fisher, Antarctica** – 515 km (320 miles)
**2 Novaya Zemlya, Russia** – 418 km (260 miles)
**3 Arctic Institute, Antarctica** – 362 km (225 miles)
**4 Nimrod-Lennox-King, Antarctica** – 290 km (180 miles)
**5 Denman, Antarctica** – 241 km (150 miles)

## Glaciers

Glaciers hold about 75 per cent of the world's fresh water. If all the glaciers melted, the world's sea level would rise about 70 m (230 ft).

# Greatest rivers

The volume of water flowing from the mouth of a river varies according to the season. The figures given are highest averages. The outflow of the Amazon would fill almost two million baths every second.

**1 Amazon** flows into the South Atlantic, Brazil at 219,000 m³/sec (286,441 yd³/sec)
**2 Ganges** flows into the Bay of Bengal, Bangladesh at 43,900 m³/sec (57,419 yd³/sec)
**3 Zaïre (Congo)** flows into the South Atlantic, Angola/Congo at 41,800 m³/sec (54,672 yd³/sec)
**4 Chang Jiang** flows into the Yellow Sea, China at 31,900 m³/sec (41,724 yd³/sec)
**5 Orinoco** flows into the South Atlantic, Venezuela at 31,900 m³/sec (41,724 yd³/sec)
**6 Plata-Paraná-Grande** flows into the South Atlantic, Uruguay at 25,700 m³/sec (33,614 yd³/sec)
(Based on rate of discharge at mouth)

## Lake fact file

● **Largest lake by volume and area**
The Caspian Sea (Russia, Kazakhstan, Turkmenistan, Azerbaijan and Iran) has a volume of 78,200 cubic km (18,760 cubic miles) and an area of 374,000 sq km (144,402 sq miles), making it the world's largest body of inland water. It would take 400 years for the entire contents of the Caspian to flow over Niagara Falls!

● **Largest freshwater lake by area**
Some geographers think that Lake Michigan and Lake Huron are one lake. They have a combined area of 117,612 sq km (45,410 sq miles) and have a larger area than half the world's countries.

● **Largest freshwater lake by volume and deepest lake**
Lake Baikal, Russia, contains 22,995 cubic km (5,517 cubic miles) of water. It has an average depth of 730 m (2,395 ft) and is 1,741m (5,712 ft) at its deepest point – deep enough to cover more than four Empire State Buildings piled on top of one another.

● **Fastest-shrinking lake**
In 1960, The Aral Sea (Kazakhstan and Uzbekistan) was 64,501 sq km (24,904 sq miles). Since then, feeder rivers have been diverted for irrigation and the lake has shrunk to about 28,000 sq km (10,811 sq miles). It is now in danger of disappearing.

## Wave height scale

The wave height scale describes the sort of waves that sailors might meet at sea. Wave height varies according to wind speed. High waves can be very dangerous, especially to small boats which can be turned over and even smashed.

**0 Glassy** – 0.0 m (0.0 ft)
**1 Calm** – 0.0–0.30 m (0.0–1.0 ft)
**2 Rippled** – 0.30–0.60 m (1.0–2.0 ft)
**3 Choppy** – 0.60–1.2 m (2.0–4.0 ft)
**4 Very choppy** – 1.2–2.4 m (4.0–7.9 ft)
**5 Rough** – 2.4–4.0 m (8.0–13.0 ft)
**6 Very rough** – 4.0–6.0 m (13.0–20.0 ft)
**7 High** – 6–9 m (20.0–30.0 ft)
**8 Very high** – 9.0–14 m (30.0–45.0 ft)
**9 Ultra high** –14.0 m+ (45.0 ft+)

Huge waves breaking over a lighthouse in Havana, Cuba during a hurricane

## Tsunami

The word tsunami comes from the Japanese *tsu* (meaning port) and *nami* (meaning wave). A tsunami is not a tidal wave, but a powerful surge of moving water caused by an earthquake or volcanic eruption beneath the sea bed.

There may be advance warning signs, such as bubbling water, a roaring noise and a sudden rise in water temperature. Tsunamis are rarely as high as tidal waves. However, powerful ones can cross huge distances, raising the sea level and destroying entire islands and coastal areas in their path. Lisbon, the capital of Portugal, was almost completely destroyed in 1755 by the combined effects of an earthquake, tsunami and fire. The worst recorded tsunami occurred in 2004 in South East Asia.

### Animal survivors

Amazingly, few animals died in the tsunami that hit Sri Lanka and other areas in 2004. Elephants, buffalo and tigers, as well as smaller animals, moved to high ground in time. Scientists think that they sensed soundwaves and changes in air pressure in advance of the wave and this gave them time to escape.

## Iceberg fact file

An iceberg is a large piece of ice that has broken away from a glacier or ice shelf. Icebergs in the North Atlantic mostly come from glaciers on Greenland, and those in the South Atlantic from the Antarctic.

● The word iceberg probably comes from the Dutch *ijsberg*, or ice hill.

● Icebergs float because they are made of fresh water, which is less dense than sea water.

● Seven-eighths of an iceberg is below the surface of the sea, hence the expression "the tip of the iceberg", which means that more is hidden than can be seen.

● The tallest iceberg measured was 168 m (551 ft) high. It was seen in 1958 off Greenland and was as tall as a 50-storey skyscraper.

● Icebergs less than 1 m (3.25 ft) high and 5 m (16.25 ft) wide are known as growlers because of the noise they make.

● Icebergs larger than growlers are called bergy bits; then they are graded small, medium, large or very large. Very large icebergs are those measuring more than 75 m (246 ft) high and 213 m (699 ft) wide.

● One of the biggest icebergs of recent times, known as B-15, broke away from the Ross Ice Shelf, Antarctica, in March 2000. It had an average length of 295 km (183 miles) and width of 37 km (23 miles), making it about the size of Jamaica!

● About 10,000 to 15,000 new icebergs are formed every year. The process is called "calving".

● The air trapped in icebergs is "harvested" and sold for use in drinks. It may be 3,000 years old.

# Longest coastlines

The coastline of Canada, including all its islands, is more than six times as long as the distance round the Earth at the Equator (40,076 km [24,902 miles]). Greenland (Kalaalit Nunaat) is not in this list as it is part of Denmark, not a separate country, but its coastline is 44,087 km (27,394 miles) long.

**1 Canada** – 265,523 km (164,988 miles)

**2 USA** – 133,312 km (82,836 miles)

**3 Russia** – 110,310 km (68,543 miles)

**4 Indonesia** – 95,181 km (59,143 miles)

**5 Chile** – 78,563 km (48,817 miles)

**6 Australia** – 66,530 km (41,340miles)

**7 Norway** – 53,199 km (33,056 miles)

**8 Philippines** – 33,900 km (21,064 miles)

**9 Brazil** – 33,379 km (20,741 miles)

**10 Finland** – 31,119 km (19,336 miles)

**11 China** 30,017 km (18,652 miles)

**12 Japan** 29,020 km (18,032 miles)

# Deepest oceans and seas

The Pacific Ocean is the deepest ocean. Its greatest depth is 10,924 m (35,837 ft) with an average depth of 4,028 m (13,215 ft). The Indian Ocean is 7,455 m (24,460 ft) at its deepest point and has an average depth of 3,963 m (13,002 ft). The Atlantic Ocean comes next with a greatest depth of 9,219 m (30,246 ft) and an average depth of 3,926 m (12,880 ft).

Giant feather stars live 198 m (650 ft) deep in Cayman Trench, Caribbean.

## Deep-sea trenches

There are about 20 deep trenches in the world's oceans. The eight deepest would be deep enough to submerge Mount Everest. The Marianas Trench is the deepest point in the deepest ocean, the Pacific. It was discovered in 1951 and explored in 1960 when Jacques Piccard (Switzerland) and Donald Walsh (USA) descended in their bathyscaphe *Trieste 2* to a depth that has since been calculated as 10,916 m (35,813 ft).

# Oceans and seas

Ocean is the term used for the world's sea water, except for landlocked seas such as the Caspian.

More than 70 per cent of the planet's surface is occupied by oceans – the Pacific Ocean alone is more than 25 per cent larger than the planet's entire land area. Smaller divisions of some oceans are separately named as seas.

**Pacific Ocean** – 166,240,000 sq km (64,185,629 sq miles)

**Atlantic Ocean** – 86,560,000 sq km (33,421,006 sq miles)

**Indian Ocean** – 73,430,000 sq km (28,351,484 sq miles)

**Arctic Ocean** – 13,230,000 sq km (5,108,132 sq miles)

**South China Sea** – 2,974,600 sq km (1,148,499 sq miles)

**Caribbean Sea** – 2,753,000 sq km (1,062,939 sq miles)

**Mediterranean Sea** – 2,510,000 sq km (969,116 sq miles)

**Bering Sea** – 2,261,000 sq km (872,977 sq miles)

**Gulf of Mexico** – 1,542,985 sq km (595,749 sq miles)

**Sea of Okhotsk** – 1,527,570 sq km (589,798 sq miles)

**East China Sea** – 1,249,150 sq km (482,299 sq miles)

**Sea of Japan** – 1,012,945 sq km (391,100 sq miles)

**Andaman Sea** – 797,700 sq km (307,993 sq miles)

**Hudson Bay** – 730,380 sq km (282,001 sq miles)

Global warming is melting the world's ice shelves. As ice floes shrink and drift apart, polar bears are forced to swim up to 97 km (60 miles) between them in search of prey. Some never make it and drown.

## See also

Worst natural disasters: page 47

● At least 500 incidents have been recorded of ships striking icebergs. In 1875, the crew of the schooner *Caledonia* was rescued after the ship sank and the men spent a night on an iceberg. The worst disaster involving an iceberg happened when the *Titanic* struck one on 14 April 1912 and 1,503 people died.

● During World War II, Lord Mountbatten led a programme to build artificial icebergs to use as aircraft carriers, but the project, codenamed Habbakuk, was abandoned.

www.oceansatlas.org          search

ARCTIC
OCEAN

*Beaufort
Sea*

Greenland

*Baffin
Bay*

*Bering
Sea*

*Gulf of
Alaska*

Rocky Mountains

NORTH
AMERICA

*Hudson
Bay*

*Labrador
Sea*

Great
Basin

Mojave
Desert

Sierra Madre

*Gulf of
Mexico*

## Climate

Weather and climate are not the
same. Weather is how hot, cold
or wet a place is at a particular time.
Climate is the average weather of an
area over time.

Several things decide the climate of an area, including
how far it is from the Equator, how far from the sea, its
height above sea level and its wind systems. The position
of a place on an area of land and the size of that land
area also affects the climate. Scientists divide the world
into different climate regions: polar and tundra,
temperate, tropical, desert and mountain.

## Warm temperate

These areas have mild winters and
warm to hot summers. There is rain all
year round, but there are plenty of sunny
days. This is an ideal climate for growing
crops such as citrus fruits, grapes and olives.

*Caribbean
Sea*

ATLANTIC
OCEAN

SOUTH
AMERICA

PACIFIC
OCEAN

Andes

Atacama Desert

Patagonian Desert

### Climate change

Climates have changed naturally
throughout history. But scientists think
that human activities, such as burning
fossil fuels, are producing greenhouse
gases such as carbon dioxide, and these
are causing global warming. The effects
include ocean currents altering, ice
sheets melting, sea levels rising and
severe weather, such as cyclones
and floods, becoming
more common.

The sea affects
the climate of
coastal regions,
keeping them
warmer than
inland areas in
winter and
cooler in
summer.

Key

Polar and Tundra

Cool temperate

Desert

Warm temperate

Tropical

Mountains

## Mountain

The climates of mountain
areas vary according to
altitude. The higher the
mountain, the colder it is. At a
certain point, called the tree
line, trees can no longer grow.
The climate in mountain
areas is usually wetter than in
the lowlands around them.

ARCTIC OCEAN

*Barents Sea*

*Kara Sea*

Arctic Circle

**Cool temperate**

These areas have warm summers and cool winters. In the northern areas the winters can be very cold. Rain falls all year round. Much of this area was once covered with forest.

*Kölen*

*Baltic Sea*

EUROPE

*Alps*

*nees*

*Black Sea*

*Caucasus*

*Caspian Sea*

*Mediterranean Sea*

*Kirghiz Steppe*

*Altai Mts*

ASIA

*Tien Shan*

*Kara Kum*

*Takla Makan*

*Gobi Desert*

*Hindu Kush*

*Kunlun Mts*

*Zagros Mts*

*The Gulf*

*Plateau of Tibet*

*Himalayas*

*Thar Desert*

S a h a r a
D e s e r t

*Red Sea*

*Arabian Peninsula*

*Ethiopian Highlands*

AFRICA

*Arabian Sea*

*Bay of Bengal*

*Sea of Okhotsk*

*Sea of Japan*

**Polar and tundra**

The areas around the North and South Pole are called the Arctic and Antarctic. Both have an average temperature of 0°–10°C (32°–50°F) in summer and as little as -50°C (-58°F) in winter. Few plants can grow. The tundra is land surrounding the Arctic. In summer small plants grow here.

Tropic of Cancer

*Philippine Sea*

*South China Sea*

PACIFIC OCEAN

Equator

INDIAN OCEAN

*Java Sea*

*Arafura Sea*

*Coral Sea*

*Great Sandy Desert*

*Gibson Desert*

*Simpson Desert*

AUSTRALIA

*Great Victoria Desert*

Tropic of Capricorn

*Namib Desert*

*Kalahari Desert*

*Tasman Sea*

*Southern Alps*

**Tropical**

These areas are hot all year round. In some parts there is heavy rain all year round, too, and that is where rainforests grow. Rainforest plants fruit and flower all year. In other tropical areas, such as savannas and scrubland, there are dry seasons and rainy seasons, when most of the year's rain falls.

**Desert**

True deserts are very hot – 40°C (104°F) or more – during the day, but cold at night. They are very dry and what little rain there is falls in short sudden bursts and evaporates quickly. Few plants can grow in deserts but some animals manage to survive.

SOUTHERN OCEAN

Antarctic Circle

ANTARCTICA

http://www.wmo.ch          search

# The Beaufort scale

The Beaufort scale was introduced in 1806 by British Admiral Sir Francis Beaufort (1774–1857) to describe wind effects on a fully rigged man-of-war ship. It was later extended to describe how winds affect land features such as trees.

The Beaufort scale is divided into values from 0 for calm winds to 12 and above for hurricanes. Forecasters often describe winds by their force number – for example, a force 10 gale. Wind speed can also be measured in knots: 1 knot = 1.85 km/h (1.15 mph).

**0 Calm**: 0–2 km/h (> 1 mph)  Smoke rises vertically; the sea is mirror smooth

**1 Light air**: 3–6 km/h (1–3 mph)  Smoke indicates the direction of the wind

**2 Slight breeze**: 7–11 km/h (4–7 mph)  Wind felt on the face and leaves rustle in trees

**3 Gentle breeze**: 12–19 km/h (8–12 mph)  Wind extends a light flag

**4 Moderate breeze**: 20–28 km/h (13–18 mph)  Loose paper blows around; frequent whitecaps at sea

**5 Fresh breeze**: 29–38 km/h (19–24 mph)  Small trees sway

**6 Strong breeze**: 39–49 km/h (25–31 mph)  Wind whistles in telephone wires; some spray on the sea's surface

**7 High wind**: 50–61 km/h (32–38 mph)  Large trees sway

**8 Gale**: 62–74 km/h (39–46 mph)  Twigs break from trees; long streaks of foam on the sea

**9 Strong gale**: 75–88 km/h (47–54 mph)  Branches break from trees

**10 Whole gale**: 89–102 km/h (55–63 mph)  Trees uprooted; sea takes on a white appearance

**11 Storm** At a speed of 103–117 km/h (64–72 mph)  Widespread damage

**12 Hurricane** At speeds of more than 118 km/h+ (73 mph+)  Structural damage on land; storm waves at sea

A satellite image of Earth shows a hurricane over the Caribbean Sea.

**Altocumulus** 2,000–7,000 m (6,562–22,966 ft)

**Cirrocumulus** 5,000–13,500 m (16,404–44,291 ft)

**Cirrus** 5,000–13,500 m (16,404–44,291 ft)

**Cirrostratus** 5,000–13,500 m (16,404–44,291 ft)

**Cumulonimbus** 450–2,000 m (1,476–6,562 ft)

## Cloud layers
There are ten types of clouds. Each has a characteristic shape and appears at certain levels in the sky. All types would not appear together as in this diagram.

**Altostratus** 2,000–7,000 m (6,562–22,966 ft)

**Stratus** below 450 m (1,476 ft)

**Stratocumulus** 450–2,000 m (1,476–6,562 ft)

**Cumulus** 450–2,000 m (1,476–6,562 ft)

**Nimbostratus** 900–3,000 m (2,953–9,843 ft)

## Hottest and coldest

The hottest place where people live is Djibouti, in the Republic of Djibouti, Africa. The average temperature is 30°C (86°F). Next hottest are Timbuktu in Mali and Tirunelevi in India, both 29.3°C (84.7°F). The coldest place where people live is Norilsk, Russia, with an average temperature of -10.9°C (12.38°F). Next coldest is Yakutsk in Russia, at -10.1°C (13.8°F).

# World extremes

### Windiest place on Earth
Commonwealth Bay, Antarctica, has some consistently high wind speeds, occasionally reaching 320 km/h (200 mph). The highest individual gust of wind measured was 371 km/h (231 mph) at Mt Washington, USA, on 12 April 1934.

### Tornado wind speed
Fastest 450 km/h (280 mph) at Wichita Falls, Texas, USA, on 2 April 1958.

### Hurricane wind speed
The fastest sustained winds in a hurricane in the USA measured 322 km/h (200 mph), with 338 km/h (210 mph) gusts, on 17–18 August 1969, when Hurricane Camille hit the Mississippi/Alabama coast.

### Hottest place on Earth
Dallol in Ethiopia had an average temperature of 34.4°C (94°F) during 1960–66.

### Highest shade temperature recorded
Al'Aziziyah, Libyan desert, 57.8°C (136°F) on 13 September 1922. A temperature of 56.6°C (134°F) was recorded at Death Valley, California, USA, on 10 July 1913.

### Least sunshine
At the South Pole there is no sunshine for 182 days every year, and at the North Pole the same applies for 176 days.

### Driest place
Atacama Desert, Chile, where average annual rainfall is officially nil (also longest drought – 400 years up to 1971). The average rainfall on the Pacific coast of Chile between Arica and Antofagasta is less than 1 mm (0.04 in).

### Coldest place
Vostok, Antarctica, -89.2°C (-129°F) on 21 July 1983.

## Tornados

Tornadoes, or twisters, are columns of air that spin violently, reaching speeds of over 420 km/h (260 mph). They destroy crops and any houses or vehicles in their path. Tornadoes are rare in the UK, but one struck Kensal Rise, London, on 7 December 2006, damaging houses and cars. In the book and film of *The Wizard of Oz* (1939) Dorothy is carried by a tornado from her Kansas home to the magical land of Oz.

## Tools of the trade

Weather forecasters use a range of instruments. Balloons, radar stations and orbiting satellites also provide increasingly accurate weather information, and computer programs are able to make detailed forecasts.

### Anemometer

Wind speed is measured by a cup anemometer. This has three or four cups that rotate round a vertical rod. The speed at which the wind spins the cups round is recorded by a counter. A wind vane shows the direction of wind, and an anemograph records the speed on a chart.

### Rain gauge

Rain gauges – containers that measure the amount of rain that has fallen – date from ancient China and India. In 1662, British architect Sir Christopher Wren invented a tipping bucket rain gauge, which emptied itself when full.

### Thermometer

Galileo invented the thermsocope, a form of thermometer. Later, sealed thermometers using mercury, which expands in a narrow tube as the temperature rises, were developed. Gabriel Fahrenheit's scale dates from 1714, and that of Anders Celsius from 1742. The maximum and minimum thermometer, which records the highest and lowest temperatures reached over a period of time, was invented by James Six at Cambridge in 1780.

A tornado sets down in a field.

www.metoffice.gov.uk        search

### Greatest snowfall in 12 months
31,102 mm (1,224 in) at Mt Rainier, Washington, USA, from 19 February 1971 to 18 February 1972. This is an incredible 31 m (102 ft), equivalent to 17 people standing on each other's heads!

### Greatest depth of snow
11.46 m (38 ft) at Tamarac, California, USA, in March 1911.

### Freak snow storm
In the Sahara Desert, Algeria, 18 February 1979.

### Heaviest hailstones
Coffeyville, Kansas, USA, 0.75 kg (1.65 lb), 3 September 1970. The largest hailstone – 17.8 cm (7 in) diameter – fell in Aurora, Nebraska on 22 June 2003.

### Most rainfall in 24 hours
Cilaos, La Réunion, 1,870 mm (74 in), 15–16 March, 1952.

### Greatest annual rainfall (extreme example)
Cherrapunji, Assam, India, 26,461 mm (1,042 in) between 1 August 1860 and 31 July 1861 – which is close to the length of a tennis court! Also, at the same place, the greatest in one calendar month – 9,300 mm (366 in) – fell in July 1861. That's about the same as five people standing on each other's heads.

### Greatest annual rainfall (annual average)
Mawsynram, India, with 11,870 mm (467 in) a year; and Tutunendo, Colombia, 11,770 mm (463 in).

### Most rainy days in a year
Mt Waialeale, Kauai, Hawaii, USA, up to 350 days a year. The total rainfall is about 11,684 mm (460 in), which approaches the annual record.

# Volcanic eruptions

## Santorini
The eruption of the Greek island of Santorini in c1450 BC is believed to have been one of the most powerful ever.

## Vesuvius, Italy
On 24 August AD 79 Vesuvius erupted with little warning, engulfing the Roman city of Herculaneum in a mud flow. Nearby Pompeii was buried under a vast layer of pumice and volcanic ash. This preserved the city, including the bodies of many of its inhabitants, until it was excavated by archaeologists in the 19th and 20th centuries. As many as 20,000 people died. Vesuvius erupted again in 1631, killing up to 18,000 people.

## Laki, Iceland
Iceland is one of the most volcanically active places on Earth, but the population is small so eruptions seldom cause many deaths. On 11 June 1783 the largest lava flow ever recorded engulfed many villages in a river of lava up to 80 km (50 miles) long and 30 m (98 ft) deep. It released poisonous gases that killed those who managed to escape the lava flow – up to 20,000 people.

## Unsen, Japan
On 1 April 1793 the volcanic island of Unsen, or Unzen, completely disappeared, killing all 53,000 inhabitants.

## Tambora, Indonesia
On the island of Sumbawa the eruption of Tambora between 5 and 12 April 1815 killed about 10,000 islanders immediately. A further 82,000 died later from disease and famine. This made it the worst-ever eruption for loss of human life.

## Krakatoa, Sumatra/Java
The uninhabited island of Krakatoa exploded on 27 August 1883 with what may have been the biggest bang ever heard by humans. People heard it up to 4,800 km (2,980 miles) away!

## Mont Pelée, Martinique
Mont Pelée began to erupt in April 1902, after lying dormant for centuries. The 30,000 residents of the main city, St Pierre, were told that they were not in danger, so stayed in their homes. They were there on 8 May when the volcano burst apart and showered the port with molten lava, ash and gas, destroying all buildings and killing as many as 40,000 people.

## Nevado del Ruiz, Colombia
In 1985 this Andean volcano gave warning signs that it was about to erupt, but the local people were not evacuated soon enough. On 13 November the hot steam, rocks and ash ejected from Nevado del Ruiz melted its icecap, causing a mudslide. This completely engulfed the town of Armero, killing 22,940 people.

## Earthquake detector
Chinese astronomer Chan Heng (AD 78–139) invented an earthquake detector made of a vase adorned with dragons' heads and surrounded by metal frogs. In each of the dragons' jaws was a carefully balanced ball. When the first tremors of an earthquake made the device vibrate, the balls fell into the frogs' mouths, making a noise to warn of the coming danger.

Mount St Helens erupting in 1980

## Avalanche!
An avalanche caused by the eruption of the Mount St Helens volcano, Washington, USA, on 18 May 1980, was reckoned to have travelled at 400 km/h (249 mph).

A volcano erupts on Réunion Island in the Indian Ocean. (Inset) Lava pouring from an erupting volcano

www.earthquake.usgs.gov/4kids          search

## The Richter scale

Seismic waves are vibrations from earthquakes that travel through the Earth. Sensitive instruments called seismographs can record the waves, even at great distances, and calculate their strength and location.

The Richter scale indicates the magnitude or strength of an earthquake based on the size of the seismic waves (the distance the ground moves). The biggest earthquake (9 on the Richter scale) is a billion times greater than the smallest.

**0** Detected by sensitive seismographs (some can detect magnitudes of less than zero!)

**1** Detected by instruments

**2** Lowest felt by humans

**3** Slight vibration; more than 100,000 a year around the world

**4** Up to 15,000 a year; at 4.5, would be detected by seismographs worldwide, but cause little damage

**5** 3,000 a year; the 1960 earthquake in Agadir, Morocco was 5.6

**6** 100 a year worldwide

**7** 20 a year; the 1995 earthquake in Kobe, Japan was 7.2

**8** Major destructive earthquakes; average two a year; the 1904 San Francisco earthquake was probably 8.25

**9** No quake higher than 8.9 has been recorded, but 9.0 or even higher is theoretically possible

## Earthquake

Earthquakes are movements of the Earth's surface, often as a result of a fault, or fracture, in the crust. They happen more often in some parts of the world than others. In heavily populated areas, they cause great damage to buildings and loss of life.

### Worst ever
An earthquake affecting the Middle East and North Africa on 20 May 1202 may have been the worst in human history. Up to 1,000,000 people were killed, 110,000 in Cairo, Egypt alone.

### Most powerful
The worst earthquake affecting an inhabited area was in Assam, India on 12 June 1897. It is reckoned to have reached 8.7, killing about 1,500. The Colombia/Ecuador earthquake of 31 January 1906 was 8.9 on the Richter scale. Fortunately, it was 300 km (200 miles) off the coast, and so resulted in fewer than 1,000 deaths on land.

### Worst modern earthquakes
An earthquake in Tang-shan, China, on 28 July 1976, killed 242,419. The Kashmir quake of 8 October 2005 officially killed 87,350 people, but it may have been more than 100,000.

### Longest-lasting
Most earthquakes last only a minute or two, but the Alaska earthquake of 27 March 1964 continued for at least five minutes and registered 8.6 on the Richter scale. It killed only 131 people but caused more than $450 million (£162 million) worth of damage.

## Worst natural disasters

### Drought
Serious droughts kill people and livestock and destroy crops. The drought in Australia in 1982 cost £3.5 billion ($6 billion), and one in Spain in 1995 cost £3 billion ($4.7 billion).

### Flood
Floods caused by China's Huang He, or Yellow River, were first recorded in 2297 BC. The river has flooded at least 1,500 times since. In 1887 floods killed between 1.5 and 7 million people, making it the worst flood ever.

### Tsunami
On 26 December 2004 a tsunami created by an undersea earthquake caused catastrophic floods in Indonesia, Sri Lanka, Myanmar, the Maldives, Malaysia, India and parts of Africa. More than 283,100 people died.

### Hurricane
The worst hurricanes of the 21st century are Hurricane Jeanne (2004), which killed over 3,000 in Haiti, and Katrina (2005), which killed 1,417 in Louisiana, USA, and neighbouring states.

# Life
## Sciences

### Clouded leopard

The clouded leopard is found in south-east Asia. Little is known about its behaviour in the wild, due to its reclusive nature. In 2007 scientists identified the Bornean clouded leopard, which inhabits the islands of Borneo and Sumatra, as an entirely new species of big cat.

# TREES AND PLANTS

## Top food plants

Every year the people of the world eat more than 2 billion tonnes of cereals, 888 million tonnes of vegetables and 512 million tonnes of fruit. These figures come from the Food and Agriculture Organization of the United Nations, or FAO, which is based in Rome. The aim of the FAO is to help people around the world grow more food and eat a better diet.

**Sugar cane** 1,285,388,292 tonnes per annum
**Maize** 711,762,871 tonnes p.a.
**Wheat** 630,556,602 tonnes p.a.
**Rice** 621,588,528 tonnes p.a.
**Potatoes** 324,491,141 tonnes p.a.
**Sugar beet** 251,289,226 tonnes p.a.
**Soybeans** 213,976,284 tonnes p.a.
**Cassava** 213,024,811 tonnes p.a.
**Barley** 139,220,431 tonnes p.a.
**Tomatoes** 124,663,053 tonnes p.a.
**Sweet potatoes** 122,728,053 tonnes p.a.
**Watermelons** 97,497,401 tonnes p.a.
**Bananas** 74,236,885 tonnes p.a.
**Cabbages** 68,133,011 tonnes p.a.
**Grapes** 66,901,419 tonnes p.a.
**Apples** 62,356,095 tonnes p.a.
**Oranges** 60,188,121 tonnes p.a.
**Sorghum** 59,722,088 tonnes p.a.
**Onions** 59,512,356 tonnes p.a.
**Coconuts** 54,254,232 tonnes p.a.

### Important crops

These are the most important crops grown for uses other than food.

**Cotton** (clothing, household items)
67,803,392 tonnes a year
**Rubber** (tyres, shoes, balls, erasers)
8,965,567 tonnes a year
**Tobacco** (cigarettes, cigars)
6,603,571 tonnes a year
**Jute** (sacks, rope)
3,113,336 tonnes a year

A woman going to work in rice fields in Vietnam

## American plants

As many as 30 per cent of the world's most useful plants originally came from North, Central and South America. Early European explorers discovered the plants while on their travels and took them back home to grow.

This was not always easy. Pineapples were so difficult and expensive to cultivate in Europe that they became a symbol of wealth – carved stone pineapples are often seen on the gateposts of many grand houses.

### US plants

Here are some of the plants that originally came from America – avocado, beans (kidney, French, etc), cashew nut, cassava, chilli pepper, cocoa, corn, cranberry, loganberry, peanut, pecan, pineapple, potato, pumpkin, quinine, rubber, squash/gourd, sunflower, tobacco, tomato, vanilla

 avocado

chilli pepper

peanut

tomato

 squash

## World forests

Forests cover 29.6 per cent of Earth's land and almost a quarter of these are in Russia. There are three main types of forest which grow in particular climates in different parts of the world.

● Tropical forests or rainforests grow near the Equator where it is always hot and wet. Here, temperatures are about 20–25°C (68–77°F) and there is more than 200 cm (79 in) of rain a year.

● Temperate forests grow in places that have hot summers and cold winters. The summers can be as hot as 30°C (86°F) and winters as cold as -30°C (-22°F). Average rainfall is about 75–150 cm (30–59 in) a year. Many trees are deciduous (drop their leaves in autumn).

● Boreal or taiga forests grow in Russia, Canada and elsewhere in the far north. Winters are long and very cold. There is rainfall of 40–100 cm (16–39 in) a year, but most falls as snow. Most trees are evergreen conifers (cone-producing trees with needle-like leaves).

## Dangerous plants

● Potatoes are safe to eat when cooked, but the stems and leaves of the plants contain a poison called solanine. If potatoes turn green, they may also contain solanine.

● Ricin is extracted from the seeds of the castor oil plant and is more poisonous than cyanide or snake venom. Even minute doses of ricin can be fatal.

● Opium is extracted from the juice of a poppy and contains morphine. Small quantities of both are used legally as painkillers and illegally as drugs. Both can easily cause death.

● The death cap is a highly poisonous mushroom. It is responsible for almost 90 per cent of deaths from eating fungi. The poison causes severe diarrhoea and vomiting.

● Curare is extracted from the bark of certain trees and is used by South American Indian tribes to tip their poison arrows when they go hunting.

● Deadly nightshade is also known as belladonna. It contains a poison called atropine. Less than 10 milligrams (0.0004 oz) could kill a child.

● Nicotine is a yellow oily liquid found in tobacco. About 50 milligrams (0.002 oz) of nicotine would kill an adult within minutes.

● The leaves of the purple foxglove contain digitalis and eating just a few can be fatal. Digitalis is used in tiny doses to treat people suffering from heart disease.

Purple foxglove

### Largest and smelliest flower

The flower of the rafflesia, or stinking corpse lily, measures almost 1 m (3.3 ft) across and weighs 11 kg (24 lb). It is one of the world's smelliest flowers, with an odour like rotting flesh. The smell attracts flies, which pollinate the plant.

Children investigating a Rafflesia flower

## Record-breaking plants

● **Tallest tree**
The world's tallest tree is called the Stratosphere Giant. It grows in the Rockefeller Forest, Humboldt Redwoods State Park, California. At 112.32 m (369 ft), this redwood is almost three times the height of the Statue of Liberty in New York.

● **Biggest living thing**
The General Sherman giant sequoia in Sequoia National Park, California, USA, is the world's largest living thing. It is 83.8 m (275 ft) tall and measures 2.53 m (8.3 ft) round its mighty trunk. Including its huge root system, the tree weighs about 2,000 tonnes.

● **Oldest trees**
The bristlecone pines in California and Nevada, USA, are almost 5,000 years old and were long believed to be the oldest trees. Latest research suggests that creosote bushes in the USA's Mojave Desert may be even older – some of these plants began life nearly 12,000 years ago.

● **Smallest flowering plant**
*Wolffia*, a kind of duckweed, is just 0.6 mm (0.024 in) long and weighs about as much as two grains of salt. Its seeds are also the tiniest known – they weigh only 70 micrograms (0.0000025 oz), as much as a single grain of salt.

www.fao.org       search

# Grouping living things

Living things are organized by scientists into five groups called kingdoms. These are: Animals (Animalia); Algae and protozoans (Protoctista); Bacteria (Prokaryotae); Mushrooms, moulds and lichens (Fungi); Plants (Plantae).

The animal kingdom alone has thousands of different species. A species is a type of animal, and animals of the same species can breed successfully with each other. Similar species are grouped in a genus. Genera are grouped into families, families into orders, right up to the level of phylum. The phylum chordata contains all vertebrate animals – animals with a backbone. Here's how a human and a giant panda are classified.

|         | Human       | Giant panda  |
|---------|-------------|--------------|
| Phylum  | Chordata    | Chordata     |
| Class   | Mammalia    | Mammalia     |
| Order   | Primates    | Carnivores   |
| Family  | Hominidae   | Ursidae      |
| Genus   | *Homo*      | *Ailuropoda* |
| Species | *sapiens*   | *melanoleuca*|

## Zoo shopping list

Shopping to feed 650 different species of animals is hard work, but that is the task of keepers at London Zoo. Below is the zoo's basic shopping list for a year.

| | |
|---|---|
| **Hay** 47 tonnes | **Oranges** 4.5 tonnes |
| **Bananas** 29 tonnes | **Grapes** 4 tonnes |
| **Apples** 29 tonnes | **Potatoes** 3.1 tonnes |
| **Straw** 28 tonnes | **Tomatoes** 2.78 tonnes |
| **Clover** 26 tonnes | **Honey** 0.25 tonnes |
| **Fish** 19 tonnes | **Eggs** 38,000 (number) |
| **Food pellets** 18 tonnes | **Lettuces** 15,860 (number) |
| **Carrots** 13 tonnes | **Cabbages** 8,320 (number) |
| **Meat** 9 tonnes | **Milk** 975 litres (2,060 pt) |

# Animal species

Below is a list of the animals we know about. No one knows exactly how many species there may be altogether. New species are always being found and there may be tens of millions not yet discovered.

Some experts think there may be millions of species of insects and at least a million species of deep-sea fish that no one has ever seen. About half of all known creatures and plants live in tropical rainforests. In a study of just 19 trees in a tropical rainforest, 1,200 beetle species were found. About 80 per cent of these had not been seen before.

- **Arachnids** 75,500 (spiders, scorpions, etc)
- **Molluscs** 70,000 (snails, clams, etc)
- **Crustaceans** 40,000 (shrimps, crabs, etc)
- **Fish** 29,300
- **Nematodes** 20,000 (unsegmented worms)
- **Flatworms** 17,500
- **Segmented worms** 12,000
- **Sponges** 10,000
- **Birds** 9,934
- **Jellyfish, coral, etc** 9,000
- **Reptiles** 8,240
- **Starfish** 6,000
- **Amphibians** 5,918
- **Mammals** 5,416

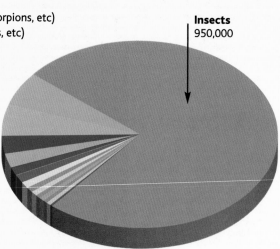

**Insects**
**950,000**

---

## Life on Earth     3,900 million years ago

The first simple life forms began to appear on Earth almost four billion years ago. More familiar animals appeared about 500 million years ago, and humans only within the past two million. We know a little about extinct creatures and early humans from fossil remains found in rocks from each period.

**3,900–2,500 million years ago**
Archaean period – the earliest marine life form (blue-green algae)

**2,500–540 million years ago**
Proterozoic period – the first many-celled organisms evolve

**540–490 million years ago**
Cambrian period – the first fossils of animals with shells and skeletons

**490–443 million years ago**
Ordovician period – molluscs, some corals and fishlike vertebrates

**443–417 million years ago**
Silurian period – fish develop jaws; first sharks

**417–354 million years ago**
Devonian period – fish dominant; amphibians (the first land animals) evolve

**354–290 million years ago**
Carboniferous period – insects; first reptiles

**290–248 million years ago**
Permian period – insects evolve into modern types; reptiles evolve

**248–206 million years ago**
Triassic period – early dinosaurs; marine reptiles

## How fast?

Most of the creatures in this list can keep up these speeds for only a short time – less than an hour. The peregrine falcon achieves its speed as it dives through the air to catch prey, not in level flight.

**Peregrine falcon** (diving speed) 298 km/h (185 mph)

**Spine-tailed swift** 171 km/h (106 mph)

**Eider duck** 113 km/h (70 mph)

**Sailfish** (fastest fish) 110 km/h (68 mph)

**Cheetah** (fastest on land) 105 km/h (65 mph)

**Pronghorn antelope** 89 km/h (55 mph)

**Racing pigeon** 80 km/h (50 mph)

**Lion** (charging) 80 km/h (50 mph)

**Brown hare** 72 km/h (45 mph)

**Ostrich** (fastest flightless bird) 72 km/h (45 mph)

**Blue shark** 69 km/h (43 mph)

**Horse** 69 km/h (43 mph)

**Greyhound** 68 km/h (42 mph)

**Killer whale** 56 km/h (35 mph)

**Death's head hawkmoth** (fastest-flying insect) 53 km/h (33 mph)

**Guano bat** (fastest-flying mammal) 51 km/h (32 mph)

**Butterfly** 48 km/h (30 mph)

**California sea lion** 40 km/h (25 mph)

**Dolphin** 40 km/h (25 mph)

**Fastest man over 100 m (328 ft)** 37km/h (23 mph)

Peregrine falcon

### Oldest creature?

On 23 March 2006 a giant tortoise called Adwayita died at the Alipore Zoo, Kolkata (Calcutta). He was brought to the zoo in the 1860s from the estate of Lord Robert Clive. He may even have been up to 250 years old when he died.

## How long do they live?

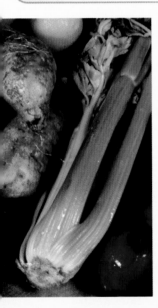

Who would have thought that a sea anemone could live for 80 years? All these figures are the longest ever recorded. Most of these animals have much shorter lives.

**Marine clam** 200
**Giant tortoise** 150
**Human** 122
**Killer whale** 90
**Sea anemone** 80
**Asiatic elephant** 78
**American alligator** 66
**Blue macaw** 64
**Horse** 62
**Chimpanzee** 56

**Hippopotamus** 54
**Slow-worm** 54
**Beaver** 50
**Bactrian camel** 50
**Grizzly bear** 50
**Blue whale** 45
**Boa constrictor** 40
**Domestic cat** 34
**Lion** 30
**Pig** 27

**Common rabbit** 18
**Queen ant** 18
**Giant centipede** 10
**Millipede** 7
**House mouse** 6
**Bedbug** 6 months
**Common housefly** (male) 2 weeks

A mouse can live for up to six years

**2000s**

**206–144 million years ago**
Jurassic period – reptiles dominate land, sea and air; *Archaeopteryx* (first bird) appears; first mammals

**144–65 million years ago**
Cretaceous period – dinosaurs become extinct; snakes and lizards appear

**65–55 million years ago**
Palaeocene period – first large land mammals

**55–34 million years ago**
Eocene period – modern land mammals and whales appear

**34–24 million years ago**
Oligocene period – modern mammals dominant

**24–5 million years ago**
Miocene period – modern mammals eg primates; birds

**5–1.8 million years ago**
Pliocene period – human-like apes appear

**1.8–10,000 million years ago**
Pleistocene period – humans appear

**10,000 million years ago to present**
Holocene period – human civilization

http://animaldiversity.ummz.umich.edu     search

# Types of mammal

A mammal is a warm-blooded vertebrate (animal with a backbone) with some hair on its body. Female mammals feed their young on milk from their mammary glands. Most mammals give birth to live young which develop inside the mother's body, but echidnas and the platypus lay eggs.

Marsupial mammals such as kangaroos give birth to live young, but they are very small and weak. They finish their development in a pouch on the mother's body. There are 21 main groups, or orders, of mammals. Listed below are the names of the main mammal groups, examples of the animals and the approximate number of known species. Common names are given where possible.

**Rodents** Beavers, squirrels, mice, rats, porcupines, voles, guinea pigs, chinchillas 2,052

**Chiroptera** Bats 977

**Insectivores** Shrews, moles, hedgehogs, tenrecs 440

**Marsupials** Opossums, koalas, bandicoots, kangaroos, wallabies, numbat 292

**Primates** Lemurs, lorises, tarsiers, marmosets, monkeys, gibbons, apes, humans 270

**Carnivores** Dogs, foxes, wolves, cats, bears, hyenas, raccoons, civets, mongooses, weasels, pandas 249

**Even-toed ungulates** Pigs, peccaries, giraffe, okapi, hippopotamuses, deer, camels, llamas, antelopes, cattle 225

**Cetacea** Whales, dolphins, porpoises 83

**Lagomorphia** Rabbits, hares, pikas 80

**Pinnipedia** Seals, sea-lions, walruses 34

**Edentates** Anteaters, sloths, armadillos 29

**Odd-toed ungulates** Horses, asses, zebras, rhinos, tapirs 19

**Scandentia** Tree shrews 19

**Macroscelidea** Elephant-shrews 15

**Monotremes** Duck-billed platypus, echidnas 5

**Hyracoidea** Hyraxes 8

**Pholidota** Pangolins 7

**Sirenia** Manatees, dugong 4

**Proboscidea** Elephants 3

**Dermoptera** Flying lemurs 2

**Tubulidentata** Aardvark 1

## Big babies

The African elephant has the longest pregnancy of any mammal. She carries her baby for an average of 660 days. When the baby is born it weighs 90–120 kg (198–265 lb). A baby blue whale is even bigger. It weighs 2,000 kg (4,409 lb) and is 7 m (23 ft) long. It puts on weight at the astonishing rate of 90 kg (198 lb) a day.

African elephant

## Biggest and smallest

The following are the biggest land mammals according to weight:

**African elephant** 7,000 kg (14,432 lb)
**White rhinoceros** 3,600 kg (7,937 lb)
**Hippopotamus** 2,500 kg (5,512 lb)
**Giraffe** 1,600 kg (3,527 lb)
**American bison** 1,000 kg (2,205 lb)
**Arabian camel** (dromedary) 690 kg (1,521 lb)
**Polar bear** 600 kg (1,521 lb)

The following are the smallest land mammals, according to length:

**Kitti's hog-nosed bat** 2.9 cm (1.1 in)
**Pygmy shrew** 3.6 cm (1.4 in)
**Pipistrelle bat** 4.0 cm (1.6 in)
**Little brown bat** 4.0 cm (1.6 in)
**Masked shrew** 4.5 cm (1.8 in)
**Southern blossom bat** 5.0 cm (2.0 in)
**Harvest mouse** 5.8 cm (2.3 in)

## Big cats

Big cats like lions are perhaps the most powerful of all mammal predators. These measurements are from the nose to the tip of the tail. The length of tail varies – a leopard's tail can be as long as 110 cm (43 in) and a jaguar's tail as short as 45 cm (18 in).

**Tiger** (Asia) 330 cm (130 in)
**Leopard** (Asia, Africa) 320 cm (126 in)
**Lion** (Africa, Asia) 280 cm (110 in)
**Jaguar** (North, Central and South America) 271 cm (107 in)
**Mountain lion** (North, Central and South America) 245 cm (96 in)
**Snow leopard** (Asia) 240 cm (94 in)
**Cheetah** (Africa, Asia) 220 cm (87 in)
**Clouded leopard** (Asia) 197 cm (75 in)

# Bears of the world

Scientists have long argued about whether the giant panda should be grouped with the raccoon family or the bears. DNA tests have now proved that it belongs with the bears. The koala, often called koala bear, is actually a marsupial not a bear.

**Polar bear** (Arctic) Length up to 257cm (101 in); weight 200–800 kg (440–1,760 lb)

**Brown (grizzly) bear** (North America, Europe, Asia) Length up to 290 cm (114 in); weight 136–390 kg (300–860 lb)

**American black bear** (North America) Length 127–191 cm (50–75 in); weight 60–300 kg (130–660 lb)

**Asiatic black bear** (Southern Asia) Length 127–188 cm (50–74 in); weight 100–200 kg (220–440 lb)

**Sloth bear** (Asia) Length 152–191 cm (60–75 in); weight 80–140 kg (175–310 lb)

**Giant panda** (China) Length 122–152 cm (48–60 in); weight up to 125 kg (275 lb)

**Spectacled bear** (South America) Length 152–183 cm (60–72 in); weight 70–113 kg (150–250 lb)

**Sun bear** (Asia) Length 122–152 cm (48–60 in); weight 27–65 kg (60–145 lb)

# Champion divers

Lots of mammals can dive underwater, including humans, but whales are the champions. All have to hold their breath. These are average dives.

**Northern bottlenose whale** 120 mins

**Sperm whale** 112 mins

**Greenland whale** 60 mins

**Seal** 22 mins

**Beaver** 20 mins

**Dugong** 16 mins

**Hippopotamus** 15 mins

**Porpoise** 15 mins

**Muskrat** 12 mins

**Duck-billed platypus** 10 mins

**Sea otter** 5 mins

**Human pearl diver** 2.5 mins

**Human** 1 min

Western lowland gorilla

## Intelligence

Edward O. Wilson, professor of Zoology at Harvard, researched the intelligence of mammals. He defined intelligence on the basis of how fast and how well an animal can learn a wide range of tasks. He also took into account the size of the animal's brain compared with its body. His top ten most intelligent mammals, in order are: human, chimpanzee, gorilla, orang-utan, baboon, gibbon, monkey, small-toothed whale, dolphin and elephant.

## Monkeys and apes

Monkeys and apes (and humans) belong to the group of mammals called primates. There are 256 known species of primate. The smallest is the pygmy mouse lemur, which weighs only 30 g (1 oz). The largest is the gorilla, which weighs 220 kg (485 lb). The human comes next at 77 kg (170 lb).

Siberian tiger cubs in the snow

# Reptiles

A reptile is a vertebrate animal with a body covered in tough scales. Most reptiles live on land, but turtles and some kinds of snake live in water.

Crocodiles and their relatives spend time on land and in water. There are more than 8,000 species of reptiles, which are divided into the following groups.

**Lizards** 4,765 species
**Snakes** 2,978 species
**Turtles and tortoises** 307 species
**Amphisbaenians (worm lizards)** 165 species
**Crocodiles, alligators, caimans** 23 species
**Tuataras** 2 species

## Deadly snakes

The coastal taipan of Australia injects the most venom per bite with 120 mg (0.004 oz). Just 1 mg (0.00004 oz) would be enough to kill a person. The common krait's venom is even more dangerous – only 0.5 mg (0.00002 oz) can be fatal.

# Alligators and crocodiles

The crocodile family contains 23 species, including alligators, caimans and gavials. All are large reptiles with long bodies and short legs. Most crocodiles have narrow V-shaped snouts, but alligators and caimans have wider, U-shaped snouts. The gavial has long slender jaws – just right for catching fish.

In alligators and caimans the teeth of the lower jaw fit into pits in the upper jaw and cannot be seen when the mouth is closed. In crocodiles the fourth tooth on each side of the lower jaw fits into a notch on the upper jaw, so they are always visible. Crocodiles are generally bigger and more aggressive than alligators.

## Alligators
**American alligator** (southern USA) 4–4.5 m (13.1–14.8 ft)
**Chinese alligator** (China) 2 m (6.6 ft)
**Spectacled caiman** (South America) 2–2.5 m (6.6–8.2 ft)
**Broad-snouted caiman** (South America) 2 m (6.6 ft)
**Yacaré caiman** (South America) 2.5–3 m (8.2–9.8 ft)
**Black caiman** (South America) 4–6 m (13.1–19.7 ft)
**Cuvier's dwarf caiman** (South America) 1.5–1.6 m (4.9–5.2 ft)
**Schneider's or Smooth-fronted caiman** (South America) 1.7–2.3 m (5.6–7.5 ft)

## Crocodiles
**American crocodile** (southern USA, Mexico, Central and South America) 5 m (16.4 ft)
**Slender-snouted crocodile** (West Africa) 2.5 m (8.2 ft)
**Orinoco crocodile** (northern South America) 6 m (19.7 ft)
**Australian freshwater crocodile** (Australia) 2.5–3 m (8.2–9.8 ft)
**Philippine crocodile** (Philippines) 3 m (9.8 ft)
**Morelet's crocodile** (Central America) 3 m (9.8 ft)
**Nile crocodile** (Africa) 5 m (16.4 ft)
**New Guinea crocodile** (New Guinea) 3.5 m (11.5 ft)

**Mugger or marsh crocodile** (India, Sri Lanka) 4–5 m (13.1–16.4 ft)
**Estuarine or saltwater crocodile** (Southeast Asia, Australia) 6–7 m (19.7–23 ft)
**Cuban crocodile** (Cuba) 3.5 m (11.5 ft)
**Siamese crocodile** (Southeast Asia, very rare) 3–4 m (9.8–13.1 ft)
**African dwarf crocodile** (Central and West Africa) 1.9 m (6.2 ft)
**False gharial or gavial** (Southeast Asia) 5 m (16.4 ft)

## Gavials
**Indian gavial or gharial** (India, Pakistan, Bangladesh, Nepal) 5–6 m (16.4–19.7 ft)

Estuarine or saltwater crocodile

# Amphibians

An amphibian is a vertebrate animal that spends at least some of its life in water. Its skin is not scaly. There are about 5,578 species of amphibian, divided into:

**Frogs and toads** 4,896 species
**Newts and salamanders** 517 species
**Caecilians (legless amphibians)** 165 species

Caecilian

Salamander

## Snake facts

### Largest snakes
Many people believe that the South American anaconda is the longest snake. There are reports of anacondas up to 36.5 m (120 ft) long, but this has never been proved. The reticulated or royal python is probably the longest snake at up to 10.7 m (35 ft), but the anaconda may be the heaviest at up to 230 kg (500 lb).

### Smallest snake
The thread snake is rarely longer than 108 mm (4.3 in). The spotted dwarf adder is the smallest venomous snake at 22.8 cm (9 in) long.

## Turtles and tortoises

These reptiles all have a hard shell that protects the body. There are about 250 species, some of which live in the sea, others in fresh water and the rest on land.

### Biggest
● Fossils of the extinct turtle *Stupendemys geographicus* have been found with shells up to 3 m (10 ft) long. They would have weighed more than 2,040 kg (4,497 lb).

● The largest living turtle is the leatherback. A male washed up on the coast of Wales in 1988 holds the record – he was 291 cm (113.5 in) long and weighed 916 kg (2,019 lb).

● The Aldabra giant tortoise, which lives on an island in the Seychelles, weighs up to 304 kg (670 lb) and is the largest land-living tortoise. It is also one of the slowest tortoises. It moves at an average speed of 0.27 km/h (0.17 mph).

### Smallest
The smallest turtle or tortoise is the common musk turtle which is 7.62 cm (3 in) long and weighs 227 g (8 oz).

Blue poison arrow frog

## Fantastic frogs and toads

### Largest frogs and toads
● The world's largest known frog is the goliath frog, which lives in central Africa. It measures up to 87.63 cm (34.5 in) long and weighs as much as 3.66 kg (8.1 lb).

● The largest tree frog is *Hyla vasta*, which lives only on the island of Hispaniola. It is more than 12 cm (4.7 in) long and has huge round finger and toe disks which grip like superglue.

● The world's largest toad is the South American marine toad. It can have a body length of over 23 cm (9.1 in) and weigh up to 1.2 kg (2.6 lb).

### Smallest frog
The smallest frog and the world's smallest amphibian is the *Eleutherodactylus limbatus* frog, which measures only 8.5–12 mm (0.3–0.5 in).

### Newest frogs
In 2006, 20 previously unknown frog species were discovered in an expedition to Indonesia (see page 69) including a tiny microhylid frog that measures less than 14 mm (0.6 in).

### Egg laying
The marine toad lays 35,000 eggs a year, but the Cuban arrow-poison frog lays only one egg.

### Highest and lowest homes
The green toad has been seen at 8,000 m (26,247 ft) in the Himalayas and toads have been discovered more than 3,048 m (10,000 ft) down a coal mine.

### Most poisonous
The poison-arrow frogs of Central and South America are the most deadly. The world's most poisonous amphibian is the golden poison-arrow frog of western Colombia. One adult contains enough highly toxic poison in its skin to kill 1,000 people.

### Smelliest
The smelliest frog is the Venezuela skunk frog, which was discovered in 1991. It warns off its enemies by releasing a bad-smelling chemical identical to the one produced by skunks.

### Longest jumps
● On 21 May 1977, a female sharp-nosed frog leaped 10.2 m (33.5 ft) in three consecutive jumps at a frog derby at Larula Natal Spa, Paulpietersburg in South Africa.

● The cricket frog is only 3.5 cm (1.4 in) and can jump 36 times its own length. If an adult human jumped 36 times his own length, the long-jump record could stand at 65.8 m (216 ft)!

## The lig

● **Hydroge**
Hydrogen is t
atoms in the
– only 5 of ev
hydrogen com
This is why it
on 1 Decembe
until 6 May 19
Lakehurst, Nev

● **Helium**
Helium is twic
of air. Unlike h

● **Lithium**
Lithium was dis
although it is a
cut with a knife
types of wood.

# Science
## &Technology

### Solar power
The world is increasingly
looking towards using renewable
sources of energy. Europe's largest
solar furnace at Font-Romeu, France,
uses mirrors to focus the Sun's
rays, reaching temperatures of
up to 4,000°C (7,232°F). The
heat is used to generate
electricity.

THE ELEMENTS

TELECOMMUNICATIONS

The first telegraph message was sent by Morse code using a hand-operated key.

## From fixed cables to satellites

In the early years of telecommunications, the only way of linking one telephone with another was by fixed cables. Links between continents relied on cables under the sea. The invention of radio brought the first wireless communications, but because the surface of the Earth is curved these signals could not travel far.

Satellites changed everything. They sit at an exact height above the Earth's equator (usually around 35,000 km/22,000 miles) and they rotate at the same speed as the Earth spins. This means that they stay in a fixed position. Telephone signals can be sent to the satellites and bounced back to Earth. Everywhere on the planet can be covered by only five or six satellites, except for the poles and surrounding areas, which are out of their range.

## Cables under the sea

Soon after telegraph cables came into use in the 1840s, attempts were made to lay them across rivers and between islands and mainlands. Most didn't work. In 1850 the first cable was laid across the English Channel. It had to resist attack by salt water, ocean currents and water pressure, so had a thick, water-resistant, steel cover. Inside were copper wires that carried the power and signal.

Technical improvements and the demand for faster communications led to cables being laid over ever greater distances. Several attempts to lay them across the Atlantic failed when the cables snapped, but one was completed in 1858. To mark the occasion, Queen Victoria sent a telegraph message to President Buchanan in the USA. It took almost 18 hours. Attempts were made to increase the pace by raising the voltage, but this burned out the cable. In 1865 the world's largest ship at the time, the *Great Eastern*, laid the first continuous cable across the Atlantic.

During the 20th century, telegraph cables, which transmitted Morse code were steadily replaced by telephone cables, which could transmit voices. Hundreds of thousands of kilometres of underwater cables were laid across the world's oceans and seas. These have been replaced by fibre-optic cables, which offer faster transmission and many more connections.

## The
## ele

● Osı
Osmiı
[13.07
It was
becaus
and is
such as

● Plat
Platinu
that it
much a

## Telecom timeline    1850s                                                    1870s

| | | | |
|---|---|---|---|
| **1793** Word "telegraph" first used (in France) | **1852** First telegraph line in India; there are now 37,015 km (23,000 miles) of telegraph line in USA | **1876** Alexander Graham Bell patents the telephone – beating his rival Elisha Gray by a matter of hours. He makes his historic first call to his assistant, Thomas Watson, who is in the next room: "Mr Watson, come here, I want to see you." The invention is demonstrated at the Centennial Exposition, Philadelphia, USA where Emperor Don Pedro of Brazil hears Bell recite the "To be or not to be" speech from *Hamlet* over the phone. | **1877** Bell makes the first long-distance call between Boston and Salem, Massachusetts, 22.5 km (14 miles) away |
| **1837** Charles Wheatstone and William Cooke set up first electric telegraph in London | **1854** First Australian telegraph line (Melbourne to Williamstown) | | **1878** Bell demonstrates his telephone to Queen Victoria at Osborne House on the Isle of Wight. She becomes the first European monarch to use a phone |
| **1843** Morse code inventor Samuel Morse (USA) sends first telegraph message between Washington and Baltimore | **1858** First transatlantic telegraph cable laid, but fails | | **1884** First telephone handset is launched |
| **1850** Telegraph cable laid between England and France across English Channel, but fails; 19,312 km (12,000 miles) of telegraph line in USA | **1861** First USA transcontinental telegraph | | **1889** First coin-in-the-slot public phone, USA |
| | **1862** 51,500 km (32,000 miles) of telegraph line and more than 5 million messages sent in USA | | **1891** France and England are connected by telephone cable |
| **1851** Thomas Crampton lays successful Dover-Calais cable | **1867** First theory suggests using radio waves for telecommunication | | |

## Telephone Bell

Alexander Graham Bell (1847–1922) is often called the father of the telephone. He was born in Edinburgh, Scotland, moved to Canada in 1870, and later to the USA. He became an expert on the science of speech and his first inventions helped deaf people to hear sounds. During his research, Bell developed a method of transmitting voice messages along a wire. In 1876 he patented the device, which he called the harmonic telegraph. This was the first telephone.

Alexander Graham Bell making the first telephone call between New York and Chicago

## Countries with most mobile phones

China 408,000,000
USA 170,000,000
Japan 141,000,000
Russia 130,000,000
India 101,000,000

In 2006, India joined the list of countries with more than 100 million mobile phones. It is predicted that by the end of 2008, it will be second in the list with 250 million subscribers.

## 2000s

**1894** Guglielmo Marconi invents wireless telegraphy

**1897** There are seven phones per 1,000 people in the USA

**1901** Marconi sends a radio signal across the Atlantic

**1902** The trans-Pacific telephone cable connects Canada, New Zealand and Australia

**1907** There are an estimated 1,653,356 km (1,027,348 miles) of land telecommunications lines and 376,302 km (233,823 miles) of submarine cable worldwide

**1914** The first radio message is sent to an aircraft; the first transcontinental telephone call is made in the USA

**1919** Rotary dial telephones are invented

**1945** British writer Arthur C. Clarke proposes putting communications satellites in orbit above the Earth, which move at the same speed as the Earth spins; this means they stay in a fixed position, and communication with the ground is not interrupted.

**1956** The first transatlantic telephone cable is laid

**1965** Intelsat I (*Early Bird*), the first commercial telecommunications satellite, is launched

**1967** The first cordless telephones go on sale

**1975** The first handheld mobile phones are sold

**1988** The first transatlantic fibre optic cable is laid

**2004** There are 1.2 billion telephone lines around the world: 538,981,500 in Asia,

327,657,500 in Europe, 295,292,700 in North and South America, 25,929,800 in Africa and 13,773,000 in Oceania

**2005** Mobile phone users now number more than 2 billion worldwide

**2006** US company Western Union ends its telegraph service after 150 years, as e-mails replace telegrams

**2007** More than 3 billion worldwide use mobile phones. Apple's iPhone is launched

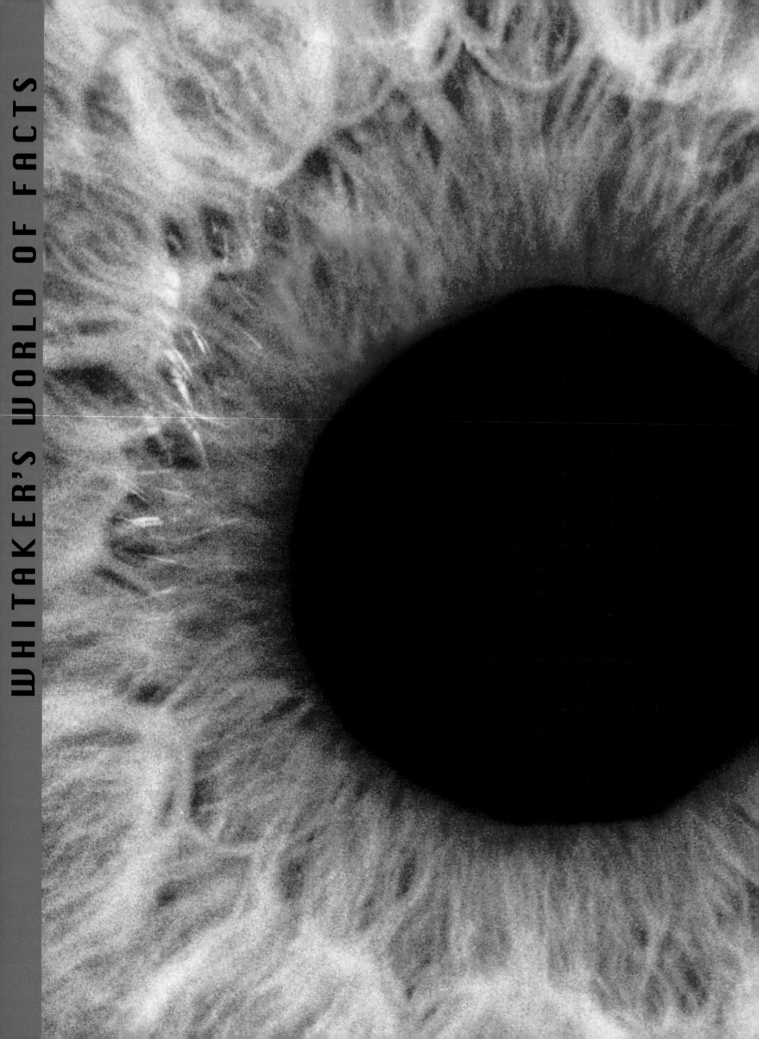

# Human Body

### Bionic eye

"Bionic eyes" are currently being developed and in 2007 six blind patients had their sight partially restored by artificial eyes surgically implanted onto their retinas. Scientists have also created robotic limbs, including a bionic arm that can be controlled by the owner's thoughts.

# HUMAN BODY

# Your amazing body

## Blood
An adult man's body contains about 5 l (10.5 pt) of blood. A woman's contains about 4.3 l (9.1 pt). The blood travels along 100,000 km (62,137 miles) of blood vessels. It contains 25,000,000,000 to 30,000,000,000 red cells. The life span of red cells is only about 120 days, and 1,200,000 to 2,000,0000 of them are made every second.

## Brain power
You lose 100,000 brain cells every day! Luckily you have 100 billion altogether. If the surface area of your brain could be ironed out it would measure 2,090 sq cm (324 sq in).

## Breathing
The average person inhales 6 l (12.6 pt) of air per minute, or 8,640 l (18,260 pt) a day. You take 13–17 breaths a minute when sitting still and up to 80 during vigorous exercise.

## Cells
There are 50 trillion cells in your body and 3 billion of them die every minute (4,320,000,000,000 a day). Most of these are replaced. You make 10 billion new white blood cells each day. You have a total of 1,000,000,000,000 white cells, which help fight germs and infections.

## Chemicals
There is enough carbon in your body to fill 900 pencils, enough fat to make 75 candles, enough phosphorus to make 220 match heads and enough iron to make a 7.5 cm (3 in) nail.

## Digestive system
Your stomach produces up to 2 l (4.2 pt) of hydrochloric acid a day. It does not damage the stomach walls because 500,000 cells in your stomach lining are replaced every minute. The small intestine is about 5 m (16.4 ft) long. The large intestine is thicker, but only about 1.5 m (4.9 ft) long.

## Eyes
You blink about 20,000 times a day.

## Gas
On average, you release 2 l (4.2 pt) of gases from your intestines as burps or farts.

## Hair
Hair grows about 0.5 mm (0.02 in) a day.

## Heartbeats
Your heart pumps 13,640 l (28,800 pt) of blood around your body in a day. An average heartbeat rate of 70 beats a minute adds up to more than 100,000 beats a day.

## Mouth
You will produce 37,800 l (79,900 pt) of saliva in your life.

## Nerves
Your body has about 13,000,000,000,000 nerve cells, transmitting messages at speeds of 290 km/h (180 mph).

## Sweat
You lose about 0.5 l (1.1 pt) of water a day through 3,000,000 sweat glands. In hot climates you may lose as much as 13.5 l (28.5 pt) a day.

## Urine
You will pass 400 to 2,000 ml (0.8 to 4.2 pt) of urine every day, depending on your age, your size and outside conditions, especially temperature.

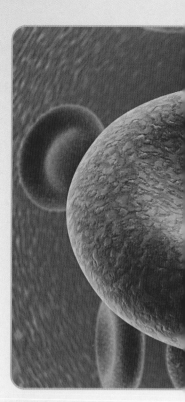

Highly magnified image of red blood cells

# Largest human organs

The weights listed below are all averages, but sometimes organs are much larger. Some brains have weighed more than 2,000 g (4.4 lb), but that doesn't mean the owners were super-intelligent!

**Skin** 10,886 g (384 oz)
**Liver** 1,560 g (55 oz)
**Brain male** 1,408 g (49.7 oz)
**Brain female** 1,263 g (44.6 oz)
**Lungs right** 580 g (20.5 oz)
**Lungs left** 510 g (18 oz)
**Heart male** 315 g (11.1 oz)
**Heart female** 265 g (9.3 oz)
**Kidney left** 150 g (5.3 oz)
**Kidney right** 140 g (4.9 oz)

**Spleen** 170 g (6 oz)
**Pancreas** 98 g (3.5 oz)
**Thyroid** 35 g (1.2 oz)
**Prostate** (male only) 20 g (0.7 oz)
**Adrenals left** 6 g (0.2 oz)
**Adrenals right** 6 g (0.2 oz)

## One and only
The only bone in the human body that is not connected to another bone is the hyoid bone, a U-shaped bone at the base of the tongue. It is supported by the muscles in the neck, but it is not connected to any other bone.

# What's your body made of?

Most of the human body is made up of water, or $H_2O$, which is a combination of hydrogen and oxygen. As much as 99 per cent of the body is made up of oxygen, carbon, hydrogen, nitrogen, calcium and phosphorus. There are also small amounts of other elements.

| Element | Avg. in 70 kg (154 lb) person g (oz) | Element | Avg. in 70 kg (154 lb) person g (oz) |
|---|---|---|---|
| Oxygen | 43,000 (1,1517) | Potassium | 110–140 (4–5) |
| Carbon | 16,000 (564) | Sodium | 100 (3.5) |
| Hydrogen | 7,000 (247) | Chlorine | 95 (3.35) |
| Nitrogen | 1,800 (64) | Magnesium | 25 (0.8) |
| Calcium | 1,200 (42) | Iron | 4 (0.1) |
| Phosphorus | 780 (28) | Zinc | 2.3 (0.08) |
| Sulphur | 140 (5) | Silicon | 1 (0.03) |

Skull
28 bones

Throat
1 bone

Shoulders
4 bones

The ear bones
are the smallest
in the body.

Sternum
(breastbone)
3 bones

Ribs
24 bones

Vertebrae
(backbone)
26 bones

Pelvis
2 bones

Arms and
hands
60 bones

## Human skeleton

The skeleton is the body's framework. The bones of the skeleton support the body, protect the internal organs such as the heart and lungs, and allow you to move.

## Longest bones in the body

These are the average measurements of the longest bones of an adult male. The same bones in the female skeleton are usually 6–13 per cent smaller, except the breastbone which is almost the same.

**Femur** (thighbone, upper leg) 50.50 cm (19.88 in)

**Tibia** (shinbone, inner lower leg) 43.03 cm (16.94 in)

**Fibula** (outer lower leg) 40.50 cm (15.94 in)

**Humerus** (upper arm) 36.46 cm (14.35 in)

**Ulna** (inner lower arm) 28.20 cm (11.10 in)

**Radius** (outer lower arm) 26.42 cm (10.40 in)

**7th rib** 24.00 cm (9.45 in)

**8th rib** 23.00 cm (9.06 in)

**Hipbone** (one half of pelvis) 18.50 cm (7.28 in)

**Sternum** (breastbone) 17.00 cm (6.69 in)

### Nails

Your fingernails grow 0.05 cm (0.02 in) a week, four times faster than your toenails.

### How heavy?

The human skeleton makes up about one-fifth of a person's entire weight. An average adult weighing 70 kg (154 lb) will have a skeleton that weighs 14 kg (31 lb).

### Skin

Your skin weighs up to 4 kg (8.8 lb) and covers up to 1.3–1.7 sq m (14–18.3 sq ft). Getting dressed and undressed, rubbing body parts together and even breathing cause microscopic flakes of skin to fall off at the rate of 50,000 flakes a minute. In a lifetime you will shed 18 kg (39.7 lb) of skin.

Legs and feet
58 bones

www.innerbody.com          search

## Weighty wonder

Daniel Lambert (1770–1809) was one of the heaviest British people of all time. At his largest, he weighed 330 kg (727.5 lb) and measured 2.8 m (9.2 ft) round his body and 94 cm (37 in) round his leg. Lambert used to charge visitors to his house a shilling (five pence) just to look at him.

When he died in 1809, it took 34 m (111.5 ft) of elm planking to make his coffin, which looked like a gigantic packing case. A window and part of the wall of his house had to be removed to get the coffin out, and it had to be mounted on wheels to trundle it to the cemetery.

Daniel Lambert

## Body records

### Longest beard
Hans Langseth (1846–1927) had a beard that measured 5.33 m (17 ft 6 in). It has been in the Smithsonian Institution, Washington DC, USA, since 1967.

### Longest nails
Shridhar Chillal of Pune, India (1937– ) has not cut the nails on his left hand since 1952. By 2000 the total length of his nails on that hand was over 600 cm (236 in).

### Longest moustache
Kalyan Ramji Sain of Sundargath, India, holds the record. His moustache is 3.29 m (11 ft 11.5 in) from tip to tip.

### Longest hair
Swami Pandarasannadhi was the head of a monastery in Madras, India. When his hair was measured in 1949 it was 7.9 m (26 ft) long.

### Longest sneezing bout
Donna Griffiths of Pershore, Worcestershire, started sneezing on 13 January 1981 and continued for 978 days.

### Maths genius
When he was only eight years old, American Zerah Colburn (1804–40) worked out how many seconds had elapsed since the birth of Christ. He did this in his head

Hans Langseth

within seconds. When Zerah was asked whether 4,294,967,297 was a prime number (one that cannot be divided evenly by another number), he instantly replied that it was not – it is equal to 641 times 6,700,417.

### Longest hiccuping
Charles Osborne of Anthon, Iowa, USA, hiccuped from 1922 to 1990.

### Infant prodigy
By the age of four, Kim Ung-Yong of Korea (1963– ) could speak fluent Korean, English, Japanese and German, and could solve calculus problems.

### Memory
Gon Yang-ling of Harbin, China, has memorized more than 15,000 telephone numbers.

## World's oldest people

Below is a list of the world's longest-living people, or supercentenarians. It includes only those for whom there are accurate records of their birth and death dates.

Although Christian Mortensen is ninth in the list, he is the world's oldest man. The others in the list are women.

**Jeanne Calment (1875–1997), France:** 122 years and 164 days
**Sarah DeRemer Knauss (1880–1999), USA:** 119 years and 97 days
**Lucy Hannah (1875–1993), USA:** 117 years and 248 days
**Marie-Louise Meilleur (1880–1998), Canada:** 117 years and 229 days
**Maria Capovilla (1889–2006) Ecuador:** 116 years and 347 days
**Tane Ikai (1879–1995), Japan:** 116 years and 175 days
**Elizabeth Bolden (1890–2006) USA:** 116 years and 118 days
**Maggie Barnes (1882–1998), USA:** 115 years and 319 days
**Christian Mortensen (1882–1998), Denmark/USA:** 115 years and 252 days
**Charlotte Hughes (1877–1993), UK:** 115 years and 228 days

## Oldest living person

Yone Minagawa of Japan was born on 29 January 1893 and celebrated her 114th birthday in 2007, making her the oldest person alive in the world.

## Tom Thumb and friends

American showman Phineas T. Barnum first met Charles Sherwood Stratton (USA, 1838–83) when he was four years old. He was 61cm (24 in) tall and weighed 6.8 kg (15 lb). Barnum persuaded Charles's parents to allow him to exhibit their son for a fee of $3 a week. He was advertised as "General Tom Thumb, a dwarf eleven years of age, just arrived from England". By the time he died, he had grown to 1 m (3 ft 3 in) and weighed 32 kg (70 lb). Lavinia Warren (USA, 1841–1919) was 79 cm (31 in) tall. Her first husband was Tom Thumb.

"Commodore" Nutt (USA, 1844–81) was 74 cm (29 in) tall. Like Tom Thumb he was exhibited by Phineas T. Barnum.

# Amazing feats

● In 1997, at Sydney Airport, Australia, David Huxley pulled a 187-tonne Boeing 747-400 a distance of 91 m (298.5 ft). He had previously hauled a Boeing 737 and a Concorde.

● In 2005, US arm-wrestler Ed Shelton ripped up 55 telephone directories, each 1,044 pages thick. It took him three minutes.

● Sri-Lankan born Arulanantham Suresh Joachim currently holds 30 endurance records, including a drumming marathon (84 hours), the longest time standing still (76 hours 40 minutes), running 100 miles/161 km on a treadmill (42 minutes 33 seconds) and crawling one mile/1.6 km (37 minutes 17 seconds). In 2006 he announced his intention to run a mega-marathon through 54 countries in 181 days – over 6,000 km (3,729 miles).

## Tallest real giants

These are the most reliable records. All are men, except Trijntje Keever and Jeng Jinlian.

**Robert Pershing Wadlow (1918–40), USA:** 2.72 m (8 ft 11.1 in)
**John William Rogan (1868–1905), USA:** 2.68 m (8 ft 9.8 in)
**John Aasen (1887–1938), USA:** 2.67m (8 ft 9.8 in)
**John F. Carroll (1932–69), USA:** 2.64 m (8 ft 7.6 in)
**Al Tomaini (1918–62), USA:** 2.55 m (8 ft 4.4 in)

**Trijntje Keever (1616–33), Netherlands:** 2.54 m (8 ft 3.3 in)
**Edouard Beaupre (1881–1904), Canada:** 2.50 m (8 ft 2.5 in)
**Bernard Coyne (1897–1921), USA:** 2.49 m (8 ft 1.2 in)
**Don Koehler (1925–81), USA:** 2.49 m (8 ft 1.2 in)
**Jeng Jinlian (1964–82), China:** 2.48 m (8 ft 1.1 in)
**Väinö Myllyrinne (1909–63), Finland:** 2.48 m (8 ft 1.1 in)
**Louis Moilanen (1885–1913), Finland/USA:** 2.46 m (8 ft 1 in)
**Gabriel Estavo Monjane (1944–90), Mozambique:** 2.46 m (8 ft 0.75 in)

## Life expectancy

Life expectancy is the average number of years people in different countries are likely to live. Conditions can improve or sometimes get worse, so life expectancy can get higher or lower.

The country with the highest life expectancy is Andorra at 83.5 years. The country with the lowest life expectancy is Swaziland with 36.2 years. People who live in the UK and the USA have an average life expectancy of 78.8 years and 78.1 years respectively.

Commodore Nutt, Miss Warren, normal-sized man and Tom Thumb

### Run-up records

In the annual Empire State Building Run-Up, runners race up the famous skyscraper's 1,576 steps. In 2006 Andrea Mayr of Austria set a new women's record of 11 minutes 23 seconds. The overall record-holder is Australian athlete Paul Crake. In 2003, he got to the top in 9 minutes 33 seconds. He also holds the record for the Australian Sydney Tower Run-Up.

Robert Wadlow

A fear of snakes is called ophidiophobia.

## Common phobias

A phobia is a strong fear of a particular animal, object, situation or activity. The fear is often out of proportion to the reality and may make people vomit, sweat, tremble and even faint. People may go to great lengths to avoid the subjects of their phobias.

### Most common phobias

**Fear of snakes** is called ophidiophobia
**Fear of flying** is called aerophobia or aviatophobia
**Fear of open spaces** is called agoraphobia, cenophobia or kenophobia
**Fear of confined spaces** is called claustrophobia, cleisiophobia, cleithrophobia or clithrophobia
**Fear of spiders** is called arachnephobia or arachnophobia
**Fear of heights** is called acrophobia, altophobia, hypsophobia or hypsiphobia

### Unusual phobias

**Fear of beards** is called pogonophobia
**Fear of chickens** is called alektorophobia
**Fear of dancing** is called chorophobia
**Fear of dolls** is called pediophobia
**Fear of fish** is called ichthyophobia
**Fear of frogs** is called batrachophobia
**Fear of hair** is called chaetophobia
**Fear of mirrors** is called eisoptrophobia
**Fear of the number 13** is called triskaidekaphobia
**Fear of string** is called linonophobia
**Fear of teeth** is called odontophobia

## Calorie counts

A Calorie (with a capital C) is a unit that measures the amount of energy in foods. It is also known as a kilocalorie and is equal to 1,000 calories (with a small c). A calorie is the amount of heat needed to raise the temperature of 1 gram (0.035 oz) of water by 1°C (1.8°F).

An adult might eat up to 3,000 Calories a day. Eating too many Calories that the body does not use for energy may make you fat. The figures below are based on the average number of Calories a 70 kg (155 lb) adult burns when doing an activity for one hour. A lighter person uses fewer Calories; a heavier person more.

**Squash** 844 Calories
**Rugby, skipping, swimming** 704 Calories
**Basketball, cycling, running, walking upstairs** 563 Calories
**Canoeing or rowing** 493 Calories
**Football, ice skating, roller skating, skiing, tennis** 493 Calories
**Aerobics** 422 Calories
**Mowing lawn** 387 Calories

**Cricket (batting or bowling), gardening, skateboarding** 352 Calories
**Dancing** 317 Calories
**Golf, table tennis** 281 Calories
**Housework, walking dog** 246 Calories
**Frisbee, surfing** 211 Calories
**Playing piano** 176 calories
**Standing** 120 calories
**Sitting** 90 calories
**Sleeping** 65 calories

## Causes of death worldwide

There are big differences between the causes of death in developing countries and in developed countries. In developing countries, many more deaths are caused by infectious diseases and illnesses spread by insects such as malaria.

In developed countries more people become ill from being overweight and eating rich diets. There are about 57,029,000 deaths a year worldwide.

**Heart diseases** 16,733,000 per year
**Cancers** 7,121,000 per year
**Respiratory infections** 3,963,000 per year
**Lung diseases** 3,702,000 per year
**HIV/AIDS** 2,777,000 per year
**Digestive diseases** 1,968,000 per year
**Diarrhoeal diseases** 1,798,000 per year
**Tuberculosis** 1,566,000 per year
**Malaria** 1,272,000 per year
**Road traffic injuries** 1,192,000 per year
**Neuropsychiatric disorders** 1,112,000 per year

## Medical milestones       1800s

**c. 460 BC** The first medical studies were carried out by Hippocrates (Greece)
**AD 1543** Accurate anatomical drawings were made by Andreas Vesalius (Belgium)
**1628** Blood circulation was discovered by William Harvey (UK)
**1683** Bacteria were first described by Antonie van Leeuwenhoek (the Netherlands)

**1796** The first smallpox vaccination was carried out by Edward Jenner (UK)
**1805** Morphine was used as a painkiller by Friedrich Sertürner (Germany)
**1810** Homeopathy was used by Samuel Hahnemann (Germany)
**1816** The stethoscope was invented by René Laënnec (France)
**1818** The first blood transfusion was carried out by Thomas Blundell (UK)

**1842** Ether was administered as an anaesthetic by Crawford Long (USA)
**1844** Nitrous oxide (laughing gas) was used as an anaesthetic by Horace Wells (USA)
**1846** Ether vapour was used as an anaesthetic by William Morton (USA)
**1847** Chloroform was used as an anaesthetic by John Bell/James Simpson (UK)
**1864** The Red Cross was founded by Henri Dunant (Switzerland)

**1867** Antiseptic was used before surgery by Joseph Lister (UK)
**1885** Rabies vaccine was developed by Louis Pasteur (France)
**1895** X-rays were discovered by William von Röntgen (Germany)
**1895** Psychoanalysis was used by Sigmund Freud (Austria)
**1898** Aspirin was made by Felix Hoffman (Germany)
**1901** Blood groups were identified by Karl Landsteiner (Austria)

# Sleep fact file

● About one-third of our lives are spent sleeping, but very little is really known about it.

● We sleep in different stages. These range from light sleep to deep sleep, with periods of REM (Rapid Eye Movement) in between, during which we dream.

● The connection between REM and dreaming was discovered in 1953. It usually begins about 90 minutes after falling asleep and occurs in bursts, totalling about two hours a night, or 20 per cent of total sleep time.

● At least 30 per cent of adults snore. Many inventors have come up with anti-snoring gadgets to solve the problem. These include mouth or nose devices that alter breathing by blasting the snorers with sound, giving them electric shocks or shaking their beds.

● Trains have a "dead man's handle", which must be held at all times. If the driver falls asleep and loses his grip, the train stops.

● The scientific word for stretching and yawning is pandiculaton.

● Newborn babies can sleep for up to 21 hours out of 24. Children and teenagers need about 10 hours of sleep a night, while most adults need only 7–9 hours. Those over 65 need the least of all – about six hours. Older people also have less deep sleep and less REM sleep than young people.

## First face transplant

The world's first face transplant was carried out in 2005 on Isabelle Dinoire (born 1967) of Valenciennes, France. Her nose, lips and chin had been seriously injured when she was attacked by her dog. In an operation that lasted 15 hours, she was successfully given the face of a brain-dead donor.

LET US FORWARD TOGETHER"

Sir Winston Churchill

● It is claimed that several famous people have existed on polyphasic sleep – short naps of a few minutes – instead of one long period of sleep. These include Leonardo da Vinci and Winston Churchill.

## 2000s

**1906** Vitamins were discovered by Frederick Hopkins (UK)

**1922** Insulin was used to treat diabetes by Frederick Banting and John Macleod (Canada) and Charles Best (USA)

**1927** Iron lung was invented by Philip Drinker (USA)

**1928** Penicillin was discovered by Alexander Fleming (UK)

**1940** Penicillin was first used by Howard Florey (Australia) and Ernest Chain (UK)

**1952** The first artificial heart valve was used by Charles Hufnagel (USA)

**1953** DNA structure was identified by Francis Crick (UK) and James Watson (USA)

**1955** Kidney dialysis machine was invented by Willem J. Kolff (the Netherlands/USA)

**1957** First heart pacemaker was used by Clarence Lillehie (USA)

**1967** The first human heart transplant was performed by Christiaan Barnard (S. Africa)

**1970** First artificial heart was used by Robert Jarvik (USA)

**1971** CAT scanner was first used by Godfrey Hounsfield (UK)

**1978** First test-tube baby (Louise Brown) was born after procedure perfomed by Patrick Steptoe (UK)

**1980** Smallpox was eradicated by World Health Organization

**1984** Genetic fingerprinting was invented by Alec Jeffreys (UK)

**1984** AIDS virus was first identified by Centers for Disease Control (USA)

**1996** First mammal was cloned (Dolly, a sheep) by Ian Wilmut, Roslin Institute (UK)

**2000** Human DNA genome sequence was completed

**2006** Robot heart surgery was performed by Carlo Pappone (Italy)

# World History

## Royal tomb

In 2007 archaeologists announced the discovery of a tomb at Herodium, Israel, believed to be that of King Herod. Herod was the king of Judea under Roman rule who is said to have condemned Jesus to death.

# US presidents

US presidents are elected for a term of four years. George Washington was the first president of the USA and he served two terms. Only Franklin Delano Roosevelt served three terms. He died shortly after he was elected for a fourth term.

In 1951 the 22nd Amendment to the US Constitution ruled that two terms are the most any president may serve. The two main political parties in the USA today are the Democratic Party and the Republican Party.

The heads of presidents Washington, Jefferson, Lincoln and Roosevelt are carved into the face of Mt Rushmore in South Dakota, USA.

Abraham Lincoln on a US 1-cent coin

**1 George Washington** (Federalist party) first elected 1789
**2 John Adams** (Federalist party) first elected 1797
**3 Thomas Jefferson** (Dem-Rep party) first elected 1801
**4 James Madison** (Dem-Rep party) first elected 1809
**5 James Monroe** (Dem-Rep party) first elected 1817
**6 John Quincy Adams** (Dem-Rep party) first elected 1825
**7 Andrew Jackson** (Democratic party) first elected 1829
**8 Martin Van Buren** (Democratic party) first elected 1837
**9 William Henry Harrison** (Whig party) first elected 1841
**10 John Tyler** (Whig party) first elected 1841
**11 James Knox Polk** (Democratic party) first elected 1845
**12 Zachary Taylor** (Whig party) first elected 1849
**13 Millard Fillmore** (Whig party) first elected 1850
**14 Franklin Pierce** (Democratic party) first elected 1853
**15 James Buchanan** (Democratic party) first elected 1857
**16 Abraham Lincoln** (Republican party) first elected 1861
**17 Andrew Johnson** (Democratic party) first elected 1865
**18 Ulysses Simpson Grant** (Republican party) first elected 1869
**19 Rutherford Birchard Hayes** (Republican party) first elected 1877
**20 James Abram Garfield** (Republican party) first elected 1881
**21 Chester Alan Arthur** (Republican party) first elected 1881
**22 Grover Cleveland** (Democratic party) first elected 1885
**23 Benjamin Harrison** (Republican party) first elected 1889

**24 Grover Cleveland** (Democratic party) first elected 1893
**25 William McKinley** (Republican party) first elected 1897
**26 Theodore Roosevelt** (Republican party) first elected 1901
**27 William Howard Taft** (Republican party) first elected 1909
**28 Woodrow Wilson** (Democratic party) first elected 1913
**29 Warren Gamaliel Harding** (Republican party) first elected 1921
**30 Calvin Coolidge** (Republican party) first elected 1923
**31 Herbert Clark Hoover** (Republican party) first elected 1929
**32 Franklin Delano Roosevelt** (Democratic party) first elected 1933
**33 Harry S. Truman** (Democratic party) first elected 1945
**34 Dwight David Eisenhower** (Republican party) first elected 1953
**35 John Fitzgerald Kennedy** (Democratic party) first elected 1961
**36 Lyndon Baines Johnson** (Democratic party) first elected 1963
**37 Richard Milhous Nixon** (Republican party) first elected 1969
**38 Gerald Rudolph Ford** (Republican party) first elected 1974
**39 Jimmy Carter** (Democratic party) first elected 1977
**40 Ronald Reagan** (Republican party) first elected 1981
**41 George Bush** (Republican party) first elected 1989
**42 Bill Clinton** (Democratic party) first elected 1993
**43 George W. Bush** (Republican party) first elected 2001

# World monarchies

A monarchy is a country where the head of state is a king, queen or other hereditary ruler – someone who inherits the throne from a family member. In some countries, such as Malaysia, the monarch is elected.

**Bahrain** Shaikh Hamad bin Isa al-Khalifa succeeded to the throne in 1999
**Belgium** King Albert II succeeded to the throne in 1993
**Bhutan** King Jigme Singye Wangchuck succeeded to the throne in 1972
**Brunei** Sultan Haji Hassanal Bolkiah succeeded to the throne in 1967

**Cambodia** King Norodom Sihamoni succeeded to the throne in 2004
**Denmark** Queen Margrethe II succeeded to the throne in 1972
**Japan** Emperor Akihito succeeded to the throne in 1989
**Jordan** King Abdullah II succeeded to the throne in 1999

**Kuwait** Shaikh Sabah al-Ahmad al-Sabah succeeded to the throne in 2006
**Lesotho** King Letsie III succeeded to the throne in 1996
**Liechtenstein** Prince Hans Adam II succeeded to the throne in 1989
**Luxembourg** Grand Duke Henri succeeded to the throne in 2000

# Amazing monarchs

## Oldest monarch to ascend the British throne

William IV (ruled 1830–37) was 64 when he was crowned.

## British monarchs with the most children

Edward I had 16 children (6 sons and 10 daughters). Both George III and James II had 15.

## Most-married British monarch

Henry VIII had six wives who suffered various fates. They were: Catherine of Aragon (divorced), Anne Boleyn (beheaded), Jane Seymour (died 1537), Anne of Cleves (divorced), Catherine Howard (beheaded) and Catherine Parr, who survived Henry.

Henry VIII

## Youngest British monarchs

Henry VI was just eight months old when he became king on 1 September 1422 after the death of his father, Henry V. When his grandfather, Charles VI, died 50 days later on 21 October 1422, Henry also became king of France.

## Shortest-reigning British monarchs

Queen Jane (Lady Jane Grey), ruled for only nine days in 1553, before being sent to the Tower of London. She was executed the following year. Edward V ruled for 75 days. He was one of the Princes in the Tower, who were allegedly murdered on the orders of their uncle, Richard III. Edward VIII abdicated (gave up the throne) on 11 December 1936, before his coronation. He had ruled for just 325 days.

## Longest-reigning world monarch

King Louis XIV of France became king at the age of five. He ruled for 72 years, from 1643–1715.

## Longest-reigning British monarch

Queen Victoria was 18 years old when she became queen in 1837 and she ruled for 63 years.

## Richest world ruler

Although no longer the richest man in the world, the Sultan of Brunei is estimated to have a fortune of $28 million.

## Monarchies with the most rulers

Japan's monarchy dates from 40 BC. Since then, it has had 125 rulers.

### Oldest king to be crowned

The British crown usually passes to the next in line when the king or queen dies. Charles, Prince of Wales, is Queen Elizabeth II's oldest son and heir. If he becomes king before his 59th birthday on 14 November 2007, he will be the third oldest king to be crowned. Only Edward VII was older (aged 59 years, 2 months) and William IV, who was the oldest king to be crowned in British history (aged 64 years, 10 months). Queen Elizabeth II celebrated her 80th birthday on 21 April 2006.

Henry VII was the first Tudor. He devised the Tudor Rose to symbolize unity between the House of York (white rose) and the House of Lancaster (red rose).

See also
Types of government:
pages 110–111

---

**Malaysia** Sultan Mizan Zainal Abidin succeeded to the throne in 2006

**Monaco** Prince Albert II succeeded to the throne in 2005

**Morocco** King Mohammed VI succeeded to the throne in 1999

**Nepal** King Gyanendra Bir Bikram Shah Dev succeeded to the throne in 2001

**Netherlands** Queen Beatrix succeeded to the throne in 1980

**Norway** King Harald V succeeded to the throne in 1991

**Oman** Sultan Qaboos Bin Said al-Said succeeded to the throne in 1970

**Qatar** Shaikh Hamad bin Kaalifa al-Thani succeeded to the throne in 1995

**Samoa** King Susaga Malietoa Tanumafili II succeeded to the throne in 1963

**Saudi Arabia** King Abdullah ibn Abdul Aziz al-Saud succeeded to the throne in 2005

**Spain** King Juan Carlos I succeeded to the throne in 1975

**Swaziland** King Mswati III succeeded to the throne in 1986

**Sweden** King Carl XVI Gustaf succeeded to the throne in 1973

**Thailand** King Bhumibol Adulyadej succeeded to the throne in 1946

**Tonga** George Tupou V succeeded to the throne in 2006

**United Kingdom** Queen Elizabeth II succeeded to the throne in 1952

# WORLD POLITICS

## Votes for women

The Isle of Man was the first place to give women the vote, in 1880, but the island is part of the UK and not a separate country. Until 1920 the only European countries that allowed women to vote were Sweden (1919) and Czechoslovakia (1920).

In the USA women were granted the vote in 1920, although some states allowed it earlier. Women could not vote in France or Italy until 1945, in Switzerland until 1971 or in Liechtenstein until 1984. Women were granted the right to vote in Kuwait for the first time in 2005, but they are still not allowed to vote in Brunei, Saudi Arabia and the United Arab Emirates. There are other countries where women have no vote – but neither do men.

**1** The first country to give women the vote was New Zealand in 1893.

**2** Australia followed suit in 1902 although women had the vote in South Australia in 1894 and in Western Australia in 1898 before the separate states were united in 1901.

**3** Finland (then a Grand Duchy under the Russian Crown) granted women the vote in 1906.

**4** Norway gave some women the vote in 1907. It was not until 1913 that all women over 25 could vote.

**5** Denmark and Iceland (a Danish dependency until 1918) allowed women to vote in 1915.

**6** The Netherlands and the USSR both gave women the vote in 1917.

**8** Austria, Canada, Germany, Poland, Great Britain and Ireland all gave women the vote in 1918. (In Ireland, part of the UK until 1921, only women over 30 got the vote in 1918. This was lowered to 21 in 1928.)

🔍 www.rulers.org     **search**

British poster demanding votes for women

## Types of government

There have been many different types of government around the world throughout history. Many of the names for them end in the term -cracy, from a Greek word meaning power.

**Aristocracy**
Rule by a small group of members of a privileged class.

**Autocracy**
Government by one person with unrestricted power; also known as despotism and dictatorship.

2007 was Fidel Castro's 48th year as President of Cuba.

**Communist**
Government of a classless state in which private ownership is abolished and the state controls all means of production, as in China and Cuba.

**Democracy**
Government by the people directly or through elected representatives, as in the UK and USA.

## Roosevelt's Four Freedoms

On 6 January 1941 during World War II, US President Roosevelt made a famous speech to the US Congress. He proclaimed that four freedoms are essential to a democracy: freedom of speech, freedom of worship, freedom from want, and freedom from fear. He looked forward to these freedoms being possible after the defeat of Hitler and the Axis powers. In 1997 a memorial park was opened in Washington DC, honouring Roosevelt. It contains The Four Freedoms fountain as a symbol of his ideas.

# Major international organizations

A number of international organizations have been set up to deal with issues that concern the world in general, rather than the interests of individual countries. These organizations are not linked to political parties but often become involved in political matters.

Flags flying outside the United Nations, New York

## Women in parliament

There are 49 countries with at least 20 per cent of their parliament made up of women – but a number of countries still do not have any women representatives at all.

Based on the most recent general election results, these countries have the highest percentages of women in parliament: Rwanda 48.8 per cent, Sweden 47.3 per cent, Costa Rica 38.6 per cent, Finland 38 per cent, Norway 37.9 per cent.

### United Nations

The UN was founded in 1945. Most countries of the world – a total of 192 – are members. The General Assembly of the UN makes decisions about peacekeeping and human rights.

**Meritocracy**
Government by leaders selected according to their ability.

**Monarchy**
Government in which power is held by a king (or queen, emperor or empress) who can pass power on to their heirs.

**Oligarchy**
Government by a small group of people.

**Plutocracy**
A government or state in which wealthy people rule.

**Theocracy**
Government ruled by or subject to religious authority.

### Amnesty International (AI)
Amnesty International is a charitable organization set up in 1961. It campaigns for human rights throughout the world and against the detention of political prisoners.

### International Monetary Fund (IMF)
The IMF was established in 1944 and promotes world trade. It has 184 member countries.

### International Red Cross and Red Crescent Movement
These organizations help the victims of such events as warfare and natural disasters.

### Organization for Economic Co-operation and Development (OECD)
The OECD was formed in 1961. It aims to encourage economic and social development in industrialized countries and provide aid to developing countries.

### United Nations Children's Fund (UNICEF)
UNICEF was set up in 1947. It works to improve the health and welfare of children and mothers in developing countries.

### United Nations Educational, Scientific and Cultural Organization (UNESCO)
UNESCO was set up in 1946. It encourages countries to get together on matters such as education, culture and science.

### World Bank
The World Bank was founded in 1944 and has 184 member countries. It helps developing countries by giving loans.

### World Health Organization
The WHO is part of the UN. It promotes health matters worldwide and aims to raise medical standards and monitor diseases.

### World Trade Organization (WTO)
The Swiss-based WTO encourages international trade by establishing trade agreements between countries.

### World Wildlife Fund (WWF)
The WWF was set up in 1961 and is the world's largest conservation organization. Its main aims are to protect endangered animals and the places where they live.

### NATO
The North Atlantic Treaty Organization (NATO) was founded in 1949. Ten countries signed a defence treaty that committed them to helping each other in the event of attack. There are now 26 country members, and the NATO headquarters are based in Belgium.

### G8
The Group of 8 (G8) is made up of the world's leading industrial countries (Canada, France, Germany, Italy, Japan, the UK, the USA and Russian Federation). The heads of the G8 countries meet each year to discuss global issues such as world poverty and security.

# Countries
## of the
# World

## Bustle in Bangalore

There will be approximately 6.8 billion people in the world in 2008. In about 2026, India is set to overtake China as the country with the world's highest population.

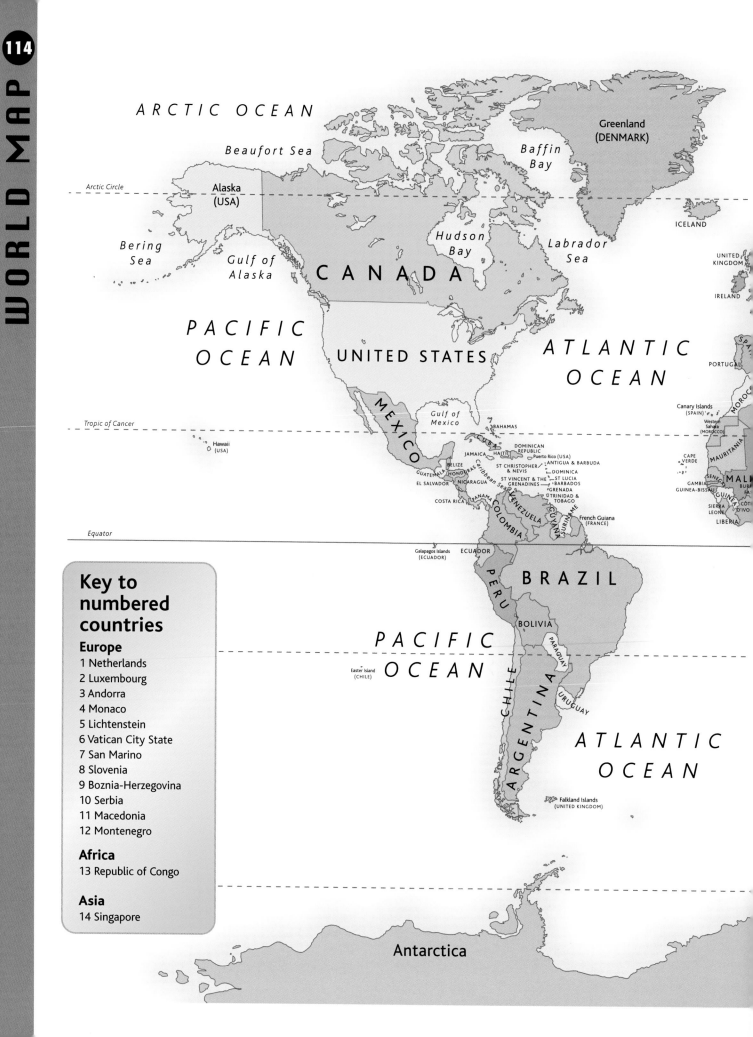

ARCTIC OCEAN

Beaufort Sea

Greenland
(DENMARK)

Baffin
Bay

Arctic Circle

Alaska
(USA)

ICELAND

Bering
Sea

Gulf of
Alaska

Hudson
Bay

Labrador
Sea

UNITED
KINGDOM

C A N A D A

IRELAND

PACIFIC
OCEAN

UNITED STATES

ATLANTIC
OCEAN

SPAIN

PORTUGAL

MEXICO

Gulf of
Mexico

Canary Islands
(SPAIN)

MOROCCO

Tropic of Cancer

BAHAMAS

Western
Sahara
(MOROCCO)

MAURITANIA

Hawaii
(USA)

CUBA

DOMINICAN
REPUBLIC

Puerto Rico (USA)

HAITI

MALI

ANTIGUA & BARBUDA

BELIZE

ST CHRISTOPHER
& NEVIS

DOMINICA

CAPE
VERDE

GUATEMALA HONDURAS

ST LUCIA
BARBADOS

SENEGAL

JAMAICA

Caribbean Sea

ST VINCENT & THE
GRENADINES

GAMBIA

GUINEA

EL SALVADOR

NICARAGUA

GRENADA

GUINEA-BISSAU

TRINIDAD &
TOBAGO

COSTA RICA

PANAMA

VENEZUELA

SIERRA
LEONE

CÔTE
D'IVO

COLOMBIA

GUYANA

LIBERIA

SURINAME

French Guiana
(FRANCE)

Galapagos Islands
(ECUADOR)

ECUADOR

P E R U

B R A Z I L

PACIFIC
OCEAN

BOLIVIA

PARAGUAY

Easter Island
(CHILE)

CHILE

ARGENTINA

URUGUAY

ATLANTIC
OCEAN

Falkland Islands
(UNITED KINGDOM)

## Key to numbered countries

**Europe**

1 Netherlands
2 Luxembourg
3 Andorra
4 Monaco
5 Lichtenstein
6 Vatican City State
7 San Marino
8 Slovenia
9 Boznia-Herzegovina
10 Serbia
11 Macedonia
12 Montenegro

**Africa**

13 Republic of Congo

**Asia**

14 Singapore

Antarctica

ARCTIC OCEAN

Svalbard (NORWAY)

Barents Sea

Kara Sea

Arctic Circle

NORWAY
SWEDEN
FINLAND
DENMARK
LATVIA
LITHUANIA
BELARUS
POLAND
UKRAINE
MOLDOVA
ROMANIA
BULGARIA
Black Sea
TURKEY
GREECE
CYPRUS
LEBANON
ISRAEL
SYRIA
Mediterranean Sea
MALTA
Corsica (FRANCE)
Sardinia (ITALY)
ITALY
allorca (SPAIN)

RUSSIA

Sea of Okhotsk

KAZAKHSTAN

MONGOLIA

Sea of Japan

NORTH KOREA
SOUTH KOREA
JAPAN

UZBEKISTAN
KYRGYZSTAN
TURKMENISTAN
TAJIKISTAN

CHINA

Caspian Sea
GEORGIA
ARMENIA
AZERBAIJAN

IRAQ
IRAN
AFGHANISTAN
PAKISTAN
KUWAIT
BAHRAIN
QATAR

NEPAL
BHUTAN

INDIA

TAIWAN

PACIFIC OCEAN

Tropic of Cancer

ALGERIA
TUNISIA
LIBYA
EGYPT
SAUDI ARABIA
UNITED ARAB EMIRATES
OMAN
YEMEN
Red Sea
ERITREA
DJIBOUTI

Philippine Sea

PHILIPPINES

NIGER
CHAD
SUDAN
NIGERIA
CAMEROON
CENTRAL AFRICAN REPUBLIC
EQUATORIAL GUINEA
GABON
TOMÉ NCIPÉ

Arabian Sea

Bay of Bengal

South China Sea

MARSHALL ISLANDS

MICRONESIA

PALAU

ETHIOPIA
SOMALIA
DEMOCRATIC REPUBLIC OF CONGO
KENYA
UGANDA
RWANDA
BURUNDI

SRI LANKA

MALDIVES

THAILAND
CAMBODIA
MYANMAR
LAOS

MALAYSIA
BRUNEI

Equator

NAURU
KIRIBATI

Angola
SEYCHELLES

INDONESIA

PAPUA NEW GUINEA

SOLOMON ISLANDS

TUVALU

TANZANIA
COMOROS
ANGOLA
ZAMBIA
ZIMBABWE
MOZAMBIQUE
MADAGASCAR
MAURITIUS
NAMIBIA
BOTSWANA
SWAZILAND
LESOTHO
SOUTH AFRICA

EAST TIMOR

Coral Sea
VANUATU
New Caledonia (FRANCE)
FIJI
SAMOA
TONGA

INDIAN OCEAN

AUSTRALIA

Tropic of Capricorn

Tasman Sea

NEW ZEALAND

SOUTHERN OCEAN

Antarctic Circle

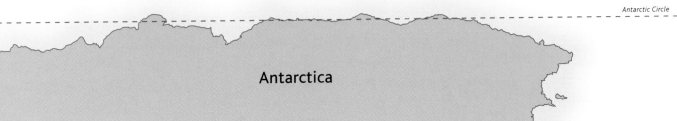

Antarctica

St Peter's, Vatican City

## Largest countries

These figures are based on total land area, including inland water, such as rivers and lakes. If the water area was not taken into account, China would be second largest, at 9,326,410 sq km (3,600,947 sq miles), the USA third with 9,161,923 sq km (3,537,439 sq miles) and Canada fourth at 9,093,507 sq km (3,511,023 sq miles).

### Largest countries

| Country | Area sq km (sq miles) |
| --- | --- |
| Russia | 17,075,200 (6,592,772) |
| Canada | 9,984,670 (3,855,103) |
| USA | 9,826,630 (3,794,083) |
| China | 9,596,960 (3,705,407) |
| Brazil | 8,511,965 (3,286,488) |
| Australia | 7,686,850 (2,967,910) |

### Smallest countries

| Country | Area sq km (sq miles) |
| --- | --- |
| Vatican City | 0.44 (0.17) |
| Monaco | 2 (0.77) |
| Nauru | 21 (8) |
| Tuvalu | 26 (10) |
| Bermuda | 53 (20) |
| San Marino | 61 (24) |
| Liechtenstein | 160 (62) |

## Biggest landlocked countries

A landlocked country has no coastline. This means that it has no direct access to the sea and fishing. Also, people and goods travelling to and from the country must go through another country. This may be difficult or expensive.

There are more than 40 landlocked countries in the world. The largest, Kazakhstan, has a coast on the Caspian Sea – which is a landlocked sea. The largest landlocked European country is Hungary (92,300 sq km [35,637 sq miles]). Europe also contains the world's smallest landlocked countries – Andorra, Liechtenstein, San Marino and Vatican City. All are less than 500 sq km (193 sq miles) in size. Liechtenstein and Uzbekistan are both double-landlocked. This means that they are surrounded by other landlocked countries.

**Kazakhstan** 2,717,300 sq km (1,049,155 sq miles)
**Mongolia** 1,564,116 sq km (603,908 sq miles)
**Chad** 1,284,000 sq km (495,755 sq miles)
**Niger** 1,267,000 sq km (489,191 sq miles)
**Mali** 1,240,000 sq km (478,766 sq miles)
**Ethiopia** 1,127,127 sq km (435,186 sq miles)
**Bolivia** 1,098,580 sq km (424,164 sq miles)

## Longest and shortest frontiers

A country's frontier is made up of the combined length of all its land borders.

**Longest**
**China** 22,117 km (13,743 miles)
**Russia** 20,097 km (12,488 miles)
**Brazil** 16,885 km (10,488 miles)
**India** 14,103 km (8,763 miles)
**USA** 12,034 km (7,478 miles)

**Shortest**
**Vatican City** 3.2 km (2.0 miles)
**Monaco** 4.4 km (2.7 miles)
**Cuba** 29.0 km (18 miles)
**San Marino** 39.0 km (24 miles)
**Qatar** 60 km (37 miles)

# Biggest and smallest populations

In most countries, more people are born every day than die, so population figures are going up all the time. China has the biggest population, but India is catching up fast.

| Biggest population | | Smallest population | |
|---|---|---|---|
| **Country** | **Population** | **Country** | **Population** |
| China | 1,313,973,713 | Vatican City | 821 |
| India | 1,095,351,995 | Tuvalu | 11,992 |
| USA | 298,444,215 | Nauru | 13,287 |
| Indonesia | 245,452,739 | Palau | 20,579 |
| Brazil | 188,078,227 | San Marino | 29,251 |
| Pakistan | 165,803,560 | Monaco | 32,543 |
| Bangladesh | 147,365,352 | Liechtenstein | 33,987 |
| Russia | 142,893,540 | St Christopher and Nevis | 39,129 |
| Nigeria | 131,859,731 | Marshall Islands | 60,422 |
| Japan | 127,463,611 | Antigua and Barbuda | 69,481 |

Crowded shopping street in Shanghai, China

## Country development

These rankings from the United Nations are based on a range of factors, including how long people can expect to live, how much money they earn, education level and quality of life.

| Most developed | Least developed |
|---|---|
| **1** Norway | **1** Niger |
| **2** Iceland | **2** Sierra Leone |
| **3** Australia | **3** Mali |
| **4** Ireland | **4** Burkina Faso |
| **5** Sweden | **5** Guinea-Bissau |
| *8* USA | **6** Central African Republic |
| *18* UK | |

# Population density

In densely populated countries, lots of people live on a small amount of land, usually in cities. The least densely populated countries are usually difficult for people to live in. The climate may be very cold or very hot, or there may be large areas of mountain, desert or forest.

## Most densely populated countries
**Monaco** 16,272 people per sq km (42,264 per sq mile)
**Singapore** 6,482 people per sq km (21,701 per sq mile)
**Vatican City** 1,866 people per sq km (4,829 per sq mile)
**Malta** 1,267 people per sq km (3,280 per sq mile)
**Maldives** 1,197 people per sq km (3,095 per sq mile)

## Least densely populated countries
**Mongolia** 1.81 people per sq km (4.69 per sq mile)
**Namibia** 2.48 people per sq km (6.41 per sq mile)
**Australia** 2.64 people per sq km (6.83 per sq mile)
**Suriname** 2.69 people per sq km (6.97 per sq mile)
**Botswana** 2.73 people per sq km (7.07 per sq mile)

Monaco

www.census.gov/main/www/popclock.html    search

# Changing names

Many cities change their names after the countries they are in become independent. Others are renamed after political changes, such as those ending the former Soviet Union. Some changes come from variations in the way in which foreign languages are translated from one alphabet to another.

| Was called/country | Now called (since) |
|---|---|
| Batavia, Indonesia | Jakarta (1949) |
| Bombay, India | Mumbai (1995) |
| Christiana, Norway | Oslo (1924) |
| Byzantium/Constantinople, Turkey | Istanbul (1930) |
| Danzig, Poland | Gdansk (1945) |
| Leningrad, USSR | St Petersburg, Russia (1991) |
| Léopoldville, Belgian Congo | Kinshasa, Zaire (1960) |
| New Amsterdam, America | New York, USA (1664) |
| Pretoria, South Africa | Tshwane (2005) |
| Rangoon, Burma | Yangon, Myanmar (1989) |
| Saigon, Vietnam | Ho Chi Minh City (1975) |
| Salisbury, Rhodesia | Harare, Zimbabwe (1980) |
| Santa Isabel, Equatorial Guinea | Malabo (1973) |
| Tsaritsyn/Stalingrad, USSR | Volgograd, Russia (1961) |

# Cities with the most people*

| | |
|---|---|
| 1 Tokyo, Japan | 37,037,743 |
| 2 Mexico City, Mexico | 22,752,357 |
| 3 New York, USA | 22,747,604 |
| 4 Seoul, South Korea | 22,596,020 |
| 5 Mumbai (Bombay), India | 20,426,991 |
| 6 São Paulo, Brazil | 19,637,518 |
| 7 Manila, The Philippines | 18,491,668 |
| 8 Jakarta, Indonesia | 18,267,156 |
| 9 New Delhi, India | 18,031,488 |
| 10 Los Angeles, USA | 17,989,605 |

*Estimated figures for city and adjoining populated areas 2007

www.citypopulation.de/cities.html    search

# Highest towns and cities

Some towns and cities are in surprisingly high places. The Chinese city of Wenchuan, founded in 1955, is at more than half the height of Everest. Even the towns and cities at the bottom of this list are at more than a third the height of Everest.

1 Wenchuan, China – 5,099 m (16,729 ft)
2 Potosí, Bolivia – 3,976 m (13,045 ft)
3 Oruro, Bolivia – 3,702 m (12,146 ft)
4 Lhasa, China – 3,684 m (12,087 ft)
5 La Paz, Bolivia – 3,632 m (11,916 ft)
6 Cuzco, Peru – 3,399 m (11,152 ft)
7 Huancayo, Peru – 3,249 m (10,659 ft)
8 Sucre, Bolivia – 2,835 m (9,301 ft)
9 Tunja, Colombia – 2,820 m (9,252 ft)
10 Quito, Ecuador – 2,819 m (9,249 ft)

La Paz, the world's highest capital city

# What is a city?

A city is a large town. In some countries, a city has a special status. In the UK it may have been given a royal charter. In the USA it is an urban area with its own government.

A town is a densely populated area with a defined boundary and its own government. A town is smaller than a city and larger than a village.

A village is a small group of houses and other buildings in a country area.

A hamlet is a small village or a cluster of houses in a country area. In the UK a village is a hamlet if it does not have a church.

A settlement is a small group of inhabited buildings, or a small countryside community, such as a ranch or farm with a few dwellings.

The legendary city of Troy

# Lost cities

There are some cities that were very famous in the past but have since been destroyed or abandoned.

### Angkor, Cambodia
Angkor was once the largest city in the world and more than a million people lived there. The city had an area of more than 78 sq km (30 sq miles) and was surrounded by a water-filled moat. It was abandoned in about AD 1100. Frenchman Henri Mouhot was the first westerner to discover the city, in 1861.

## One and only

The only city in two continents: Istanbul, Turkey, is partly in Europe and partly in Asia.

The only city centre with no cars: Venice. Its only traffic is boats on the canals.

The only non-US capital city named after a US president: Monrovia, the capital of Liberia, in Africa, was named after US president James Monroe.

### Atlantis
Some people believe that there was a city and island of Atlantis, perhaps in the Mediterranean, that was destroyed by an earthquake and flooding almost 12,000 years ago. No one knows exactly where it was or even whether it really existed.

### Chichén Itzá, Mexico
Chichén Itzá was once the centre of the Mayan empire. It was built in about AD 400 and had many buildings used in Mayan rituals. The city was abandoned in AD 1200.

### Cliff Palace (Mesa Verde), Colorado, USA
This Native American Indian city was built on a cliff side, but was abandoned during a long drought in the late 13th century. It lay unknown until 18 December 1888, when Richard Wetherill, a local farmer, spotted it while looking for stray cattle.

### Machu Picchu, Peru
The fortified Inca city on top of a mountain was stumbled on in 1911 by American explorer Hiram Bingham. He was searching for Vilcabamba, another lost Inca city.

### Pompeii, Italy
The entire city was buried by volcanic ash when Mount Vesuvius erupted in AD 79. Nearby Herculaneum was buried at the same time. Excavations began in 1748, and many treasures have been uncovered, including beautifully preserved murals (wall paintings). Plaster casts have been made of the bodies of inhabitants who were buried beneath the debris.

### Troy, Turkey
Troy was once thought to have existed only in legends, but its site was discovered in the 1870s.

### Ur, Iraq
Ur was once one of the greatest cities in the world, but was abandoned in the 4th century BC. Its magnificent royal tombs and other sites were excavated by archaeologists in 1922–34 and many treasures discovered.

**See also**
World civilizations and empires: pages 106–107

Grand Canal, Venice

# Canada

Canada is the second largest country in the world, after Russia. Almost half of Canada's land area is covered by forest and it exports more timber, pulp and newsprint than any other country. Canada also has a successful fishing industry and lots of natural resources, such as minerals and metals. Its varied landscape attracts millions of tourists each year. Famous Canadian landmarks include Niagara Falls and the Rocky Mountains.

**Area** 9,984,670 sq km
(3,855,103 sq miles)
**Country population** 33,098,932
**Capital city (pop)**
Ottawa (1,142,548)
**Official languages** French/English
**Currency**
Canadian dollar

Banff National Park, Alberta, Canada

# United States

The USA is made up of 50 states (including Alaska and Hawaii) and the District of Columbia, which contains the capital city, Washington. It includes a huge variety of landscapes, from hot deserts to snow-covered mountains. The country was once a colony under British rule but has been independent since 1776. It is now the world's wealthiest country and a great economic and military superpower.

**Area** 9,826,630 sq km (3,794,083 sq miles)
**Country population** 298,444,125
**Capital city (pop)** Washington DC (6,423,470)
**Official language** English
**Currency** US dollar

# Mexico

Some of the world's oldest civilizations have lived in Mexico, such as the Aztecs and Mayans. Nowadays, many tourists visit and it has plenty of natural resources. However, almost half the people are very poor and many try to cross the border into the USA every year. Some of them are arrested by border patrols.

**Area** 1,972,550 sq km (761,606 sq miles)
**Country population** 107,449,525
**Capital city (pop)** Mexico City (22,752,357)
**Official language** Spanish
**Currency** Peso

# Guatemala

Guatemala is one of Central America's most beautiful countries, with a dramatic landscape of forests, lakes and volcanoes. It is also one of the poorest and most violent. The country is still suffering from the after-effects of a long civil war (1960–96). Two-thirds of Guatemalan children live in poverty.

**Area** 108,890 sq km (42,043 sq miles)
**Country population** 12,293,545
**Capital city (pop)** Guatemala City (3,122,458)
**Official language** Spanish
**Currency** Quetzal

# Honduras

Honduras lies in Central America between the Caribbean Sea and the Atlantic Ocean. It is one of the world's poorest countries, although it has valuable stocks of timber. In 1998 Hurricane Mitch caused four billion dollars' worth of damage.

**Area** 112,090 sq km (43,278 sq miles)
**Country population** 7,326,496
**Capital city (pop)** Tegucigalpa (1,765,626)
**Official language** Spanish
**Currency** Lempira

# El Salvador

The tiny country of El Salvador is on Central America's Pacific coast. It often suffers hurricanes and earthquakes. Coffee is a major crop, but El Salvador relies heavily on aid money from other countries.

**Area** 21,040 sq km (8,124 sq miles)
**Country population** 6,822,378
**Capital city (pop)** San Salvador (1,881,584)
**Official language** Spanish
**Currency** US dollar

# Nicaragua

Nicaragua is the largest country in Central America. It is one of the poorest countries in the Western world and half its people are very poor indeed. In 1998, Hurricane Mitch caused great damage and left 20 per cent of Nicaraguans homeless.

**Area** 129,494 sq km (49,998 sq m)
**Country population** 5,570,129
**Capital city (pop)** Managua (1,713,807)
**Official language** Spanish
**Currency** Córdoba

# Panama

Panama is a narrow strip of land stretching between North and South America. It has coastlines on the Atlantic Ocean and the Pacific Ocean and has a canal, which connects the two oceans. Panama receives money from the many ships that use the canal each year and has other successful industries, but nearly 40 per cent of the people are poor.

**Area** 78,200 sq km (30,193 sq miles)
**Country population** 3,191,319
**Capital city (pop)** Panama City (1,233,204)
**Official language** Spanish
**Currency** Balboa

# Costa Rica

Costa Rica is one of the most successful Central American countries and has a good standard of living. Its landscape is beautiful, with many mountains and tropical forests, and tourism is increasing. However, the country is also becoming more and more involved in the illegal drugs trade.

**Area** 51,100 sq km (19,730 sq miles)
**Country population** 4,075,261
**Capital city (pop)** San José (1,648,870)
**Official language** Spanish
**Currency** Costa Rican colón

# St Christopher and Nevis

The Caribbean islands of St Christopher (also known as St Kitts) and Nevis became independent of the UK in 1983. Most of the people are descended from slaves brought from West Africa to work on the islands. Sugar has always been the islands' main crop, but tourism and financial services are now important industries.

**Area** 261 sq km (101 sq miles)
**Country population** 39,129
**Capital city (pop)** Basseterre (12,849)
**Official language** English
**Currency** East Caribbean dollar

# The Bahamas

The Bahamas is made up of more than 700 islands, which lie southeast of Florida in the Atlantic Ocean. The islands were ruled by the British, but became independent in 1973. Queen Elizabeth II is still the head of state. About 40 per cent of people work in tourism, but banking and finance are also important.

**Area** 13,940 sq km (5,382 sq miles)
**Country population** 303,770
**Capital city (pop)** Nassau (235,105)
**Official language** English
**Currency** Bahamian dollar

# Jamaica

The Caribbean island of Jamaica became independent of the UK in 1962, but has remained in the Commonwealth. Tourism is its main industry, but many visitors are put off by the island's poverty and violence. Jamaica has one of the world's highest murder rates.

**Area** 10,991 sq km (4,244 sq miles)
**Country population** 2,731,832
**Capital city (pop)** Kingston (949,235)
**Official language** English
**Currency** Jamaican dollar

# Dominican Republic

The Dominican Republic makes up the eastern two-thirds of the island of Hispaniola, sharing it with Haïti. It is the oldest European settlement in America. The Dominican Republic is one of the Caribbean's poorest countries, but it is now very popular with tourists.

**Area** 48,730 sq km (18,815 sq miles)
**Country population** 9,183,984
**Capital city (pop)** Santo Domingo (3,165,031)
**Official language** Spanish
**Currency** Dominican Republic peso

# Belize

Belize was a British colony called British Honduras, but became independent in 1981. Queen Elizabeth II is still the head of state. The coral reef off the coast is the world's second largest after Australia's Great Barrier Reef. Belize is now popular with tourists.

**Area** 22,966 sq km (8,867 sq miles)
**Country population** 287,730
**Capital city (pop)** Belmopan (15,940)
**Official language** English
**Currency** Belize dollar

# Antigua and Barbuda

The Caribbean islands of Antigua and Barbuda were settled by the Spanish, the French and the British before becoming independent in 1981. They are still part of the Commonwealth and Queen Elizabeth II is the head of state. The islands are popular with tourists.

**Area** 443 sq km (171 sq miles)
**Country population** 69,481
**Capital city (pop)** St John's (25,498)
**Official language** English
**Currency** East Caribbean dollar

# Haïti

Haïti shares the island of Hispaniola with the Dominican Republic. In 1804, Haïti was the first Caribbean state to become independent. Now Haïti is the poorest country in the Americas, after years of dictatorship and violence. Financial help from the EU and US was stopped in 2000 after unfair elections, and drug-trafficking is a big problem.

**Area** 27,750 sq km (10,714 sq miles)
**Country population** 8,308,504
**Capital city (pop)** Port-au-Prince (2,327,326)
**Official languages** Haïtian Creole/French
**Currency** Gourde

# Cuba

Cuba is 150 km (93 miles) south of Florida and is the largest island in the Caribbean. It has a Communist government, which has been led by Fidel Castro since 1959. Cuba attracts more and more tourists, but the collapse of the Soviet Union and trade restrictions put on Cuba by the USA have caused financial problems.

**Area** 110,860 sq km (42,803 sq miles)
**Country population** 11,382,820
**Capital city (pop)** Havana (2,164,362)
**Official language** Spanish
**Currency** Cuban peso

A street in Havana, Cuba

## St Vincent and the Grenadines

This Caribbean nation includes 33 small islands. It became independent from Britain in 1979, but it is still a member of the Commonwealth. Bananas are the main crop. Many tourists visit the islands.

**Area** 389 sq km
(150 sq miles)
**Country population** 117,848
**Capital city (pop)** Kingstown (18,323)
**Official language** English
**Currency** East Caribbean dollar

Boats moored near the island of St Vincent

## Dominica

This tropical, mountainous Caribbean island was once under British rule. It became independent in 1978. Dominica's main exports are bananas and fruit juices, but the crops are often destroyed by hurricanes.

**Area** 750 sq km (291 sq miles)
**Country population** 68,910
**Capital city (pop)** Roseau (16,582)
**Official language** English
**Currency** East Caribbean dollar

## Barbados

This Caribbean island became an independent state in 1966, but it remains part of the Commonwealth. Queen Elizabeth II is the head of state. The main industries are tourism and sugar manufacturing.

**Area** 431 sq km (166 sq miles)
**Country population** 98,947
**Capital city (pop)**
Bridgetown (98,947)
**Official language** English
**Currency** Barbados dollar

## Grenada

Grenada lies between the Caribbean Sea and the Atlantic Ocean, north of Trinidad and Tobago. Nearly 400,000 tourists visit Grenada every year. The island exports spices, and about a quarter of the world's nutmegs come from there.

**Area** 344 sq km (133 sq miles)
**Country population** 89,703
**Capital city (pop)** St George's (4,298)
**Official language** English
**Currency** East Caribbean dollar

## Trinidad and Tobago

The Caribbean islands of Trinidad and Tobago lie northwest of Venezuela. They have large reserves of oil and natural gas and are among the richest of all Caribbean nations. Tobago is quieter than Trinidad. Both islands are popular with tourists.

**Area** 5,128 sq km (1,980 sq miles)
**Country population** 1,065,842
**Capital city (pop)** Port of Spain (49,865)
**Official language** English
**Currency** Trinidad and Tobago dollar

## St Lucia

This mountainous island lies between the Atlantic Ocean and the Caribbean Sea. It is famous for its two large, cone-shaped peaks known as the Pitons. Bananas are the island's main crop, but banking and tourism are also important.

**Area** 616 sq km
(238 sq miles)
**Country population** 168,458
**Capital city (pop)**
Castries (70,389)
**Official language** English
**Currency** East Caribbean dollar

# South America

## Argentina

Argentina was once ruled by Spain, but it became independent in 1816. This South American country is famous for its beef and has large mineral deposits.

**Area** 2,766,890 sq km (1,068,302 sq miles)
**Country population** 39,921,833
**Capital city (pop)** Buenos Aires (13,615,412)
**Official language** Spanish
**Currency** Peso

## Venezuela

Venezuela is a land of great natural beauty in northern South America. Angel Falls is the world's highest waterfall, and Maracaibo is the largest lake in South America. Venezuela has large reserves of oil, coal and gold, but almost half of Venezuelans live in poverty.

**Area** 912,050 sq km (352,145 sq miles)
**Country population** 25,730,435
**Capital city (pop)** Caracas (3,849,469)
**Official language** Spanish
**Currency** Bolívar

## Suriname

This is the smallest independent nation in South America. It was governed by the Netherlands but became independent in 1975. Suriname has large amounts of timber as well as bauxite and gold, but 70 per cent of the people are still very poor.

**Area** 163,270 sq km (63,039 sq miles)
**Country population** 439,117
**Capital city (pop)** Paramaribo (226,124)
**Official language** Dutch
**Currency** Suriname dollar

# Colombia

Colombia is in the northwest of South America. The main crops are coffee, bananas and sugar, and the country has oil and mineral reserves. Colombia is also the world's leading producer of cocaine.

**Area** 1,138,910 sq km (439,736 sq miles)
**Country population** 43,593,635
**Capital city (pop)** Bogotá (8,090,883)
**Official language** Spanish
**Currency** Colombian peso

 # Uruguay

Uruguay is the second smallest country in South America. It is wealthier than most South American nations because of its livestock, tourism and banking industries. It has a good welfare system and its people are well educated.

**Area** 176,220 sq km (68,039 sq miles)
**Country population** 3,431,932
**Capital city (pop)**
Montevideo (1,765,436)
**Official language**
Spanish
**Currency**
Uruguayan peso

 # Ecuador

Ecuador lies on the Equator and stretches across the Andes Mountains. The country's main exports are fish, bananas, cocoa and coffee. Oil was discovered there in 1972.

**Area** 283,560 sq km (109,483 sq miles)
**Country population** 13,547,510
**Capital city (pop)** Quito (2,049,473)
**Official language** Spanish
**Currency** US dollar

 # Bolivia

The Andes mountain range crosses Bolivia. The Bolivian capital La Paz is in the Andes and is the highest capital city in the world. Bolivia is one of only two landlocked countries in South America.

**Area** 1,098,580 sq km (424,164 sq miles)
**Country population** 8,989,046
**Capital city (pop)** La Paz (1,965,974)
**Official language** Spanish
**Currency** Boliviano

# Peru

Peru lies on South America's Pacific coast. It has been home to famous ancient civilizations, including the Inca Empire. Peru has important natural resources, including gold and oil, but they have not yet been developed.

**Area** 1,285,220 sq km (496,226 sq miles)
**Country population** 28,302,603
**Capital city (pop)** Lima (7,979,965)
**Official languages** Spanish/Quechua
**Currency** New sol

 # Paraguay

The Republic of Paraguay is landlocked. It has one of the smallest populations in South America. Alfredo Stroessner, the region's longest-ruling dictator, was overthrown in 1989, but Paraguay is still struggling with political and financial problems.

**Area** 406,750 sq km (157,047 sq miles)
**Country population** 6,506,464
**Capital city (pop)** Asunción (1,944,445)
**Official languages** Spanish/Guaraní
**Currency** Guaraní

 # Guyana

Guyana is the only country in South America where English is the official language. Its natural resources include gold and diamonds, but it is very poor and has political problems. The country has many fascinating animals and plants and is popular with tourists interested in nature.

**Area** 214,970 sq km (83,000 sq miles)
**Country population** 767,245
**Capital city (pop)** Georgetown (238,747)
**Official language** English
**Currency** Guyana dollar

Statue of Christ,
Rio de Janeiro, Brazil

 # Chile

Chile is an extremely long, narrow country, which lies between the Andes Mountains and the Pacific Ocean. It is one of the most successful nations in South America and has many natural resources, including minerals and timber, as well as thriving agriculture and fishing industries.

**Area** 756,950 sq km (292,260 sq miles)
**Country population** 16,134,219
**Capital city (pop)** Santiago (4,949,540)
**Official language** Spanish
**Currency** Chilean peso

# Brazil

**Area** 8,511,965 sq km (3,286,488 sq miles)
**Country population** 188,078,227
**Capital city (pop)** Brasília (2,314,172)
**Official language** Portuguese
**Currency** Real

Brazil covers nearly half of South America. It contains the world's second longest river, the Amazon, and vast tropical rainforests. About 82 per cent of Brazil's population lives in cities, which are mostly on the coast in the south and southeast of the country. Brazil is the leading nation in South America but there are wide divisions between rich and poor.

## Norway

Norway is famous for its fjords. The population is small and has a very good standard of living, thanks to the country's plentiful natural resources. Only Russia and Saudi Arabia export more oil than Norway, and it is the world's biggest exporter of seafood.

**Area** 323,802 sq km (125,021 sq miles)
**Country population** 4,610,820
**Capital city (pop)** Oslo (830,380)
**Official language** Norwegian
**Currency** Krone

Oil rig supply boat in Bergen harbour, Norway

## Ireland

Ireland was divided in the 1920s, when 26 counties in the south gained independence from the United Kingdom. Since then there has been conflict in Northern Ireland between those who want to remain part of the United Kingdom and those who want a united, independent Ireland. Since Ireland joined the European Community in 1973 it has become a modern, high-tech nation with successful industry. It began using the Euro in January 1999, along with ten other nations.

**Area** 70,200 sq km (27,135 sq miles)
**Country population** 4,062,235
**Capital city (pop)** Dublin (1,036,724)
**Official languages** Irish/English
**Currency** Euro

## Denmark

Denmark shares a border with Germany and is the smallest, most southerly Scandinavian nation. It is a wealthy, high-tech country and has all the oil and natural gas it needs. The standard of living is high. Denmark is a monarchy and the kingdom includes the Faeroe Islands and Greenland.

**Area** 43,094 sq km (16,639 sq miles)
**Country population** 5,450,611
**Capital city (pop)** Copenhagen (1,093,954)
**Official language** Danish
**Currency** Danish krone

## Finland

Since the end of World War II, Finland has changed from being a rural country covered with dense forest into a modern nation. It has very successful industries and an excellent welfare system. Finland joined the European Union in 1995 and adopted the Euro as its currency in 2002.

**Area** 338,145 sq km (130,559 sq miles)
**Country population** 5,231,372
**Capital city (pop)** Helsinki (1,248,122)
**Official languages** Finnish/Swedish
**Currency** Euro

## Luxembourg

Luxembourg is landlocked by Belgium, Germany and France. Its inhabitants have an amazingly high standard of living. Steel was once the main industry, but financial services have now become more important.

**Area** 2,586 sq km (999 sq miles)
**Country population** 474,419
**Capital city (pop)** Luxembourg (76,330)
**Official languages** French/German
**Currency** Euro

Window in Heidelberg Castle Germany

## Sweden

Sweden is a rich country with a high standard of living. Swedes have one of the world's longest life expectancies. The country has many natural resources including iron ore, lead, granite, zinc and forests. Forests cover about half the land and there are important timber and paper industries.

**Area** 449,964 sq km (173,732 sq miles)
**Country population** 9,016,596
**Capital city (pop)** Stockholm (1,721,758)
**Official language** Swedish
**Currency** Swedish krona

## Germany

Germany was divided after World War II. The Soviet Union and Poland claimed the East, and the USA, UK and France controlled the West. The East became a Communist state and the West became a democracy. Thousands of East Germans fled to the West. The Berlin Wall was built in 1961 to close the border and stop the flow of people. The decline of the USSR led to the fall of the Berlin Wall in 1989 and Germany was reunited in 1990. Today, 80 per cent of Germany's people live in the West, and the effects of Communism are still felt in the East.

**Area** 357,021 sq km (137,847 sq miles)
**Country population** 82,422,299
**Capital city (pop)** Berlin (4,025,873)
**Official language** German
**Currency** Euro

People bathing in the Blue Lagoon, Iceland

# Iceland

Iceland is a volcanic island and is the most westerly country in Europe. Its capital city is the furthest north in the world. Iceland is a wealthy country with low unemployment and a good welfare system. Fishing provides 70 per cent of its exports, which could cause problems as fish stocks decline.

**Area** 103,000 sq km (39,769 sq miles)
**Country population** 299,388
**Capital city (pop)** Reykjavík (115,214)
**Official language** Icelandic
**Currency** Icelandic króna

# The Netherlands

The Netherlands is a low-lying country and much of it has been reclaimed from the sea. Nearly a quarter of the land lies below sea level, which makes it vulnerable to flooding, despite coastal defences and a network of dykes and canals. Banking, shipping and fishing all are important industries. The Netherlands is the sixth largest exporter in the world.

**Area** 41,526 sq km (16,033 sq miles)
**Country population** 16,491,461
**Capital city (pop)** Amsterdam (746,685)
**Official language** Dutch
**Currency** Euro

# Belgium

Belgium is divided into Flanders (in the northwest), and Wallonia (in the southeast). Brussels is the headquarters of the European Union. This has brought wealth to the country as multinational companies have settled in the city. Belgium is well known for its fine chocolates and beer – and Tintin!

**Area** 30,528 sq km (11,787 sq miles)
**Country population** 10,379,067
**Capital city (pop)** Brussels (2,129,024)
**Official languages** Flemish/French/German
**Currency** Euro

# France

France is the largest country in Western Europe and a key member of the European Union. It has a varied landscape ranging from coastal plains to the Alps in the southeast. Farms and forests cover a large proportion of the country, and agricultural products – particularly wine and liqueurs – are major exports. France once had one of the world's largest empires. Most of its former colonies are now independent, but French Guiana, Guadeloupe, Martinique, Réunion, Mayotte, St Pierre and Miquelon, French Polynesia, New Caledonia, Wallis and Futuna and the Southern and Antarctic Territories all still have links with France.

**Area** 643,427 sq km (248,428 sq miles)
**Country population** 62,752,136
**Capital city (pop)** Paris (11,695,134)
**Official language** French
**Currency** Euro

# United Kingdom

The United Kingdom is made up of Great Britain (England, Scotland and Wales) and Northern Ireland. Although it is a small country, the UK has had a huge influence on the world because of its cultural, military and industrial strengths. At one time, it controlled a vast empire of lands across the globe and was the world's leading industrial nation. Traditional manufacturing industries are now less important. In the 21st century the UK's main industries are technology, tourism and services such as banking, and it is still an important economic power.

**Area** 244,820 sq km (94,526 sq miles)
**Country population** 60,609,153
**Capital city (pop)** London (12,629,020)
**Language** English
**Currency** British pound

# Monaco

Monaco is a principality – it is ruled by a prince. It is surrounded by France and is the second smallest independent state in the world. It has no income tax and low business taxes so rich people flock there to escape taxes.

**Area** 2 sq km (0.77 sq miles)
**Country population** 32,543
**Capital city (pop)** Monaco (965)
**Official language** French
**Currency** Euro

Plaza de España in Seville, Spain

# Spain

Spain covers most of the Iberian peninsula. The country has many cultures. Basque, Catalan, Galician and Valencian are spoken in different regions, but Castilian Spanish is the official language. There are 19 regions with their own elected authorities. There is a campaign for independence by the Basque country in the north, which has caused ongoing problems for the government. Spain is the world's second most popular tourist destination (after France) and has more than 50 million visitors every year. The fishing industry is one of the biggest in Europe, but unemployment is high.

**Area** 504,782 sq km (194,897 sq miles)
**Country population** 40,397,842
**Capital city (pop)** Madrid (6,097,994)
**Official language** Castilian Spanish
**Currency** Euro

# Portugal

Portugal lies to the west of Spain on the Iberian peninsula. It is one of the European Union's least developed countries and has the highest number of people working on the land. Portugal's economy has grown rapidly since it joined the European Union in 1986. Tourism is one of its fastest growing industries. Portugal once had a vast empire, stretching across the Americas, Africa and Asia. Over 177 million people worldwide speak Portuguese.

**Area** 92,391 sq km (35,672 sq miles)
**Country population** 10,605,870
**Capital city (pop)** Lisbon (2,618,411)
**Official language** Portuguese
**Currency** Euro

# Malta

Malta, which includes the neighbouring island of Gozo, used to be under British rule. It became independent in 1964, but remains a part of the Commonwealth. Malta became the European Union's smallest new member in 2004. Tourism is the island's most important industry and Malta has more than a million visitors every year.

**Area** 316 sq km (122 sq miles)
**Country population** 400,214
**Capital city (pop)** Valletta (6,703)
**Official languages** Maltese/English
**Currency** Maltese lira

# Vatican City State

The Vatican City is the smallest country in the world, both in area and population. It is surrounded by the city of Rome. The Vatican is home to the Pope and it is the spiritual centre of the Roman Catholic Church. It depends on contributions from Roman Catholics all over the world for its income, and the sale of souvenirs and publications.

**Area** 0.44 sq km (0.17 sq miles)
**Country population** 821
**Capital city (pop)** Vatican City (767)
**Official languages** Latin/Italian
**Currency** Euro

# San Marino

San Marino is entirely surrounded by Italy and it is the third smallest state in Europe. The tiny republic attracts about three million tourists every year. San Marino's inhabitants (known as Sammarinese) enjoy the world's sixth highest income per person.

**Area** 61 sq km (24 sq miles)
**Country population** 29,251
**Capital city (pop)** San Marino (4,647)
**Official language** Italian
**Currency** Euro

# Andorra

Andorra is a small principality (a state ruled by a prince), which dates from 1278. It lies in the mountains between France and Spain. Tourism is its main industry, but financial services are also becoming important.

**Area** 468 sq km (181 sq miles)
**Country population** 71,201
**Capital city (pop)** Andorra la Vella (20,209)
**Official language** Catalan
**Currency** Euro

# Estonia

The small Baltic state of Estonia regained its independence in 1991 when the Soviet Union collapsed. It was one of the Eastern European nations that joined the European Union in 2004.

**Area** 45,226 sq km (17,462 sq miles)
**Country population** 1,324,333
**Capital city (pop)** Tallinn (390,472)
**Official language** Estonian
**Currency** Kroon

# Italy

Italy is a long, narrow country reaching into the Mediterranean Sea. It includes the islands of Sicily and Sardinia among others. Italy can be divided into two: the wealthy, industrial north, and the poorer south, where most people work on the land and around 20 per cent of the population is unemployed. About 40 million foreign tourists visit Italy every year, many of them to see its beautiful cities, which include Rome, Venice and Florence.

**Area** 301,230 sq km (116,306 sq miles)
**Country population** 58,133,509
**Capital city (pop)** Rome (3,776,313)
**Official language** Italian
**Currency** Euro

# Austria

Austria is a small mountainous country. It is landlocked by the Czech Republic, Slovakia, Italy, Slovenia, Hungary, Germany, Switzerland and Liechtenstein. It was once the centre of the powerful Austro-Hungarian empire, until its defeat in World War I. It was occupied by Nazi Germany and then by the Allies after World War II. Since the war Austria has flourished, and it is now a popular holiday spot.

**Area** 83,870 sq km (32,382 sq miles)
**Country population** 8,192,880
**Capital city (pop)** Vienna (2,081,714)
**Official language** German
**Currency** Euro

# Switzerland

Switzerland is the most mountainous country in Europe. The Alps occupy 60 per cent of its land area. It has a very high income per person, low unemployment and its people have a long life expectancy. Switzerland was not involved in either World War and has not joined the European Union.

**Area** 41,290 sq km (15,942 sq miles)
**Country population** 7,523,934
**Capital city (pop)** Bern (119,197)
**Official languages** German/French/Italian/Romansch
**Currency** Swiss franc

# Belarus

Belarus became independent when the Soviet Union collapsed in 1991. It continues to have close ties with Russia. The country still suffers from the effects of nuclear fallout from the 1986 Chernobyl accident, which took place in neighbouring Ukraine.

**Area** 207,600 sq km (80,155 sq miles)
**Country population** 10,293,011
**Capital city (pop)** Minsk (1,753,245)
**Official languages** Belarusian/Russian
**Currency** Belarusian rouble

# Czech Republic

The Czech Republic was part of Czechoslovakia until it split from Slovakia in 1993. It now attracts investment from other countries and has a thriving tourism industry. The country joined the European Union in 2004.

**Area** 78,866 sq km (30,450 sq miles)
**Country population** 10,235,455
**Capital city (pop)** Prague (1,417,844)
**Official language** Czech
**Currency** Koruna

Astronomical clock in Prague, Czech Republic

# Poland

Poland is the largest nation in Central Europe and has the highest population. It was devastated by World War II, when more than six million people died – more than in any other country. In 1989 Poland was the first Eastern European nation to topple its Communist leaders. In May 2004 it joined the European Union.

**Area** 312,685 sq km (120,729 sq miles)
**Country population** 38,536,869
**Capital city (pop)** Warsaw (2,250,836)
**Official language** Polish
**Currency** Zloty

# Latvia

Latvia is bounded by the Baltic Sea, Estonia, Lithuania, Belarus and Russia. It became independent of the Soviet Union in 1991 and in 2004 it was accepted into the European Union.

**Area** 64,589 sq km (24,938 sq miles)
**Country population** 2,274,735
**Capital city (pop)** Riga (821,640)
**Official language** Latvian
**Currency** Lats

# Liechtenstein

Liechtenstein is the sixth smallest country in the world. Its low taxes have encouraged extraordinary economic growth, and thousands of foreign companies have bank accounts there.

**Area** 160 sq km (62 sq miles)
**Country population** 33,987
**Capital city (pop)** Vaduz (5,299)
**Official language** German
**Currency** Swiss franc

# Lithuania

Lithuania became independent of the Soviet Union in 1991. It used to depend on Russia, but more recently it has developed trade links with the West. It joined the European Union in 2004.

**Area** 65,200 sq km (25,174 sq miles)
**Country population** 3,585,906
**Capital city (pop)** Vilnius (541,762)
**Official language** Lithuanian
**Currency** Litas

Panoramic view of Florence, Italy

**EUROPE**

View of Rovinj, Croatia

## Croatia

Croatia was one of Yugoslavia's most advanced and prosperous areas, and declared its independence in 1991. The country borders the Adriatic Sea and its coast was popular with tourists. The Yugoslavian conflict of 1991–95 threw the country into turmoil, but visitors are now returning.

**Area** 55,542 sq km (21,831 sq miles)
**Country population** 4,494,749
**Capital city (pop)** Zagreb (702,417)
**Official language** Croatian
**Currency** Kuna

## Bulgaria

Bulgaria was Communist until 1990, when it became a democracy. It has now joined the European Union, despite organized crime, corruption, inflation and unemployment. Bulgaria is becoming popular with tourists, especially the historic capital city of Sofia.

**Area** 110,910 sq km (42,823 sq miles)
**Country population** 7,385,367
**Capital city (pop)** Sofia (1,217,465)
**Official language** Bulgarian
**Currency** Lev

## Bosnia and Herzegovina

Bosnia and Herzegovina was recognized as an independent state in 1992 after Yugoslavia collapsed in 1991. Since then clashes between Bosnia's Croats, Serbs and Muslims have caused civil war, which is still not resolved. Despite this, more tourists are beginning to visit the country again.

**Area** 51,129 sq km (19,741 sq miles)
**Country population** 4,498,976
**Capital city (pop)** Sarajevo (777,761)
**Official languages** Bosnian/Croatian/Serbian
**Currency** Convertible marka

## Slovakia

Slovakia is landlocked and mountainous. It became independent in 1993, when Czechoslovakia divided into the Czech Republic and Slovakia. It joined the European Union in 2004.

**Area** 48,845 sq km (18,859 sq miles)
**Country population** 5,439,448
**Capital city (pop)** Bratislava (421,151)
**Official language** Slovak
**Currency** Koruna

## Moldova

Moldova is Europe's poorest country. It has no natural resources and imports all its energy supplies from Russia, from which it became independent in 1991.

**Area** 33,843 sq km (13,067 sq miles)
**Country population** 4,466,706
**Capital city (pop)** Chisinau (709,085)
**Official language** Moldovan
**Currency** Moldovan leu

## Ukraine

Ukraine is a vast area between Poland and Russia. It became independent after the collapse of the Soviet Union. In 1986 it was the scene of the world's worst nuclear disaster, when a reactor at the Chernobyl nuclear plant exploded.

**Area** 603,700 sq km (233,090 sq miles)
**Country population** 46,710,816
**Capital city (pop)** Kiev (2,469,968)
**Official language** Ukrainian
**Currency** Hryvna

## Albania

Albania depends mostly on farming, and its main crops are wheat, maize, sugar beet, potatoes and fruit. It has borders with Serbia, Montenegro, Kosovo, Macedonia and Greece.

**Area** 28,748 sq km (11,100 sq miles)
**Country population** 3,581,655
**Capital city (pop)** Tirana (386,025)
**Official language** Albanian
**Currency** Lek

## Georgia

Georgia lies in a key position east of the Black Sea between Russia and Turkey. It has coal deposits, but they have not yet been exploited. The country relies on farming – particularly grapes from which wine is made.

**Area** 69,700 sq km (26,911 sq miles)
**Country population** 4,661,473
**Capital city (pop)** Tbilisi (1,234,671)
**Official language** Georgian
**Currency** Lari

The Millennium Monument in Budapest, Hungary

## Hungary

Hungary became Communist after World War II. In the 1990s, it defied the Soviet Union and began some free trade with the West. This central European country has flourished since the Soviet Union's collapse and it entered the European Union in 2004.

**Area** 93,030 sq km (35,919 sq miles)
**Country population** 9,981,334
**Capital city (pop)** Budapest (2,571,504)
**Official language** Hungarian
**Currency** Forint

# Slovenia

About half of Slovenia is covered in forest, making it the third most forested country in Europe. Slovenia became independent from Yugoslavia in 1991 and joined the European Union in 2004. Its people now have a reasonably good standard of living.

**Area** 20,273 sq km (7,827 sq miles)
**Country population** 2,010,347
**Capital city (pop)** Ljubljana (253,154)
**Official language** Slovene
**Currency** Euro

# Greece

The ancient country of Greece lies in an important position between Europe, Asia and Africa. It includes about 2,000 islands as well as the mainland. About 14 million tourists visit Greece every year. However, it has few natural resources and relies on money from the European Union.

**Area** 131,940 sq km (50,942 sq miles)
**Country population** 10,688,058
**Capital city (pop)** Athens (3,799,134)
**Official language** Greek
**Currency** Euro

Windmill on the Greek island of Santorini

# Azerbaijan

Azerbaijan regained its independence from the Soviet Union in 1991. The country has rich mineral resources as well as oil and natural gas. However, conflict and corruption have kept it from developing a healthy economy.

**Area** 86,600 sq km (33,436 sq miles)
**Country population** 7,961,619
**Capital city (pop)** Baki/Baku (2,135,335)
**Official language** Azerbaijani
**Currency** Manat

## Macedonia

Macedonia's full name is the Former Yugoslav Republic of Macedonia (FYROM), not to be confused with the Greek region of Macedonia. Macedonia became independent in 1991. Since then there have been clashes between the country's large Albanian minority and its Macedonian majority.

**Area** 25,333 sq km (9,781 sq miles)
**Country population** 2,050,554
**Capital city (pop)** Skopje (585,732)
**Official languages** Macedonian/Albanian
**Currency** Denar

## Armenia

Armenia was the first country formally to adopt Christianity in AD 301. This mountainous country is bordered by Azerbaijan, Georgia, Iran and Turkey. Its key position between Europe and Asia led to invasions by the Persian, Ottoman, Roman and Byzantine empires, among others.

**Area** 29,800 sq km (11,506 sq miles)
**Country population** 2,976,372
**Capital city (pop)** Yerevan (1,467,303)
**Official language** Armenian
**Currency** Dram

## Romania

The mountainous Republic of Romania is the largest Balkan nation. The Communist regime was overthrown in 1989 when the dictator Nicolae Ceausescu was executed. The country is still very poor, with almost half of Romanians living in poverty. It is now a member of the European Union.

**Area** 237,500 sq km (91,699 sq miles)
**Country population** 22,303,552
**Capital city (pop)** Bucharest (2,209,108)
**Official language** Romanian
**Currency** Leu

## Serbia

This landlocked country was formerly part of Yugoslavia. It was part of the state of Serbia and Montenegro from 2003 until 2006, when it declared itself independent. Its economy is based on agriculture and industry, but there is high unemployment.

**Area** 88,361 sq km (34,116 sq miles)
**Country population** 9,396,411
**Capital city (pop)** Belgrade (1,111,825)
**Official language** Serbian
**Currency** Serbian dinar

## Cyprus

The Mediterranean island of Cyprus has been divided since Turkey invaded the north of the island in 1974. The Turkish Republic of Northern Cyprus is recognized only by Turkey. Greek Cyprus attracts many tourists and was accepted into the European Union in 2004. The Turkish part depends heavily on loans from Turkey.

**Area** 9,250 sq km (3,571 sq miles)
**Country population** 784,301
**Capital city (pop)** Nicosia (204,495)
**Official languages** Greek/Turkish
**Currency** Cyprus pound

# Montenegro

Montenegro was a former part of Yugoslavia and became independent from Serbia in 2006. It is now a full member of the United Nations and, although not a member of the European Union, it has adopted the Euro as its national currency.

**Area** 14,026 sq km (5,415 sq miles)
**Country population** 630,548
**Capital city (pop)** Podgorica (163,275)
**Official language** Serbian
**Currency** Euro

# Morocco

Morocco is in northwestern Africa. The country was divided between Spanish and French rule, but gained independence in 1956. It has rich mineral deposits and nearly three-quarters of the world's phosphate. Tourism is becoming increasingly important, but almost half the population work on the land.

**Area** 446,550 sq km (172,414 sq miles)
**Country population** 33,241,259
**Capital city (pop)** Rabat (1,721,760)
**Official language** Arabic
**Currency** Dirham

## Algeria

Algeria became independent from France in 1962. Throughout the 1990s the country was torn apart by civil war, in which 100,000 people are thought to have died. Algeria is still struggling to control its religious militants.

**Area** 2,381,740 sq km (919,595 sq miles)
**Country population** 32,930,091
**Capital city (pop)** Algiers (5,937,183)
**Official languages** Arabic/Berber
**Currency** Algerian dinar

## Tunisia

The North African country of Tunisia shares borders with Algeria and Libya and has a Mediterranean coastline. About one-fifth of the people live by farming and fishing.

**Area** 163,610 sq km (63,170 sq miles)
**Country population** 10,175,014
**Capital city (pop)** Tunis (2,028,662)
**Official language** Arabic
**Currency** Tunisian dinar

## Cape Verde

Cape Verde is made up of the Windward Islands and the Leeward Islands in the Atlantic Ocean off the west coast of Africa. Their main exports are bananas and coffee.

**Area** 4,033 sq km (1,557 sq miles)
**Country population** 420,979
**Capital city (pop)** Praia (121,393)
**Official language** Portuguese
**Currency** Cape Verdean escudo

## Ethiopia

Ethiopia is Africa's oldest independent country. It has suffered many droughts and famines. These, combined with civil war and a border dispute with Eritrea, have made Ethiopia one of Africa's poorest nations. Its natural resources are underdeveloped, and 85 per cent of the people still depend upon the land for a living.

**Area** 1,127,127 sq km (435,186 sq miles)
**Country population** 74,777,981
**Capital city (pop)** Addis Ababa (2,888,248)
**Official language** There is no official language, but Amharic is the most widely used of the 70 languages
**Currency** Ethiopian birr

## Eritrea

Eritrea is in eastern Africa and has had violent border disputes with Ethiopia since 1998. The conflict has affected Eritrea's economy, but the government continues to improve the country's roads, schools and transport systems. Its Red Sea ports are an important source of income.

**Area** 121,320 sq km (46,842 sq miles)
**Country population** 4,786,994
**Capital city (pop)** Asmara (1,091,388)
**Official languages** No official language; Arabic, Tigrinya and English are the main working languages. Italian is also spoken.
**Currency** Nakfa

## Libya

Libya has large oil reserves, but its economy has suffered from sanctions imposed by the United Nations. These were in response to the bombing of an airliner over Lockerbie in Scotland in 1988. Sanctions have now been lifted and Libya's leader, Colonel Gaddafi, has promised to bring his country back into the international community.

**Area** 1,759,540 sq km (679,362 sq miles)
**Country population** 5,900,754
**Capital city (pop)** Tripoli (1,894,852)
**Official language** Arabic
**Currency** Libyan dinar

Camel and rider near the Great Pyramid in Egypt

## Egypt

Egypt lies in a key position. It has a coastline on both the Mediterranean and Red Seas, and borders with the Sudan, Libya, Israel and the Gaza Strip. Egypt also controls the vital Suez Canal. This allows about 15,000 ships each year to travel between the Mediterranean and the Indian Ocean without sailing around Africa. Famous landmarks include the pyramids.

**Area** 1,001,450 sq km (386,662 sq miles)
**Country population** 78,887,007
**Capital city (pop)** Cairo (15,907,574)
**Official language** Arabic
**Currency** Egyptian pound

Fortified town of Aït Benhaddou in the High Atlas mountains, Morocco

## Somalia

Somalia is one of the world's poorest countries and there has been conflict between different groups. The north declared independence under the name Somaliland, but is not recognized by any foreign government.

**Area** 637,657 sq km (246,201 sq miles)
**Country population** 8,863,338
**Capital city (pop)** Mogadishu (2,855,805)
**Official languages** Somali/Arabic
**Currency** Somali shilling

 ## Mauritania

Mauritania is mainly desert. It became independent from France in 1960. There is conflict between the country's African and Arab peoples. Mauritania has rich mineral deposits, but these have not yet been exploited.

**Area** 1,030,700 sq km (397,955 sq miles)
**Country population** 3,177,388
**Capital city (pop)** Nouakchott (753,187)
**Official language** Arabic
**Currency** Ouguiya

## Sudan

Sudan is the biggest country in Africa. It has large oil reserves, which have been exploited since 1999. However, the country has suffered from civil war since its independence in 1956. This war has been going on longer than any other war in Africa. Since 2003 fighting has been particularly severe in the western region of Darfur, which is one of the poorest parts of the country. The United Nations has described this as the world's worst humanitarian crisis.

**Area** 2,505,810 sq km (967,499 sq miles)
**Country population** 41,236,378
**Capital city (pop)** Khartoum (8,363,915)
**Official language** Arabic
**Currency** Sudanese dinar

 ## Djibouti

Djibouti lies in a key position between Ethiopia and the Red Sea. The country provides refuelling facilities for ships and operates a free port, which bring money into Djibouti.

**Area** 23,000 sq km (8,880 sq miles)
**Country population** 486,530
**Capital city (pop)** Djibouti (642,846)
**Official languages** Arabic/French
**Currency** Djibouti franc

 ## Senegal

Senegal is almost divided into two by The Gambia. It became independent from France in 1960. It is now popular with tourists, but has few natural resources, high unemployment and more than half its people live in poverty.

**Area** 196,190 sq km (75,749 sq miles)
**Country population** 11,987,121
**Capital city (pop)** Dakar (2,461,682)
**Official language** French
**Currency** CFA franc

## Niger

Niger is the largest nation in West Africa. It is also one of the hottest and poorest countries in the world. Niger borders the Sahara Desert and droughts often kill much of the country's vital livestock. It has one of the world's lowest literacy rates.

**Area** 1,267,000 sq km (489,191 sq miles)
**Country population** 12,525,094
**Capital city (pop)** Niamey (829,255)
**Official language** French
**Currency** CFA franc

 ## Guinea

Guinea has been placed under great strain by thousands of refugees from its war-torn neighbours, Liberia and Sierra Leone. Guinea has natural resources, including iron ore, gold and diamonds.

**Area** 245,857 sq km (94,926 sq miles)
**Country population** 9,690,222
**Capital city (pop)** Conakry (2,064,236)
**Official language** French
**Currency** Guinean franc

## Gambia

The Gambia is a sliver of land and the smallest country in mainland Africa. About 80 per cent of Gambians work on the land. It is becoming increasingly popular as a tourist destination.

**Area** 11,300 sq km (4,363 sq miles)
**Country population** 1,641,564
**Capital city (pop)** Banjul (34,125)
**Official language** English
**Currency** Dalasi

Dogon people from Mali dancing on stilts

## Mali

Mali's first democratically elected government came to power in 1992 after more than 20 years of dictatorship. This West African nation is one of the world's poorest countries. About 80 per cent of the people depend on farming for a living.

**Area** 1,240,000 sq km (478,766 sq miles)
**Country population** 11,716,829
**Capital city (pop)** Bamako (1,761,659)
**Official language** French
**Currency** CFA franc

# Kyrgyzstan

Kyrgyzstan is a picturesque country of mountains, glaciers and lakes. It became independent from the former Soviet Union in 1991. Since then it has seen many political changes.

**Area** 198,500 sq km (76,641 sq miles)
**Country population** 5,213,898
**Capital city (pop)** Bishkek (933,763)
**Official languages** Kyrgyz/Russian
**Currency** Som

# Tajikistan

Tajikistan lies west of China in Central Asia. It was part of the former Soviet Union. About 50,000 people died in the civil war of 1992–97 and the country is still violent and unsettled.

**Area** 143,100 sq km (55,251 sq miles)
**Country population** 7,320,815
**Capital city (pop)** Dushanbe (853,745)
**Official language** Tajik
**Currency** Somoni

## Bhutan

The mountainous kingdom of Bhutan lies between Tibet (China) and India in the eastern Himalayas. Its main exports are rice, machinery and diesel oil, but tourism is also important.

**Area** 47,000 sq km (18,147 sq miles)
**Country population** 2,279,723
**Capital city (pop)** Thimphu (79,334)
**Official language** Dzongkha
**Currency** Ngultrum

# Afghanistan

Afghanistan is a mountainous country in Central Asia. It has been through more than 20 years of political upheaval. The country was controlled by the Taliban from 1996 until 2001, when the Taliban was overthrown by an alliance led by the US military. At present many people are involved in the drugs trade and over one million of the population may be close to starvation.

**Area** 647,500 sq km (250,001 sq miles)
**Country population** 31,056,997
**Capital city (pop)** Kabul (3,199,091)
**Official languages** Dari (Persian)/Pashto
**Currency** Afghani

# Mongolia

Mongolia is a landlocked nation between Russia and China. It is three times the size of France and is a land of deserts, grasslands, forests and mountains. Temperatures range from summer highs of 40°C (104°F) in the Gobi Desert to -40°C (-40°F) during the winter. More than half the population are nomads – they move from place to place with their livestock. Gers (moveable tent-like huts) are the most common form of shelter, even in cities.

**Area** 1,564,116 sq km (603,908 sq miles)
**Country population** 2,832,224
**Capital city (pop)** Ulaanbaatar (881,218)
**Official language** Khalkha Mongolian
**Currency** Tugrik

# India

India is the largest democratic country in the world. It became independent from the UK in 1947 when it was divided into India and Pakistan. This division has led to three wars. India has the world's largest population, after China. In 1999 its population passed the one billion mark. Most people still live by farming and around 70 per cent of the population live in rural areas. India has a booming information technology industry and one of the most successful film industries in the world.

**Area** 3,287,590 sq km (1,269,346 sq miles)
**Country population** 1,095,351,995
**Capital city (pop)** New Delhi (18,031,488)
**Official languages** Hindi/English
**Currency** Indian rupee

# Turkmenistan

Turkmenistan borders the Caspian Sea in Central Asia. About 90 per cent of its land is desert. It has the fifth largest oil and natural gas reserves in the world, but is crippled by debt to other countries.

**Area** 488,100 sq km (188,456 sq miles)
**Country population** 5,042,920
**Capital city (pop)** Ashgabat (848,444)
**Official languages** Turkmen
**Currency** Manat

# Pakistan

Pakistan was created in 1947 as a home for Indian Muslims. It was divided into Pakistan and Bangladesh in 1972. The country is in dispute with India over ownership of the state of Kashmir. This has led to fears of an arms race, as both countries are believed to have nuclear weapons.

**Area** 803,940 sq km (310,403 sq miles)
**Country population** 165,803,560
**Capital city (pop)** Islamabad (834,432)
**Official language** Urdu
(Punjabi is the most commonly used language, and English is used in business, government and higher education)
**Currency** Pakistan rupee

# Sri Lanka

Sri Lanka was called Ceylon until 1948, when it became independent from the UK. It is a tropical island in the Indian Ocean, only 20 km (12 miles) from the south coast of India. The country has textile, food processing and telecommunications industries. It is held back, however, by nearly 20 years of conflict between some of its people, the Tamils, who want independence, and the government.

**Area** 65,610 sq km (25,332 sq miles)
**Country population** 20,222,240
**Capital city (pop)** Colombo (2,558,580)
**Official language** Sinhala
**Currency** Sri Lankan rupee

# Nepal

Nepal is home to Everest, the world's highest mountain, and tourism brings vital money into the country. In 2001, Nepal's Crown Prince murdered ten members of the royal family before taking his own life.

**Area** 147,181 sq km (56,827 sq miles)
**Country population** 28,287,147
**Capital city (pop)** Kathmandu (1,507,758)
**Official language** Nepali
**Currency** Nepalese rupee

Yak train making its way over the Khumbu glacier, Nepal

# China

China is one of the oldest civilizations in the world and has the oldest continuously used language system. It also is home to the world's largest population. The economy of China is growing rapidly and it is now the world's fifth largest exporter of goods. Tourism has also become a major industry.

**Area** 9,596,960 sq km (3,705,407 sq miles)
**Country population** 1,313,973,713
**Capital city (pop)** Beijing (7,362,426)
**Official language** Mandarin Chinese
**Currency** Renminbi (also known as the yuan)

# Taiwan

The island of Taiwan lies 150 km (93 miles) from mainland China. Taiwan has a thriving electronics industry. It is one of the world's leading producers of computer technology. Taiwan is home to the world's tallest building, the Taipei 101.

**Area** 35,980 sq km (13,892 sq miles)
**Country population** 23,036,087
**Capital city (pop)** Taipei (2,646,474)
**Official language** Chinese
**Currency** New Taiwan dollar

# Uzbekistan

Uzbekistan has the largest population in Central Asia. It has been independent of the Soviet Union since 1991. It is the second largest exporter of cotton in the world and has mineral deposits. However, its people are poor because the wealth is distributed unequally.

**Area** 447,400 sq km (172,742 sq miles)
**Country population** 27,307,134
**Capital city (pop)** Tashkent (3,171,259)
**Official language** Uzbek
**Currency** Som

# Bangladesh

Bangladesh was divided from Pakistan in 1972. About 70 per cent of the people work in farming and the country produces all its own food. The main industries include cotton, tea, leather, sugar and natural gas, and its leading export is clothing.

**Area** 144,000 sq km (55,599 sq miles)
**Country population** 147,365,352
**Capital city (pop)** Dhaka (12,361,941)
**Official language** Bengali
**Currency** Taka

# North Korea

North Korea is one of the world's few remaining Communist states. As many as three million North Koreans have probably died of starvation because of famine and financial mishandling, while the regime spends money on military equipment. North Korea's nuclear programme threatens the international food aid that keeps the population going at present.

**Area** 120,540 sq km (46,541 sq miles)
**Country population** 23,113,019
**Capital city (pop)** Pyongyang (3,059,678)
**Official language** Korean
**Currency** Won

# South Korea

During the three-year Korean War in 1953 north Korea attacked the South with Chinese support. The Korean Peninsula was then divided into two. South Korea is a democratic country and has a thriving, high-tech economy and a growing tourism industry.

**Area** 98,480 sq km (38,023 sq miles)
**Country population** 48,846,823
**Capital city (pop)** Seoul (22,596,020)
**Official language** Korean
**Currency** Won

Dochu La pass in the Himalayas, Bhutan

# Papua New Guinea

Papua New Guinea is made up of many small islands and one half of New Guinea, the world's second largest island. It has mineral deposits such as gold and copper, as well as oil and natural gas. It has been difficult to use these to the full because the country lacks good roads and transport, and there are large areas of rainforest.

**Area** 462,840 sq km (178,704 sq miles)
**Country population** 5,670,544
**Capital city (pop)** Port Moresby (295,892)
**Official language** English
**Currency** Kina

# Kiribati

Kiribati is made up of 33 islands in the Pacific Ocean, halfway between Hawaii and Australia. Kiribati's main exports are coconuts and fish.

# Solomon Islands

The Solomon Islands include several densely forested volcanic islands in the South Pacific. People live by farming, forestry and fishing, but since 1998 there has been conflict between different groups in the population. Law and order has broken down, and the islanders' average income has been halved. A peacekeeping force led by Australia arrived in 2003.

**Area** 28,450 sq km (10,985 sq miles)
**Country population** 552,438
**Capital city (pop)** Honiara (58,492)
**Official language** English
**Currency** Solomon Islands dollar

**Area** 811 sq km (313 sq miles)
**Country population** 105,432
**Capital city (pop)** Tarawa (47,437)
**Official language** English
**Currency** Australian dollar

The Olgas, natural rock formations in Australia

# Palau

The Republic of Palau is made up of 340 islands in the Pacific Ocean, southeast of the Philippines. It became independent in 1994 and is one of the world's youngest nations. The islands rely mainly on tourism. The waters around Palau are rich in marine life, and visitors come to snorkel and scuba-dive. The islands also export fish, shellfish and coconuts.

**Area** 458 sq km (177 sq miles)
**Country population** 20,579
**Capital city (pop)** Koror (11,559)
**Official languages** Palauan/English
**Currency** US dollar

# Micronesia

The Federated States of Micronesia is a group of more than 600 islands in the North Pacific Ocean. It gained independence from the USA in 1986, but the USA has kept the right to have military bases on the islands. This agreement brings Micronesia billions of dollars of financial aid.

**Area** 702 sq km (271 sq miles)
**Country population** 108,004
**Capital city (pop)** Palikir (4,462)
**Official language** English
**Currency** US dollar

# New Zealand

New Zealand lies in the Pacific Ocean, about 1,600 km (994 miles) east of Australia. It is made up of two main islands and several smaller ones. The capital, Wellington, lies further south than any other capital city. New Zealand is mountainous and relatively unspoilt, and is becoming more and more popular with tourists from all over the world.

**Area** 268,680 sq km (103,738 sq miles)
**Country population** 4,076,140
**Capital city (pop)** Wellington (379,822)
**Official languages** English/Maori
**Currency** New Zealand dollar

A view of the city of Auckland in New Zealand

# Australia

Australia was discovered by Captain James Cook in 1770. It became independent in 1931, but it is part of the British Commonwealth and Queen Elizabeth II is the head of state. Australia is the world's sixth largest country. It has important mineral resources and vast areas are given over to sheep and cattle farming. Some famous landmarks include the Great Barrier Reef and Uluru.

**Area** 7,686,850 sq km (2,967,910 sq miles)
**Country population** 20,264,082
**Capital city (pop)** Canberra (325,888)
**Official language** English
**Currency** Australian dollar

 # Tonga

Tonga is a group of 169 islands in the southern Pacific Ocean. It is the only country in the Pacific ruled by a monarchy. The islands have no natural resources and people rely on farming. Tonga exports products such as coconuts, vanilla and yams. Around half of the Tongan people live abroad, particularly in the USA and Australasia.

**Area** 748 sq km
(289 sq miles)
**Country population**
114,689
**Capital city (pop)**
Nuku'alofa (23,854)
**Official languages**
Tongan/English
**Currency** Pa'anga

Traditional Polynesian canoe on a beach in Tonga

# Samoa

Samoa is a group of islands in the South Pacific Ocean. Samoa's beaches and rainforests have led to a booming tourism industry. This now brings in a quarter of the islands' income.

**Area** 2,944 sq km (1,137 sq miles)
**Country population** 176,908
**Capital city (pop)** Apia (41,204)
**Official languages** Samoan/English
**Currency** Tala

# Vanuatu

Vanuatu is a chain of 83 volcanic islands in the South Pacific Ocean, between Hawaii and Australia. About 65 per cent of the people work on the land, but offshore banking and tourism are growing industries. However, the islands sometimes suffer earthquakes, tsunamis and cyclones, which may limit the growth of tourism.

**Area** 12,200 sq km
(4,710 sq miles)
**Country population** 208,869
**Capital city (pop)** Port Vila
(38,438)
**Official languages**
Bislama/English/French
**Currency** Vatu

# Fiji

Fiji is made up of more than 300 volcanic islands in the South Pacific Ocean, about 1,770 km (1,100 miles) north of New Zealand. Fiji's main export is sugar cane, and it has a flourishing tourism industry. However, political problems from time to time have discouraged other countries from investing in the islands.

**Area** 18,270 sq km
(7,054 sq miles)
**Country population** 905,949
**Capital city (pop)** Suva
(206,631)
**Official languages** There is no official language, but the main languages are Fijian and Hindi
**Currency** Fiji dollar

# Tuvalu

Tuvalu was a British colony until 1975. It is a group of nine coral atolls in the South Pacific Ocean. It is the second lowest country in the world and is under threat from rising sea levels. Tuvalu has the world's second smallest population. The country has no known natural resources, and has fewer than 1,000 tourists a year. The islanders rely on exporting fish, stamps and handicrafts, as well as the money sent home from Tuvaluans working abroad.

**Area** 26 sq km (10 sq miles)
**Country population** 11,992
**Capital city (pop)** Funafuti (4,921)
**Official languages** Tuvaluan/English
**Currency** Australian dollar

 # Nauru

The island of Nauru lies 53 km (33 miles) south of the Equator in the Pacific Ocean. It is the smallest independent republic in the world. At present, the people have one of the highest incomes per head in the world, thanks to the export of phosphates (fertilizer). However, Nauru's phosphate reserves are running low, and it has few other resources.

**Area** 21 sq km
(8 sq miles)
**Country population** 13,287
**Capital city (pop)** no official capital
**Official languages**
Nauruan/English
**Currency** Australian dollar

# Marshall Islands

The Marshall Islands lie in the central Pacific. The islands were occupied by the USA after World War II until 1986, and were used for nuclear weapons testing. About half the people work in farming. Coconut oil is the main export.

**Area** 11,854 sq km (4,576 sq miles)
**Country population** 60,422
**Capital city (pop)** Dalap-Uliga-Darrit (21,512)
**Official languages** Marshallese/English
**Currency** US dollar

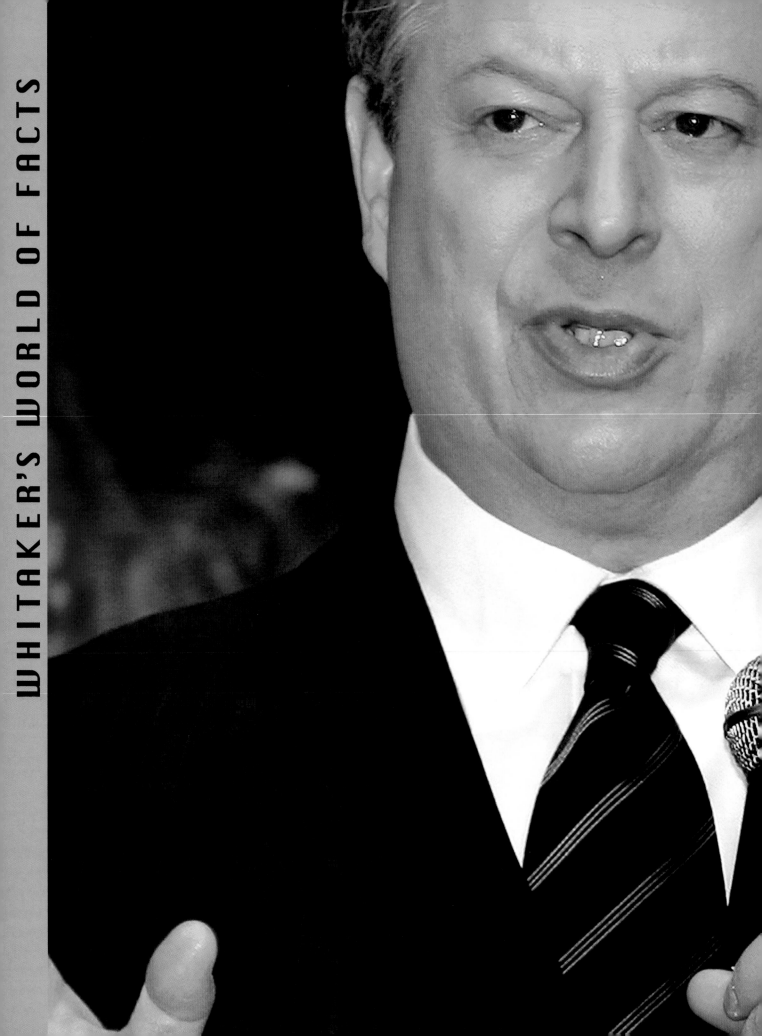

# People

## Politician to environmentalist

Former Vice-President to US President Bill Clinton, Al Gore has become a spokesman for issues such as global warming. He has made a film on the subject, *An Inconvenient Truth*, which won Best Documentary in the 2007 Oscars.

http://www.behindthename.com    **search**

## Popular first names

First name fashions change – especially those for girls. Some traditional names remain popular but new names come into use. Olivia was not in the Top 10 in the UK until 1999 or in the USA until 2001, but has kept its popularity. These are the most popular names now and 100 years ago in England and Wales and USA.

| England & Wales Girls/Boys | USA Girls/Boys | England & Wales (1904) Girls/Boys | USA (1908) Girls/Boys |
|---|---|---|---|
| 1 Jessica/Jack | 1 Emma/Aiden | 1 Mary/William | 1 Mary/John |
| 2 Emily/Thomas | 2 Madison/Jacob | 2 Florence/John | 2 Helen/William |
| 3 Sophie/Joshua | 3 Ava/Ethan | 3 Doris/George | 3 Margaret/James |
| 4 Olivia/Oliver | 4 Emily/Ryan | 4 Edith/Thomas | 4 Ruth/George |
| 5 Chloe/Harry | 5 Isabella/Matthew | 5 Dorothy/Arthur | 5 Anna/Robert |
| 6 Ellie/James | 6 Kaitlyn/Jack | 6 Annie/James | 6 Dorothy/Joseph |
| 7 Grace/William | 7 Sophia/Noah | 7 Margaret/Charles | 7 Elizabeth/Charles |
| 8 Lucy/Samuel | 8 Olivia/Nicholas | 8 Alice/Frederick | 8 Mildred/Frank |
| 9 Charlotte/Daniel | 9 Abigail/Joshua | 9 Elizabeth/Albert | 9 Alice/Edward |
| 10 Katie/Charlie | 10 Hailey/Logan | 10 Elsie/Ernest | 10 Marie/Thomas |

## Surnames around the world

Surnames were not used in Britain until after the Norman Conquest in 1066. Until then, most people were known only by their first name. People started to add extra names in order to be able to tell one William from another.

Some surnames came from where a person lived or the person's father's name – so the son of someone called John was known as Johnson. Others were based on a person's occupation (a blacksmith would be called Smith) or their appearance (a brown-haired person might be called Brown). The origins of some surnames have been forgotten.

### A very long name

Anna Pepper was born in Derby, England, on 19 December 1882. She was given 26 first names, one for each letter of the alphabet, in alphabetical order: Anna Bertha Cecilia Diana Emily Fanny Gertrude Hypatia Inez Jane Kate Louisa Maud Nora Ophelia Prudence Quince Rebecca Starkey Teresa Ulysis Venus Winifred Xenophon Yetty Zeus Pepper.

## Most common surnames

| Eng. & Wales | USA | China | Denmark | France | Germany | India | Ireland |
|---|---|---|---|---|---|---|---|
| 1 Smith | 1 Smith | 1 Lo | 1 Jensen | 1 Martin | 1 Müller | 1 Singh | 1 Murphy |
| 2 Jones | 2 Johnson | 2 Wáng | 2 Nielsen | 2 Bernard | 2 Schmidt | 2 Kumar | 2 Kelly |
| 3 Williams | 3 Williams | 3 Zhang | 3 Hansen | 3 Dubois | 3 Schneider | 3 Sharma/Sarma | 3 O'Sullivan |
| 4 Taylor | 4 Jones | 4 Liú | 4 Pedersen | 4 Thomas | 4 Fischer | 4 Patel | 4 Walsh |
| 5 Brown | 5 Brown | 5 Chén | 5 Andersen | 5 Robert | 5 Meyer | 5 Shah | 5 Smith |
| 6 Davies | 6 Davis | 6 Yáng | 6 Christensen | 6 Richard | 6 Weber | 6 Lal | 6 O'Brien |
| 7 Evans | 7 Miller | 7 Huáng | 7 Larsen | 7 Petit | 7 Schulz | 7 Gupta | 7 Byrne |
| 8 Wilson | 8 Wilson | 8 Zhào | 8 Sørensen | 8 Durand | 8 Wagner | 8 Bhat | 8 Ryan |
| 9 Thomas | 9 Moore | 9 Zou | 9 Rasmussen | 9 Leroy | 9 Becker | 9 Rao | 9 O'Connor |
| 10 Johnson | 10 Taylor | 10 Wú | 10 Jørgensen | 10 Moreau | 10 Hoffmann | 10 Reddy | 10 O'Neill |

# Known by one name

Some people are so famous they are instantly recognizable by just one name.

## Another long name!

In the late 19th century, the Reverend Ralph William Lyonel Tollemache of Grantham, Lincolnshire gave his 15 children very long names. These included Lyulph Ydwallo Odin Nestor Egbert Lyonel Toedmag Hugh Erchenwyne Saxon Esa Cromwell Orma Nevill Dysart Plantagenet Tollemache-Tollemache (1876–1961). The initial letters of his first names spell 'Lyonel the Second'.

**Aaliyah** US singer/actress Aaliyah Haughton, 1979–2001

**Barbie** US doll Barbara Millicent Roberts, 1959–

**Beyoncé** US singer Beyoncé Knowles, 1981–

**Björk** Icelandic singer/actress Björk Gudmundsdóttir, 1965–

**Bono** Irish rock band U2 singer Paul Hewson, 1960–

**Canaletto** Italian painter Giovanni Antonio Canale, 1697–1768

**Cher** US singer Cherilyn Sarkasian, 1946–

**Colette** French writer Sidonie-Gabrielle Colette, 1873–1954

**Dido** UK singer Dido Armstrong, 1971–

**Eminem** US rap singer Marshall Mathers, 1972–

**Enya** Irish singer Eithne ní Bhraonáin, 1961–

**Evita** Argentinean politician Eva Peron, 1919–52

**Flea** US Red Hot Chili Peppers bass guitarist Michael Peter Balzary, 1962–

**Hergé** Belgian Tintin cartoonist Georges Rémi, 1907–83

**Houdini** US magician Erich Weiss, 1874–1926

**Jewel** US singer Jewel Kilcher, 1974–

**Lulu** UK singer Marie McDonald McLaughlin, 1948–

**Madonna** US singer Madonna Louise Ciccone, 1958–

**Meatloaf** US singer Marvin/Michael Lee Aday, 1947–

**Michelangelo** Italian painter Michelangelo Buonarroti, 1475–1564

**Moby** US musician Richard Melville Hall, 1965–

**Pelé** Brazilian footballer Edson Arantes Nascimento, 1940–

**Pink** US singer Alecia Moore, 1979–

**Ronaldo** Brazilian footballer Ronaldo Luiz Nazario de Lima, 1976–

**Shaggy** Jamaican singer Orville Richard Burrell, 1968–

**Sting** UK singer Gordon Matthew Sumner, 1951–

# Initial impressions

These famous people are known by their initials and surnames, rather than their full first names.

**W.H. (Wystan Hugh) Auden** was a poet

**Rev. W. (Wilbert) Awdry** wrote *Thomas the Tank Engine*

**P.T. (Phineas Taylor) Barnum** was a circus proprietor

**J.M. (James Matthew) Barrie** was the author of *Peter Pan*

**T.S. (Thomas Stearns) Eliot** wrote the book on which the musical *Cats* was based

**W.C. (William Claude) Fields** was a film actor

**W.G. (William Gilbert) Grace** played cricket

**H.J. (Henry John) Heinz** manufactured food

**k.d. (Kathryn Dawn) Lang** is a singer

**D.H. (David Herbert) Lawrence** was a writer

**T.E. (Thomas Edward) Lawrence** was a soldier/writer (Lawrence of Arabia)

**C.S. (Clive Staples) Lewis** wrote *The Lion, the Witch and the Wardrobe*

**A.A. (Alan Alexander) Milne** wrote *Winnie the Pooh*

**E. (Edith) Nesbit** wrote *The Phoenix and the Carpet*

**J.K. (Joanne Kathleen) Rowling** is the author of *Harry Potter*

**O.J. (Orenthal James) Simpson** was a footballer

**R.L. (Robert Lawrence) Stine** wrote the *Goosebumps* series

**J.R.R. (John Roland Ruel) Tolkien** wrote *Lord of the Rings*

**J.M.W. (Joseph Mallord William) Turner** was a painter

**H.G. (Herbert George) Wells** was a science-fiction author

**E.B. (Elwyn Brooks) White** wrote *Charlotte's Web* and *Stuart Little*

**F.W. (Frank Winfield) Woolworth** was a retailer

Early Heinz wagon from about 1900

## Even longer!

Louis Jullien (1812–1860) was a French conductor and composer, born in Sisteron, France. His parents were persuaded by the 36 members of the local Philharmonic Society that they should all be godfathers, and Louis received all their names.

| Japan | Norway | Russia | Scotland | Spain | Sweden |
|---|---|---|---|---|---|
| 1 Sato | 1 Hansen | 1 Ivanov | 1 Smith | 1 García | 1 Johansson |
| 2 Suzuki | 2 Olsen | 2 Smirnov | 2 Brown | 2 Fernández | 2 Andersson |
| 3 Takahashi | 3 Johansen | 3 Vasilev | 3 Wilson | 3 González | 3 Karlsson |
| 4 Tanaka | 4 Larsen | 4 Petrov | 4 Campbell | 4 Rodríguez | 4 Nilsson |
| 5 Watanabe | 5 Andersen | 5 Kyznetsov | 5 Stewart | 5 López | 5 Eriksson |
| 6 Ito | 6 Nilsen | 6 Fedorov | 6 Thomson | 6 Martínez | 6 Larsson |
| 7 Yamamoto | 7 Pedersen | 7 Mikhailov | 7 Robertson | 7 Sánchez | 7 Olsson |
| 8 Nakamura | 8 Kristiansen | 8 Sokolov | 8 Anderson | 8 Pérez | 8 Persson |
| 9 Kobayashi | 9 Jensen | 9 Pavlov | 9 Macdonald | 9 Martín | 9 Svensson |
| 10 Saito | 10 Karlsen | 10 Semenov | 10 Scott | 10 Gómez | 10 Gustafsson |

Christopher Columbus landing in the New World

## Karl Marx
### (1818–83) German
Karl Marx's ideas on economic history and sociology changed the world. Marx was a social philosopher who attacked the state and predicted a future in which everyone was equal. He explained his theories in the *Communist Manifesto* (compiled with Friedrich Engels and published in 1848) and *Das Kapital* (1867–94). His ideas eventually led to the Russian Revolution and communism. By 1950 almost half of the world's people lived under communist regimes.

## Christopher Columbus
### (1451–1506) Italian
Christopher Columbus is one of the most famous of all explorers. He believed he could reach Asia by sailing west across the Atlantic Ocean and in 1492 he set sail in the *Santa Maria* to prove his theory. Instead, he landed on the islands now known as the West Indies. His discoveries led to the European exploration and settlement of the Americas.

## William Shakespeare
### (1564–1616) English
William Shakespeare is generally agreed to be the greatest playwright in the English language. He began as an actor and wrote at least 154 love poems and 37 plays, including *King Lear*, *Hamlet*, *Romeo and Juliet* and *Macbeth*. Shakespeare also probably introduced more than 1,700 new words to the English language.

A US stamp commemorating the 400th anniversary of Shakespeare's birth in 1964

## Charles Darwin
### (1809–82) English
Naturalist Charles Darwin established the theory of evolution. He began forming his ideas when he served as official naturalist on a world voyage on *HMS Beagle* (1831–36) and spent the rest of his life back in England developing them. When his famous book *The Origin of Species by Means of Natural Selection* was published in 1859 there were violent reactions against it. Darwin challenged the Bible's account of creation, and explained that human beings are descended from an ape-like ancestor. Another English naturalist, Alfred Russel Wallace, independently developed very similar ideas at the same time as Darwin.

## Emmeline Pankhurst
### (1858–1928) English
Emmeline Pankhurst was the most famous of the women who campaigned for the right to vote in the UK. From 1905 she fought for the vote by any means possible and was frequently arrested and imprisoned. She died in 1928 shortly before her aims were realized and every woman over 21 years old was granted the vote.

Emmeline Pankhurst, 1914

## Mahatma Gandhi
### (1869–1948) Indian
Gandhi began his career as a lawyer but became a great political and spiritual leader. He led the peaceful civil disobedience of Indians against British rule in India and negotiated with the British government until 1947, when India was granted independence. Gandhi became the first icon of a people's struggle against oppression. His simple lifestyle and his belief in religious tolerance have made him a symbol of decency and peace ever since.

## Albert Einstein
### (1879–1955) German/American
Einstein was one of the greatest of all physicists and his name has become a symbol of genius. When his most famous work, *The General Theory of Relativity*, was proven in 1919, Einstein became the most celebrated scientist in the world, and he won the Nobel Prize for Physics in 1921. Einstein was a firm believer in pacifism, but his scientific theories helped his adopted country, the USA, to develop the atomic bomb. A week before he died Einstein wrote to Bertrand Russell, a British philosopher and leading anti-nuclear campaigner, asking to put his name to a manifesto urging all countries to give up their nuclear weapons.

# Adolf Hitler

**(1889–1945) Austrian**

Adolf Hitler was Germany's leader from 1933 to 1945, during which time he led the world into the most devastating war in history. Hitler's hatred of Jewish people and his desire for a blue-eyed, blond-haired master race led to the murder of six million people during World War II; most died in concentration camps in Eastern Europe.

# Nelson Mandela

**(1918– ) South African**

Nelson Mandela dedicated his life to the fight against apartheid – a policy which kept black and white South Africans apart and denied black citizens the vote. He was imprisoned in 1964 for his aggressive opposition to South Africa's racist government and was held for 26 years. In 1990, after his release, Mandela was elected president of the African National Congress. In 1993 he won the Nobel Peace Prize for his work to end apartheid.

**See also**

History timeline: page 104

# Mao Zedong/ Mao Tse-tung/ Chairman Mao

**(1893–1976) Chinese**

Mao Zedong was one of the founders of the Chinese Communist Party and the first chairman of the People's Republic of China in 1949. He had an enormous influence on his country and was greatly admired for founding the Chinese republic and for changes in the early years of his rule. During his rule, Mao's image was displayed everywhere – in every school, home, factory and workplace.

# James Watson (1928– ) American and Francis Crick

**(1916–2004) English**

American biologist James Watson and English scientist Francis Crick discovered the molecular structure of DNA, using theories already written by Maurice Wilkins. Their theory helps to explain how DNA carries hereditary information and their discoveries have revolutionized our understanding of genetics and the study of disease.

# Martin Luther King, Jr

**(1929–68) American**

Martin Luther King was a Baptist minister who campaigned against the segregation of blacks in the southern states of the USA. He was influenced by Gandhi and believed in peaceful protest. He won the Nobel Peace Prize in 1964. King was assassinated in 1968, but will always be remembered for his dignified, passive resistance to an unjust society.

# Bill Gates

**(1955– ) American**

Bill Gates created his first computer program while still at high school, co-founded Microsoft in 1977, and by 1993 was the richest man on Earth. In 2000 Gates and his wife formed the Bill & Melinda Gates Foundation, which is the largest charity in the world. One of its aims is to rid the Third World of polio and other deadly diseases.

Vintage Chinese Chairman Mao lapel badges

# Beliefs & Ideas

### Burka debate

In Dubai, women wearing burkas pass a poster featuring Britney Spears. Across the world, the last year has seen increasing debate over women wearing Islamic dress, leading some countries, such as France, to ban the Islamic headscarf in schools.

# Gods and goddesses

In most of the world's major religions today only one god is worshipped. But in many ancient religions, followers worshipped a group of gods. Each god had special characteristics and responsibilities, and some could appear in a variety of forms.

The myths and legends of ancient cultures and the range of gods worshipped often changed over thousands of years as different gods and goddesses rose or fell in importance. Those listed on these pages are a selection of the most revered and long-standing gods of some of the world's ancient cultures.

## Chinese gods

The Chinese worshipped a large range of gods for more than 4,000 years, up to the coming of Chinese communism in the 20th century. Some Chinese people continue to worship these gods – often in secret – today.

**Dragon Kings** Ao-shin (North), Ao-chin (South), Ao-kuang (East) and Ao-jun (West), the gods of rain, rivers and seas

**Fu-xi** god of arts and creativity

**Guan-yin** god and goddess of compassion

**Guan-yu** god of war

**Meng-po** goddess of the underworld

**Nu-guawas** serpent goddess of creation

**Pan-gu** giant creator god

**Qi-yu** god of the rain (half bull, half giant)

**Three Pure Ones** supreme trinity of Yuan-shi-tian-zong, Ling-bao-tian-song and Lao-jun

**Xi-he** goddess of light

**Xi-wangmu** goddess of immortality

**Yi-di** god of wine

**Zao-jun** god of the household

# Ancient Egyptian gods

Egyptian religion dates back about 5,000 years and lasted until the coming of Christianity and Islam. Its huge range of gods and goddesses were believed to control almost every aspect of people's lives.

**Amun-Ra** king of the gods

**Anubis** jackal god of death and Egyptian mummies

**Aten** god of the sun-disc

**Bast/Bastet** cat goddess of fertility

**Bes** lion-like domestic god

**Hathor** cow-headed goddess of happiness

**Horus** falcon-headed sky god

**Isis** wife of Osiris, mother of Horus, goddess of motherhood and royalty

**Month** falcon-headed god of war

**Nefertum** god of the sacred blue lotus and the rising sun

**Osiris** god of the underworld and agriculture

**Ptah** creator god and patron of craftsmen

**Ra** Sun-god, ancient Egypt's most important god

**Reshef** god of war and thunder

**Sekhmet/Sakhmet** lion-headed goddess of war and destruction

**Seth** god of storms and violence

**Thoth** ibis-headed god of the Moon, arts and sciences

**See also**

World civilizations and empires: pages 106–107

Time: pages 14–16

Ancient Egyptian falcon-headed god Horus depicted on a mummy mask

## Greek and Roman gods

The ancient Greeks had 12 major gods and goddesses. They believed the gods all lived on Mount Olympus and influenced the well-being of all humans. As the Greek civilization declined and the Roman empire grew, the Romans renamed the Greek gods and took them as their own.

**Greek/Roman**
**Hera/Juno** chief goddess – marriage
**Aphrodite/Venus** goddess of beauty
**Artemis/Diana** goddess of hunting
**Athena/Minerva** goddess of wisdom

**Demeter/Ceres** goddess of the harvest, nature
**Hestia/Vesta** goddess of the hearth
**Zeus/Jupiter** chief god – sky and air
**Apollon/Apollo** god of poetry, music, Sun

**Ares/Mars** god of war
**Hephaistos/Vulcan** god of blacksmiths
**Hermes/Mercury** messenger of the gods
**Poseidon/Neptune** god of the sea

## Aztec gods

The Aztecs were based in central Mexico. They flourished from the 14th century until their conquest by Spanish invaders in 1522. They sacrificed humans to the gods, who were believed to control daily life and agriculture.

**Chalchiuhtlicue** goddess of lakes and streams, youth and beauty
**Cinteotl** god of maize
**Coyolxauhqui** goddess of the Moon
**Ehecatl** god of the wind and weather
**Huehueteotl** god of the hearth, the fire of life
**Huitzilopochtli** war god
**Ilamatecuhtli** goddess of the Earth, death and the Milky Way
**Itztlacoliuhqui** god of stone and the Morning Star
**Mayahuel** goddess of alcohol and the maguey plant (from which alcoholic drinks were made)
**Mictlantecuhtli** god of death
**Quetzalcoatl** creator god – and bringer of chocolate!
**Tepeyollotl** god of caves and earthquakes
**Tezcatlipoca** god of night and death
**Tlahuizcalpantecuhtli** god of dawn
**Tonacatecuhtli** god of food
**Xipe-totec** god of spring and agriculture, patron of goldsmiths
**Xochipilli** god of love, flowers, singing and dancing
**Xochiquetzal** goddess of love

Statue of the Aztec god Xochipilli, made between the 14th and 16th centuries

## Mayan gods

The Mayan civilization and neighbouring Olmec culture date back 3,000 years. Descendants of the Mayans still live in southern Mexico, Belize and Guatemala.

## The 12 Norse gods

The Norse people lived in ancient and medieval Scandinavia (modern Norway, Sweden, Finland, Iceland and Denmark).

The 12 Norse, or Scandinavian, gods were together called the Aesir, and their homeland was Asgard. There was also a second group of gods called the Vanir, who fought the Aesir. Later some Vanir gods, including Frey and his sister Freya, became Aesir.

● Odin, or Woden, chief god in Norse mythology

● Thor, red-haired and bearded son of Odin and Jord, god of war (his name gave us Thursday – Thor's day)

● Tyr, Tiu or Tiw, another son of Odin, god of warfare and battle (his name is commemorated in Tuesday)

● Balder or Baldur, god of sunlight

● Brag or Bragi, god of poetry

● Vidar, god of silence, stealth and revenge

● Hoder the blind

● Hermód or Hermoder the Brave, Odin's son and his messenger

● Hönir or Hoenir, a minor god

● Odnir, husband of Freya

● Loki, god of strife or mischief, capable of changing shape and performing tricks

● Vali, Odin's youngest son by Rind, a giantess. He slew Hod, who had murdered his brother Balder

## Inca gods

The Inca people lived in the part of South America that is now Peru from about 1200 to 1533. Inca gods were thought to influence natural events.

**Apocatequil** god of lightning
**Apu Illapu** god of thunder
**Ilyap'a** weather god
**Inti** Sun god
**Kon** god of rain and the southern wind
**Mama Oello** mother goddess, daughter of Inti and Mama Quilla

**Mama Quilla** Moon goddess, daughter of Viracocha and wife of Inti
**Manco Capac** creator god, Sun and fire
**Pachacamac** Earth god
**Punchau** Sun god
**Vichaama** god of death
**Viracocha** god of creation

**Bacabs** gods of the four directions – Mulac (north), Cauac (south), Kan (east) and Ix (west)
**Balu-chabtan** god of war and sacrifice
**Chak** god of rain, fertility and agriculture
**Hunahau** god of death

**Itzamna** reptile creator god
**Ix-chel** Moon goddess
**Kinichi-ahau** Sun god
**Kukulcan** feathered serpent god
**Xbalanque** god of the jaguar
**Yum-kaax** corn god

# The five pillars of Islam

The following are the five most important aspects of the Muslim faith.

**1 ash-Shahada** – profession of faith in Allah and his prophet Muhammad

**2 salat** – prayer five times a day, facing Makkah

**3 zakat** – giving alms to the poor and needy

**4 sawm** – fasting between dawn and dusk during Ramadan

**5 hajj** – pilgrimage to Makkah, at least once in one's lifetime

Jihad, meaning holy war, is sometimes added as an extra pillar.

## Major religions

**Christianity** 2,135,784,198*
**Islam** 1,313,983,654*
**Hinduism** 870,047,346*
**Chinese folk-religions** 404,922,244*
**Buddhism** 378,809,103*
**Sikkhism** 25,373,879*
**Judaism** 15,145,702*

* followers worldwide

# Religious buildings

● Abbey – a building occupied by monks or nuns and run by an abbot or abbess

● Basilica – a type of early Christian church

● Cathedral – the main church in an area and the seat of the bishop

● Chapel – a place of worship within a larger building, or a nonconformist Christian religious building

● Church – a building used for public worship by Christians

● Convent or nunnery – the home of a community of nuns

● Dagoba – a Buddhist shrine

● Friary – home to friars, members of a religious order

● Meeting house – a place where certain religious groups, such as Quakers, gather

● Monastery – the home to a religious community of monks

● Mosque – a Muslim place of worship

● Pagoda – an Eastern temple

● Priory – a religious house run by a prior; it may be under the control of an abbey

The Golden Temple, Amritsar, India

# Holy places

A holy place is somewhere that is especially revered by the followers of a religion. Examples include the birthplace of the founder of a religion, shrines and places of pilgrimage. There has been conflict in some of these holy places when members of other religions have claimed or attacked the sites.

**Amritsar, India**
This city is the Sikh religion's spiritual centre. The Golden Temple is the main shrine.

**Athos, Greece**
This is a holy mountain for the Greek Orthodox Church where there are many monasteries. Women are forbidden to go on to the mountain.

**Benares, India**
This Hindu holy city is dedicated to the god Shiva.

**Bethlehem, Israel**
The birthplace of Jesus

**Canterbury, UK**
The city was once England's most important pilgrimage centre.

**Ganges, India**
The Ganges river is sacred to Hindus, who bathe here and scatter the ashes of their dead in its waters.

**Jerusalem, Israel**
A holy city for Christians, Muslims and Jews. Sites include the Western Wall, Dome of the Rock and Church of the Holy Sepulchre.

**Karbala, Iraq**
This city is the centre of Shi'a Islam and contains the shrine of the prophet Muhammad's grandson al-Husain.

- Shrine – a place of worship connected with a sacred person or saint. It may contain sacred objects or relics
- Synagogue – a building for Jewish religious services
- Tabernacle – a house or tent used for worship, named after the tent used by the Israelites to cover the Ark of the Covenant
- Temple – a place of worship dedicated to a particular god or gods. Also sometimes used instead of synagogue

Gate of a Shinto shrine in Miyajima, Japan

# Hindu gods and goddesses

About 80 per cent of the people of India are Hindus. Most believe that God takes many different forms, so the Hindu religion has a range of gods and goddesses. Brahma, Vishnu and Shiva are the most important.

## Gods of the Vedas (sacred books)

Indra is the thunder god of battle.
Varuna is the guardian of order.
Agni is the god of fire.
Surya is the sun deity.
**Other Hindu gods**
Brahma is the creator.
Vishnu is the preserver, who has ten incarnations:
  Matsya, the fish
  Kurma, the tortoise
  Varah, the boar
  Nrisinha, half-man, half-lion
  Vamana, the dwarf
  Parasurama, Rama with the axe
  Ramachandra, Rama with bow and arrows
  Krishna, god of the Bhagavadgita
  Buddha, teacher
  Kalki, "the one to come".

Shiva is the god of destruction.
Ganesh is the elephant-headed god.
Hanuman is the monkey warrior god.
**Hindu goddesses**
Durga or Amba is the warrior god.
Parvati is the wife of Shiva.
Kali is the goddess of destruction.
Lakshmi is the wife of Vishnu, goddess of beauty, wealth and fortune.
Saraswati is the goddess of learning, arts and music.

Figure of the Hindu god Krishna

**Lhasa, Tibet (China)**
The centre of Tibetan Buddhism. The monastery here was once the home of the Dalai Lama.
**Lourdes, France**
In 1858 Bernadette Soubirous (later St Bernadette) saw visions of the Virgin Mary in a grotto at Lourdes. Since then Catholics have made pilgrimages there, seeking cures for their illnesses.

**Makkah (Mecca), Saudi Arabia**
Every year, millions of Muslims go on pilgrimage to this city. They also turn to face Makkah when they pray.
**Medina, Saudi Arabia**
This is the site of the tomb of the prophet Muhammad.
**Olympus, Greece**
The Ancient Greeks believed the mountain to be the home of Zeus and other gods.

**Salt Lake City, Utah, USA**
The headquarters of the Church of Latter-Day Saints (Mormons)
**Santiago de Compostela, Spain**
In the 9th century a tomb believed to belong to the apostle James the Greater was discovered here. Christians make pilgrimages to a shrine made on the site.

**Mount Shasta, California, USA**
A dormant volcano and a sacred site for Native Americans
**Vatican City**
The city-state in Rome, Italy, is the centre of the Roman Catholic faith.

www.adherents.com    search

# Longest-serving popes

Popes are usually chosen from among senior cardinals. They rarely live long enough to serve more than about 20 years. However, Pope Benedict IX is said to have been only 12 years old when he was elected in 1033!

Pius IX was the longest-serving pope. He was 85 years old when he died. Leo XIII was even older at 93. The shortest-serving pope was Urban VII, who died of malaria 12 days after his election in 1590.

**Pius IX** was in office for 31 years (16 June 1846 to 7 February 1878).

**John Paul II** was in office for 26 years (16 October 1978 to 2 April 2005).

**Leo XIII** was in office for 25 years (20 February 1878 to 20 July 1903).

**Pius VI** was in office for 24 years (15 February 1775 to 29 August 1799).

**Adrian I** was in office for 23 years (1 February 772 to 25 December 795).

**Pius VII** was in office for 23 years (14 March 1800 to 20 August 1823).

**Alexander III** was in office for 21 years (7 September 1159 to 30 August 1181).

## The Holy Grail

The Holy Grail was the cup that Jesus used at the Last Supper. According to legend, it was taken to England by Joseph of Arimathea but was lost, and King Arthur and his Knights of the Round Table went on a quest to find it. The cup was said to have magical powers – but only for those with a pure heart. The legend featured in many 19th-century paintings, as well as modern films, including *Monty Python and the Holy Grail* (1975), *Indiana Jones and the Last Crusade* (1989) and *The Da Vinci Code* (2006), based on the novel by Dan Brown.

*Knights of the Round Table*, a painting in the church of Trehorenteuc, France

## Largest Christian populations

1 **USA** 252,394,312
2 **Brazil** 166,847,207
3 **China** 110,956,366
4 **Mexico** 102,011,835
5 **Russia** 84,494,596
6 **Philippines** 73,987,348
7 **India** 68,189,739

## Christianity timeline

**300s**

**1000s**

c. **6-4 BC** Birth of Jesus Christ, Bethlehem

**AD c. 33** Christ crucified

c. **60-100** Gospels written

c. **64** Persecution of Christians by Roman Emperor Nero

**312** Emperor Constantine converts to Christianity, leading to it becoming sole religion in the Roman Empire

**324** Building of St Peter's Basilica, Vatican, Rome, begun on site of Circus of Nero

c. **380** Final agreement on which books should be in the Christian Bible

**635** Jerusalem and most of Middle East conquered by Muslims

**999** Most of Europe converted to Christianity

**1054** Christian church splits into Western (Catholic) and Eastern (Orthodox)

**1095–1272** Crusades (series of wars by Christians to take holy sites in Middle East away from Muslim control)

**1187** Jerusalem captured by Saladin

**1209** Franciscan order of monks started

**1382** John Wycliffe translates Bible into English

**1456** First printed Bible (Johannes Gutenberg, Germany)

**1479** Spanish Inquisition begins to persecute heretics

**1517** Martin Luther begins Protestant Reformation, Germany

# Patron saints

A patron saint is a saint chosen to be the protector of a particular person or group of people, or associated with a particular problem or situation.

Many more saints are called upon for help with problems than are linked with pleasant events. For example, at least 26 saints are connected with difficult marriages, but only one (Saint Valentine) with happy marriages.

## Patron saints for special problems

**Appendicitis** Erasmus
**Arthritis/rheumatism** James the Greater
**Broken bones** Drogo+
**Cold weather** Sebaldus
**Coughs** Blaise+
**Dog bites** Vitus

**Earache** Cornelius+
**Famine** Walburga
**Floods** Christopher+
**Headaches** Acacius+
**Insect bites** Felix+
**Knee problems** Roch+
**Lost articles** Anne+
**Natural disasters** Agatha

**Poisoning** Benedict+
**Shipwreck** Anthony of Padua
**Snake bites** Hilary of Poitiers+
**Storms** Scholastica+
**Toothache** Apollonia+
+ More than one saint

## Patron saints of professions and groups

**Accountants** Matthew the Apostle
**Actors** Genesius of Rome+
**Air travellers** Joseph of Cupertino
**Ambulance drivers** Michael the Archangel
**Architects** Barbara+
**Artists** Luke the Apostle+
**Astronauts** Joseph of Cupertino
**Athletes** Sebastian
**Authors** Francis de Sales
**Bakers** Elizabeth of Hungary+
**Beekeepers** Ambrose of Milan+
**Booksellers** John of God+
**Boys** John Bosco+
**Bricklayers** Stephen of Hungary
**Broadcasters** Gabriel the Archangel
**Cab drivers** Christopher+
**Carpenters** Joseph+
**Children** Nicholas of Myra+
**Comedians** Vitus+
**Cooks** Martha+
**Dentists** Apollonia
**Doctors** Cosmas+
**Farmers** Isidore the Farmer+
**Fathers** Joseph

**Firefighters** Florian+
**Fishermen** Andrew the Apostle+
**Gardeners** Adelard
**Girls** Agnes of Rome+
**Hairdressers** Cosmas+
**Librarians** Jerome+
**Mathematicians** Barbara
**Mothers** Monica+
**Motorcyclists** Our Lady of Grace
**Musicians** Cecilia+
**Nurses** Agatha+
**Plumbers** Vincent Ferrer
**Poets** David+
**Police officers** Michael the Archangel+
**Postal workers** Gabriel the Archangel
**Printers** Augustine of Hippo+
**Prisoners** Dismas
**Sailors** Francis of Paola+
**Scientists** Albertus Magnus+
**Sculptors** Claude de la Columbiere+
**Soldiers** George+
**Teachers** Catherine of Alexandria+
+ More than one saint

Stained glass window of Christ with Matthew, Mark, Luke and John

## One and only

According to legend, the only female saint to have grown a beard is Wilgefortis. Wilgefortis was the daughter of a king of Spain. She converted to Christianity, vowing to serve God and to remain unmarried. So when her father arranged for her to marry the king of Sicily, she prayed for a way to escape. She promptly grew a huge beard, which made her so unattractive that the wedding was called off. In a rage, her father crucified her. She became a popular saint in the Middle Ages. In Britain, she was known as Uncumber and women with troublesome husbands often prayed to her!

## 1800s

**1534** Henry VIII breaks with Rome; leads to the founding of the Church of England
**1610–1795** Baptist, Congregationalist, Presbyterian, Quaker (Society of Friends) and Methodist Churches founded
**1611** King James Bible published

**1800–1900** The Age of the Mission. Western Churches send missionaries to every country in the world. Number of Christians doubles by the end of the century
**1830** Church of the Latter-Day Saints (Mormons) founded, Fayette, New York, USA
**1872** Jehovah's Witnesses founded by Charles Taze Russell, USA

## 1900s

**1878** Salvation Army founded by William Booth, UK
**1910** International Missionary Conference marks first attempt in nearly 1,000 years to reunite churches
**1948** World Council of Churches founded
**1962–65** Second Vatican Council radically reforms the Catholic Church worldwide

**1992** Church of England votes to allow women priests
**2007** Boris Yeltsin's Russian Orthodox funeral is the first of a head of state in Russia since 1894

### See also

History timeline: page 104

# Buddhist festivals

There are a number of Buddhist traditions, and Buddhists in different countries have their own festivals on different dates. These are the most important Buddhist festivals.

● Wesak, held on the full moon in May, is the most important Buddhist festival and celebrates the birth of Buddha.

● Dharma Day celebrates Buddha's teaching and is held on the full moon of July. On Dharma Day there are readings from Buddhist scriptures, and people spend time reflecting on what they mean.

● Sangha Day is held on the full moon in November and celebrates the spiritual Buddhist community. Buddhists traditionally give presents on this day.

● Parinirvana Day, also known as Nirvana Day, marks the death of Buddha. Celebrations vary from place to place, but generally Buddhists go to temples or monasteries on this day, or meditate.

## Losar

Losar is a Tibetan Buddhist festival. It is held in February and marks the New Year. The festival lasts for three days, when people go to monasteries, visit friends and family and exchange gifts.

Tibetan monks blowing horns to celebrate the Buddhist festival of Losar

# Christian festivals

### Epiphany (also known as Twelfth Night)
6 January (18 January in Russia; 1 February in Ethiopia). The Epiphany (Epiphaneia: Greek for manifestation) celebrates three events that are all thought to have happened on this day: Jesus's appearance as a newborn to the Magi (three wise men); Jesus's baptism, when God acknowledged his son; Jesus's first public miracle, when he turned water to wine in Galilee.

### Ash Wednesday
The first day of Lent (see below). Ash Wednesday is a day of repentance for Christians, when they make amends for the year's sins before the fasting of Lent. Anglican and Roman Catholic churches hold ceremonies at which churchgoers' foreheads are marked with crosses using ash.

### Lent
The 44 days before Good Friday (including Sundays). Lent is a period of fasting when Christians identify with Jesus Christ's suffering. The day before the start of Lent is known as Shrove Tuesday or "Fat Tuesday" (Mardi Gras), when Christians traditionally eat up any leftover animal products (often in the form of pancakes), as these cannot be eaten during Lent.

### Palm Sunday
The Sunday before Easter Sunday and the first day of Holy Week. Palm Sunday commemorates Jesus's arrival in Jerusalem, when the crowd threw palm leaves in front of his donkey. Later that week, many in the cheering crowd were calling for Christ's execution.

### Maundy (or Holy) Thursday
The Thursday before Easter Sunday. Maundy Thursday commemorates the Last Supper, which established the ceremony of Holy Communion, when bread and wine became identified with Jesus's body and blood. It was also the day when Jesus washed the feet of his disciples. At Roman Catholic church services on Maundy Thursday the priest ceremonially washes 12 people's feet.

### Good Friday
The Friday before Easter Sunday. Good Friday ("good" meant "holy" in Early Modern English) commemorates the day when Jesus Christ was crucified. The symbol of the cross is an important part of church services on Good Friday, and churchgoers read the psalms and the gospels to remember Christ's experience.

### Easter Sunday
The Sunday that follows the first full moon after the 21 March (the spring equinox). Easter always falls between 22 March and 25 April in the Western calendar. Easter is up to two weeks later in Orthodox Churches. Easter Sunday is the most important day in the Christian calendar, as it celebrates Jesus's resurrection from the dead. Easter Sunday is a day of joy for Christians.

### Pentecost/Whitsunday
Fifty days after Easter Sunday. Pentecost celebrates the day the Holy Spirit entered the Apostles, enabling them to speak many new languages and spread the word of God. This event is considered by most Christians to mark the birth of the Church.

### Christmas
Christmas is the celebration of the birth of Jesus on 25 December (6 January in Russia and 17 January in Ethiopia). It comes in midwinter, a time of the year when many faiths hold festivities.

# Jewish festivals

The main Jewish festivals celebrate the great events in the history of the people of Israel. The Jewish month in which they fall is given here, with an approximate equivalent in the Gregorian calendar.

Tishri (September/October)
**Rosh Hashana**: New Year
**Yom Kippur**: Day of Atonement
**Sukkoth**: Feast of Tabernacles
**Shemini Atzeret**: 8th Day of the Solemn Assembly
**Simhat Torah**: Rejoicing of the Law

Kislev (November/December)
**Hanukkah**: Feast of Dedication

Adar (February/March)
**Tanrit Esther**: Fast of Esther
**Purim**: Feast of Lots

Nisan (March/April)
**Pesach** (Passover)
**Holocaust Remembrance Day**

Iyar (April/May)
**Lag B'Omer**: Counting Day of Barley Sheaves

Sivan (May/June)
**Shavuoth**: Feast of Weeks

Tammuz (June/July)
**Shiva Asar be-Tammuz**: Fast of 17th Tammuz

Av (July/August)
**Tisha be-Av**: Fast of 9th Av

Muslims at the Grand Mosque in Makkah before pilgrimage (Hajj) month

Sky lanterns lit up in India for the Divali festival

## Islamic festivals

Most Islamic festivals (see below) commemorate events in the life of the Prophet Muhammad. New Year's Day, for example, marks the day on which he set out from Makkah to Medina in the year 622. The month of the Islamic calendar in which the festival falls is given.

Every month starts approximately on the day of a new moon, or when a crescent is first seen after a new moon, so the calendar shifts and these festivals fall at different times every year according to the Gregorian calendar.

### Islamic festival dates

**New Year's Day** 1 Muharram
**Birthday of Muhammad, AD 572** 12 Rabi I
**Night of Ascent** (of Muhammad to Heaven) 27 Rajab
**Month of fasting during daylight hours** 1 Ramadan
**Night of Power** (sending down the Koran to Muhammad) 27 Ramadan
**Feast of Breaking of the Fast** (Eid Ul Fitr) 1 Shawwal (end of Ramadan)
**Pilgrimage** (Hajj) **month** 8–13 Dhu-al-Hijja ceremonies at Makkah
**Feast of the Sacrifice** 10 Dhu-al-Hijja

# Hindu festivals

These are the main Hindu festivals, held in honour of gods as well as to celebrate important events in mythology and in the heavens. The Hindu month in which they fall is given, with an approximate equivalent in the Gregorian calendar.

Chaitra (March/April)
**Ramanavami**: Birthday of Lord Rama

Asadha (June/July)
**Rathayatra**: Pilgrimage of the Chariot at Jaggannath

Sravana (July/August)
**Jhulanayatra**: Swinging the Lord Krishna
**Rakshabandhana**: Tying on Lucky Threads

Bhadrapada (August/September)
**Janamashtami**: Birthday of Lord Krishna

Asvina (September/October)
**Durga-puja**: Homage to Goddess Durga

**Navaratri**: Festival of Nine Nights
**Lakshmi-puja**: Homage to Goddess Lakshmi
**Diwali, Dipavali**: String of Lights

Magha (January/February)
**Sarasvati-puja**: Homage to Goddess Sarasvati
**Maha-sivaratri**: Great Night of Lord Shiva

Phalguna (February/March)
**Holi**: Festival of Fire
**Dolayatra**: Swing Festival

www.interfaithcalendar.org    search

# Conflict & Crime

### Downfall of a dictator

In 2006 Saddam Hussein, the former President of Iraq, was found guilty of crimes against humanity, following a long trial. He was hanged on 30th December, just over three years after he was captured by US soldiers following the invasion of Iraq.

# Weapons named after people

## ● Big Bertha
Big Bertha was a 144-tonne cannon used by the German army to shell Paris from a distance of 122 km (76 miles) during World War I. The name came from Bertha Krupp von Bohlen und Halbach (1886–1957), who inherited the German Krupp armaments business from her father.

## ● Browning pistol
Invented in America in 1896 by John Moses Browning (1855–1926), the Browning was an automatic pistol used by both civilians and military.

## ● Gatling gun
In 1862, Dr Richard Jordan Gatling (1818–1903) patented the hand-cranked machine gun with a fire rate of up to 350 rounds per minute. It appeared too late to be widely used in the American Civil War, and it was soon overtaken by more efficient weapons. The slang term "gat" for any gun derives from the name.

## ● Kalashnikov
This machine gun is named after its inventor, Russian Mikhail Kalashnikov (1922– ). More than 70 million have been made.

## ● Lüger
Gunmaker Georg Lüger (1849–1923) pioneered the P-08 pistol that bears his name in 1898. It was adopted by the German army and was widely used during both World Wars.

## ● Mauser
The Mauser bolt-action rifle was developed in 1898 by German brothers Wilhelm (1834–82) and Peter Paul Mauser (1838–1914). They also invented an automatic pistol.

## ● Maxim gun
American (later British) inventor Sir Hiram Maxim (1840–1916), who was also an aviation pioneer, made this machine gun in 1884.

## ● Molotov cocktail
This was a crude but effective bomb made with a petrol-filled bottle and fuse. It was given its name by the Finns in about 1940 who used it during the war against Russia. They called it a cocktail for Molotov. Vyacheslav Mikhailovich Molotov (1890–1986) was the Soviet prime minister at the time.

## ● Shrapnel
This name was given to exploding shells invented by British officer Henry Shrapnel (1761–1842). Fragments of bombs are now also called shrapnel.

## ● Tommy gun
The Thompson sub-machine gun was invented by American army general John Taliaferro Thompson and US Navy commander John N. Blish. It became known as the Tommy gun and was popular with gangsters during the 1920s.

Nuclear explosion

# Weird weapons

## Combined gun and plough
This was patented by C.M. French and W.H. Fancher of Waterloo, New York in 1862. It was designed to be used by farmers so they could quickly turn their ploughs into powerful guns if they were attacked while ploughing.

## Hard cheese
In 1865 during a war between Uruguay and Brazil, a Uruguayan ship ran out of cannon balls. Instead they fired stale Dutch cheeses, one of which dismasted an enemy vessel and killed two sailors.

## Boomerang bullets
These bullets were invented in the USA in 1870, and were designed to fire in a curved line. The danger was that if they travelled in a complete circle, they could kill the person who fired them.

# Countries with nuclear weapons

These numbers of nuclear warheads are as estimated by the Carnegie Endowment for International Peace. The total for Israel is not officially acknowledged.

**Russia:** 7,200–16,000
**USA:** 5,735–9,960
**France:** 350
**UK:** 200
**India:** 120–200
**Israel:** 75–170
**China:** 130
**Pakistan:** 30–92
**North Korea:** 1–10
**World total:** 27,600

# Weapons milestones                    1500s

**500,000 BC** Spears
**250,000 BC** Stone axes
**25,000 BC** Boomerang-like weapons (Poland) and knives
**15,000 BC** Spear-throwers
**3000 BC** Bows and arrows, shields and war chariots
**2000 BC** Armour and swords
**865 BC** Battering rams and other siege engines (Assyria)
**3rd C BC** Galleys, Crete
**397 BC** Catapults propelling darts
**332 BC** Catapults throwing stones
**7th century** Gunpowder (China)

**8th century** Viking longships
**11th century** Chain mail and crossbows
**1150** Longbows
**1221** Bombs (China)
**1242** English monk Roger Bacon first describes gunpowder
**1288** First guns (China)
**1324** Cannon used at Battle of Metz
**1346** Cannon (siege of Calais)
**1370s** Arbalests (crossbows)
**1492** Leonardo da Vinci invents giant siege crossbows

**1514** Man-of-war
**1515** Wheel-lock muskets
**1590** Bayonets made at Bayonne, France
**1776** Submarine torpedoes
**1784** Shrapnel shells
**1835** Revolvers, Samuel Colt (US)
**1838** Breech-loading rifles
**1847** Guncotton, invented by Christian Friedrich Schönbein
**1847** Nitroglycerine (explosive) invented by Ascanio Solaro
**1850** Battleships

**1860** Repeating rifle invented by Christopher Spencer (US)
**1861** Metal gun cartridges and sea mines
**1862** Gatling machine guns and Winchester repeating rifles
**1866** Dynamite invented by Alfred Nobel (Sweden)
**1872** Automatic pistols
**1884** Maxim machine guns
**1897** Dum-dum bullets (banned 1908)
**1898** Lüger pistols
**1901** Modern submarines

# Largest armed forces

The number of personnel in the armed forces listed below are all active forces, but some countries have many reserves who can be called for service if needed. South Korea may have as many as 4.5 million reserve forces, Vietnam may have 5 million and China 800,000.

**1 China** 1,600,000 army, 255,000 navy and 400,000 airforce personnel. Total: 2,255,000

**2 USA** 595,946 army, 376,750 navy and 347,400 airforce personnel. Total: 1,506,757

**3 India** 1,100,000 army, 46,000 navy and 161,000 airforce personnel. Total: 1,316,000

**4 North Korea** 950,000 army, 46,000 navy and 110,000 airforce personnel. Total: 1,106,000

**5 Russia** 395,000 army, 142,000 navy and 160,000 airforce personnel. Total: 1,027,000

Some totals include other forces

Gunner on a US army Black Hawk helicopter

## Biological warfare

The aim of biological warfare is to infect enemies with deadly diseases. It is a modern form of warfare. However, in the Middle Ages the rotting carcasses of animals were catapulted into enemy castles to infect the inhabitants. In 1500 Leonardo da Vinci suggested using bombs containing saliva from mad dogs or pigs, or the venom of animals such as toads and spiders.

## 2000s

**1902** Armoured cars

**1911** Aircraft carriers and bombers

**1914** Zeppelin airships and large multi-engined aircraft able to carry heavy bombs used in aerial warfare

**1914** Flechéttes first used – steel darts, designed to be dropped from aircraft on the enemy beneath

**1915** Aircraft machine gun invented by German manufacturer Anthony Fokker

**1915** Poisonous gases, such as mustard gas, chlorine, and tear gas, first used by German army at Ypres. Gas masks invented to combat them

**1915** Rifles with periscopic sights (allowing users to remain hidden) invented by an Australian soldier

**1917** Water-cooled Browning machine guns invented by John Browning. Tanks introduced as a way of getting through enemy barbed wire, and increasingly as a battlefield weapon

**1936** Nerve gas (Tabun) and Spitfire fighter aircraft

**1939** Military helicopters

**1940** Bazookas and radar

**1942** Napalm and V2 rockets

**1942** Dam-buster bombs

**1943** Jet bombers and fighters

**1945** Atomic bomb

**1952** Hydrogen bomb

**1955** Nuclear submarines

**1960** Harrier jump jets

**1970** Exocet missiles

**1982** Air-launched cruise missiles

**1984** Stun guns

**1988** Stealth bombers

**1988** IMINT (Imagery Intelligence) satellites

**2001** Heckler and Koch MP7 submachine guns

**2003** Multiple JDAM (Joint Direct Attack Munition) air-launched smart bombs

**2008** (Scheduled launch date) Airborne Laser weapons system capable of shooting down missiles

## Legal language

**Accessory** – someone who assists a criminal

**Accomplice** – a criminal's partner in crime

**Acquit** – to free or release from a charge, find not guilty

**Affidavit** – a written statement

**Arson** – deliberately setting a building on fire

**Assault** – is inflicting harm on another person

**Bail** – a sum of money paid to ensure a person appears in court. The money is forfeited if they fail to appear

**Battery** – unlawful assault

**Blackmail** – attempting to obtain money by threats

**Burglary** – breaking into a building to commit theft

**Capital crime** – a crime for which the penalty is death (abolished in the UK in 1965)

**Civil law** – disputes between individuals

**Criminal law** – deals with acts considered harmful to the community

**Damages** – money paid as compensation for injury or loss

**Defamation** – harming a person's reputation by libel or slander

**Evidence** – information presented to a court to prove or disprove a legal issue, such as a defendant's guilt or innocence

**Fraud** – deception to gain money, etc

**Homicide** – the unlawful killing of another person

**Indictment** – a written accusation

**Kidnap** – illegally carrying off a person, for example, to obtain ransom payment

**Libel** – defamation in writing, such as in a newspaper article

**Manslaughter** – taking another person's life without deliberate intent

**Murder** – the deliberate killing of another person

**Oath** – a promise to tell the truth in court, often sworn on a holy book such as the Bible

**Perjury** – a false statement made while under oath in a court

**Probation** – placing an offender under the supervision of a probation officer

**Receiving** – taking goods knowing that they are stolen

**Robbery** – theft with force or threat of violence

**Slander** – defamation of a person in spoken language

**Sue** – to bring legal proceedings against a person, organization, etc

**Summons** – an official order to attend court

**Trespass** – illegal entry of another person's property

**Trial** – the examination of a case in a court of law

**Vandalism** – deliberate damage to another's property

**Verdict** – the outcome of a trial, ie whether the accused is guilty or not guilty

**Warrant** – a legal document allowing for someone's arrest, the search of their property, etc

## Law courts

This is the court system in England and Wales. The system differs in Scotland. Some countries follow the English system, but most have their own procedures. In many court rooms in the UK and elsewhere there is an image of justice as a woman, which dates from Roman times.

It traditionally shows her holding scales in one hand, to show that she is impartial, and a sword to represent the power of the law. Sometimes she is blindfolded to show that justice cannot be influenced.

### County Court
Civil (non-criminal) cases are heard by a judge in a County Court.

### Magistrates' Court
Criminal and civil cases are held before Justices of the Peace or District Judges, without a jury. There are limits on the sentences and fines they can impose. Youth Courts are part of Magistrates' Courts and hear cases involving young people between 10 and 17 years of age.

A statue of justice holding scales and sword on the roof of the Old Bailey, the Central Criminal Court in London

### Crown Court
These hold trials by judge and jury for more serious criminal cases.

### High Court
The High Court tries civil cases and hears appeals in criminal cases.

### Court of Appeal
These hear appeals against civil and criminal cases following High Court and Crown Court convictions.

### House of Lords
The House of Lords is the highest court in the land and hears appeals against judgements of the Court of Appeal.

### Coroners' Courts
Coroners' courts investigate violent and unnatural deaths or sudden deaths in which the cause is unknown.

## Scottish law

Scottish law differs from English law in a number of ways. The Procurator Fiscal presents the case for the prosecution in Sheriff Courts and in District Courts (where minor cases are tried). Advocates, instead of barristers, appear in Scottish courts. In Scottish law, if a person is charged with a criminal offence, they must be brought to trial within 110 days. If that does not happen, they are set free. In English courts juries can only find defendants guilty or not guilty, but in Scotland they may find a case "not proven".

# The death penalty

The death penalty was once the most common punishment for murder and other serious crimes. It has been abolished in more than half the world's countries.

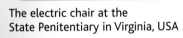
The electric chair at the State Penitentiary in Virginia, USA

● 89 countries have abolished the death penalty for all crimes.

● 10 countries have abolished the death penalty for ordinary crimes, but keep it for exceptional crimes, such as treason and war crimes.

● 29 countries keep the death penalty in law, but have not carried out any executions for the past ten years or more.

● 69 other countries and territories officially have the death penalty, but fewer than 30 of these use it.

No executions took place in the USA from 1968 to 1976, when capital punishment was re-introduced. Since 1977, more than 1,066 people have been executed, including 11 women. More than one-third of the total of US executions have been in the state of Texas.

## Ways of execution

Methods used around the world include shooting (China, Vietnam), hanging (Iran, Singapore), beheading (Saudi Arabia), lethal injection and electric chair (USA).

## Bear teeth

In Arkansas, USA, it is illegal to extract the teeth of a bear or otherwise surgically alter it.

## Strange laws

● Members of parliament are not allowed to wear suits of armour in the House of Commons.

● A law passed by Oliver Cromwell banning the eating of mince pies on Christmas Day has not yet been repealed.

● Wyoming State Legislature banned the photographing of rabbits during January, February, March and April without an official permit.

● Anyone detonating a nuclear weapon within the city limits of Chico, California, USA, is liable to a $500 fine.

● Owners of monkeys in Indonesia must have an identity card for the animal, complete with a photo of the monkey.

● In France, no pig may be called Napoleon.

● No one may eat a rattlesnake in public on a Sunday in Kansas, USA.

● It is illegal to sell a teddy bear or play with a yo-yo on a Sunday in Memphis, Tennessee, USA.

● A law in Alderson, West Virginia, USA, says that "No lions shall be allowed to run wild on the streets".

● In Spades, Indiana, USA, you may not open a can with a revolver.

● In England it is illegal to impersonate a Chelsea Pensioner.

## Who's who in court

**Accused** – a person charged with an offence.
**Barrister** – a lawyer qualified to appear in higher courts.
**Defence** – a barrister or solicitor who represents the defendant.
**Defendant** – a person accused of a crime.
**Dock officer** – an official who accompanies the defendant during a trial.
**Judge** – the public official in charge of a trial.
**Jury** – a group of 12 members of the public (jurors) chosen to hear the evidence and decide whether the defendant is guilty or not guilty.
**Logger** – a person who records the court proceedings using a stenograph or other equipment.

**Magistrate/Justice of the Peace (JP)** – a non-professional person qualified to try certain cases.
**Plaintiff** – a person bringing a civil action to court.
**Prosecution** – a barrister or solicitor who presents evidence against the defendant and has to prove his/her guilt beyond reasonable doubt (cases may be "not proven" in Scotland).
**Solicitor** – a lawyer who advises clients and prepares cases for barristers.
**Usher** – a court assistant who guides the jury and witnesses in and out of court and administers oaths.
**Witness** – a person who gives evidence in court – someone who saw the offence, a police officer, or a specialist such as a medical expert.

www.oldbaileyonline.org/schools  search

**CRIME**

# Punishments

In most countries people who break the law are either fined or imprisoned, but through the ages there have been many other forms of punishment.

### Flogging
Whipping or flogging was once common: mutinous sailors were whipped with a cat-o'-nine-tails or keelhauled (dragged beneath a ship on the end of a rope). Flogging was widely used in the USA. The last state to abolish it was Delaware – but not until 1972!

### Stoning
Even today, some countries punish people by pelting them with stones, usually resulting in the victim's death.

Alcatraz, in the bay of San Francisco, is no longer used as a prison.

Mid 19th-century ball and chain used as restraints when transporting prisoners

### Stocks and pillory
Stocks were wooden structures which held the seated victim by the ankles. People threw things at them and ridiculed them – they were literally made a laughing stock. The pillory held victims in place by the neck and wrists. It was worse than the stocks as people could not use their hands to protect their faces from things thrown at them, and could be blinded or even killed. The last person to be pilloried in England was Peter James Bossy in London on 22 June 1830. A Chinese version, a sort of heavy wooden collar, was known as the Winged Tiger.

### Ducking stool
This punishment was used in England and America. The victims were usually women. They were strapped into a special chair and plunged into a river or pond. The last person to be punished this way in England was Jenny Pipes in Leominster, Herefordshire, in 1809.

### Chain gang
Chain gangs, in which prisoners were chained together as they did heavy labour, such as breaking rocks, were used across the USA until 1955. In recent years they have been reintroduced in some prisons.

## Burning at the stake
Many famous people were burned at the stake, including the French patriot Joan of Arc in 1431 and Protestant martyrs in England. In Germany up to 100,000 people accused of witchcraft and other crimes were burned during the 16th, 17th and 18th centuries. In 1589 133 people were burned in a single day. Witches were rarely burned in England, and never in America, where hanging was the usual punishment.

## Great robberies

**Mona Lisa**
Leonardo da Vinci's famous painting was stolen from the Louvre Museum, Paris, on 21 August 1911 by Vicenzo Peruggia. He kept it for two years, but when he tried to sell it he was caught and jailed.

**Art theft**
On 18 March 1990 two thieves disguised as policemen stole 12 works of art by Rembrandt, Degas, Vermeer and others from the Isabella Stewart Gardner Museum, Boston. The paintings were valued at $300 million and have never been recovered.

**Dunbar Armored robbery**
Believed to be the USA's biggest cash robbery, an estimated $8.9 million was stolen in an armed hold-up at the Dunbar Armored facility in Los Angeles, California, on the night of 13 September 1997. The gang leader was caught and jailed for 24 years, but most of the money has not been found.

**Iraq Central Bank**
In March 2003, just before the USA-led invasion of Iraq, President Saddam Hussein removed almost $1 billion in cash from the Iraq Central Bank. About $650 million was later discovered in his palace, but the rest has never been located.

**Securitas depot robbery**
On 22 February, 2006, Britain's biggest ever robbery took place at the Securitas depot, Tonbridge. The gang kidnapped the family of the depot manager and got away with £53,116,760 in cash. Following a series of police raids, some of the cash was recovered and several people were arrested.

**See also**
History timeline:
page 104

# Science and crime detection

Modern detectives use a wide range of scientific techniques to help them identify and catch criminals.

## Fingerprinting

Fingerprints have been used for more than 100 years to prove whether someone was at a crime scene or held a weapon. Experts dust for hidden prints, which can also be revealed under special lights or on contact with certain chemicals. Faint prints can be improved by laser image enhancement.

## DNA testing

Now forensic scientists use DNA testing or genetic fingerprinting to prove or disprove a suspect's connection with a crime. Everyone's DNA is unique and even the smallest samples – a single hair or a trace of saliva – can provide evidence.

## Psychological profiling

Experts prepare profiles that suggest certain features of the killer, based on the nature of their murders. The profile may give likely age, background and habits. This builds a portrait of the criminal and helps detectives track him or her down.

## Ballistics

All guns have a unique "fingerprint" – the marks made on a bullet as it leaves the barrel. Ballistics specialists examine these with microscopes and compare bullets used in crimes with those fired from a suspect's gun to find out whether they are identical.

## Identikit

The Identikit system, which was developed in the USA in the 1940s, used transparent layers to build up a picture of a suspect's face. Witnesses' descriptions of eye colour, hair styles, etc, were laid over a basic face shape. Modern developments include Photofit and computerised E-fit (Electronic Facial Identification Technique).

## Surveillance

Crime-fighters increasingly use electronic methods to spy on suspects. They can plant bugs (hidden microphones and video cameras) and intercept telephone calls and computer data.

## Prison fact file

**Longest jail sentence**
In Thailand on 27 July 1989, fraudster Chamoy Thipyaso and her seven accomplices were each sentenced to 141,078 years.

**Longest in jail**
Paul Geidel, a New York State prisoner, was sentenced for murder on 5 September 1911 at the age of 17. He came out on 7 May 1980 at the age of 85, having served 68 years 245 days.

# Famous prisons

### Newgate

This was once London's most notorious prison. Public hangings took place outside its gates, and it features in several of Charles Dickens's novels. Newgate was rebuilt several times, and finally demolished in 1902. The Central Criminal Court (Old Bailey) was built on the site of the prison.

### Dartmoor

Dartmoor was first used for prisoners of war during the Napoleonic Wars and has served as a high-security, long-term prison ever since. The prison is miles from anywhere on a bleak Devon moor so if prisoners escape, they are usually recaptured quickly.

### Guantanamo Bay

Since 2002, the detainment camp on the US Navy base at Guantanamo Bay, Cuba, has held hundreds of al-Qaeda and other prisoners captured in Afghanistan and elsewhere. The camp has been criticized by human rights groups and legal arguments about the status of the prisoners are ongoing.

### Alcatraz

This island in San Francisco Bay, California, USA, is often known as The Rock, but was originally called Isla de los Alcatraces (Isle of the Pelicans). It was first used as a military prison, but then became a prison for the country's most dangerous criminals, among them Al Capone. Robert Stroud, a bird expert who became famous as the Birdman of Alcatraz, spent many years there.

### Sing Sing

This New York prison was named after the Sin Sinck Native Americans who originally lived there. It was built from 1825 to 1828, and from 1891 onwards many murderers were electrocuted in the electric chair at Sing Sing. In 1969 the prison was renamed Ossining Correctional Facility.

## Most wanted

Since 1950, the FBI (Federal Bureau of Investigation) in the USA, has issued a list of its "ten most wanted" criminals. Osama bin Laden, the international terrorist and al-Qaeda leader, is currently at the top of the list. There is a $25 million (£12.5 million) reward to anyone who provides information that leads to his capture.

WANTED DEAD OR ALIVE
Osama bin Laden
For mass murder in New York City

www.institutions.org.uk/prisons    search

# Work & Home

### Techno toy

Robots that help around the home and entertainment robots, such as Sony's AIBO robotic dog pictured here, are changing how we work and play. Scientists have predicted that there could be a robot in every home within the next ten years.

# Diamond fact file

- The weight of diamonds is measured in carats. The word comes from the carob which has an amazingly consistent weight of 0.2 g (0.007 oz). There are five carats to a gram and about 142 carats to the ounce.

- Fewer than 1,000 rough diamonds weighing more than 100 carats have ever been found.

- The first ever reference to diamonds is in the Bible in Exodus xxviii.18 and xxxix.11. It mentions a diamond mounted on a priest's breastplate.

- In 1796, Smithson Tennant (1761–1815), a British scientist, was the first person to show that diamonds are made of carbon. The diamond is the only gem in the world made of a single element.

- Diamonds are 180 times harder than emeralds.

- Diamonds melt at 6,900°C (12,452°F), which is two and a half times the temperature needed to melt steel.

- Diamonds come from a rock called kimberlite. About 200 tonnes of kimberlite are mined for every carat of polished diamond.

- The largest diamond ever found is called the Cullinan after Thomas Cullinan, who was president of the diamond company De Beers. The stone weighed 3,106 carats (621 g [almost 22 oz]) and was found in South Africa in about 1905. It was presented to King Edward VII, who had it cut into 105 separate diamonds. One of the largest of these weighs 317.4 carats and is set in the British Imperial State Crown.

British Imperial State Crown

## What's a million?

If you earned £100 a week, it would take you 192 years to earn £1 million. £1 million in £1 coins would weigh 9.5 tonnes. If they were in a line edge to edge they would stretch 225 km (140 miles). £1 million in 1p coins would weigh 356 tonnes.

A 2-euro coin (left) and US 1-dollar coin

## Valuable coin

In 1933, 445,500 Double Eagles, gold $20 coins, were minted. They were never officially issued and most were later melted down, but a few found their way into private hands. The only one legally sold fetched $7.59 million in 2002, the highest price ever paid for one coin. In 2005, 10 were returned to the US Mint and are the subject of a legal dispute about their ownership.

## Money facts

**The first coins** Coins made from gold and silver were used in Lydia, an ancient Middle Eastern kingdom, in about 687–652 BC. The coins were known as staters.

**Smallest coins** The silver quarter-jawa was made in Nepal in about 1740 and weighed only 0.002 g (0.00007 oz).

**Largest coins** Swedish 10-daler copper coins (made in 1644) weighed 19.71 kg (43.45 lb).

**Most coins made** The US Mint makes more than 12 billion coins every year. Almost 7 billion of them are 1 cent coins. There are nearly 25 billion UK coins in circulation.

**Banknotes** Paper money was first made in China in the 13th century. The first European notes were made in Sweden in 1548. Banknotes were issued in 1690 in America and 1695 in England.

**Largest banknotes** One-guan Chinese notes from the late 14th century measured 22.8 x 33 cm (9 x 13 in) – bigger than a page of this book.

**Smallest banknotes** Romanian 10-bani notes of 1917 had a printed area of just 27.5 x 38 mm (1.08 x 1.5 in) – not much bigger than a postage stamp.

# Golden treasures

Gold mask of Tutankhamun

## Buddha statue
A 15th-century statue of Buddha is the largest gold object in the world. It is in the Wat Traimit temple, Bangkok, Thailand, stands 3 m (10 ft) tall and weighs 5.5 tonnes.

## Gold salt cellar
This was made by Benvenuto Cellini for Francis I of France in about 1540. It is made of solid gold, elaborately decorated, and is one of the greatest works of the goldsmith's art. It is now in the Kunsthistorisches Museum, Vienna.

## Gold stores
The United States Bullion Depository at Fort Knox, Kentucky, USA, contains 4,570 tonnes of gold and the Federal Reserve Bank of New York holds about 5,000 tonnes, the largest amount of gold in one place anywhere in the world.

# Gold fact file

● People have prized gold since ancient times. It is easy to work with and makes beautiful objects that do not corrode. Even coins and jewellery that have been buried for thousands of years are as bright as the day they were made.

● Gold is rare – it is only the 73rd commonest element in Earth's crust. There are more than ten million tonnes of gold in the world's seas, but it would cost too much to get it out.

● Gold is very heavy. A cup of gold would weigh 19.3 times as much as the same cup filled with water.

● Gold can be stretched into very thin wire. Just one gram of gold makes a wire 2.4 km (1.5 miles) long and 5 microns (0.0002 in) thick.

## Tutankhamun's mask
Tutankhamun was king of Egypt in the 14th century BC. In 1922 fabulous treasures were found in his tomb by archaeologist Howard Carter. They are now in the Cairo Museum, Egypt. They include a gold mask, which weighs 10.23 kg (22.7 lb). It was found inside a solid gold coffin weighing 110.4 kg (243 lb).

● More than 90 per cent of all the gold mined in the past 6,000 years has been extracted since 1848.

● Gold is used for making coins and jewellery. It is also used in electronics, dentistry and for making special products such as the coating on astronauts' visors that protects them against harmful radiation.

● Gold bars like those in films about bank robberies are known as "London Good Delivery Bars". They measure 17.8 x 8.2 x 4.4 cm (7 x 3.6 x 1.75 in) and weigh 12.5 kg (27 lb), about six times as much as a house brick.

● The largest gold nugget ever was found at Moliagul, Australia, in 1869. It is known as Welcome Stranger and weighs 70.92 kg (156 lb).

---

**Cheques** The first cheque was issued in London on 22 April 1659. It was for £10 and made payable to the bearer by Nicholas Vanacker. It was drawn on the bank of Clayton & Morris. The original cheque was sold for £1,200 ($2,160) at Sotheby's, London in 1976.

**Credit cards** The first credit card was invented by Frank X. McNamara in the USA and issued in 1950 by Diner's Club. Holograms were first used for security on Visa cards in the US in 1984. Smart cards (cards with built-in microchips) were introduced in France in 1975. There are about 120 million credit and debit cards in the UK, about four for each adult.

**Travellers' cheques** The first were issued by American Express in the USA in 1891.

**ATM** The world's first ATM (Automated Teller Machine, or cashpoint) began operation on 27 June 1967 at Barclays Bank, Enfield, London.

**Euro** The new European currency was introduced in 1999 and was taken up by most European Union countries on 1 January 2002.

Q www.gold.org          search

# ENERGY

## Top energy users

These countries guzzle more energy than any others in the world. The figures below show the amount of gas, coal or other power needed to produce the same amount of energy as a tonne of oil. This is the standard way of comparing energy produced and consumed from different sources.

- **Other** Oil 1,677.4, Gas 1,106.5, Coal 659.7, Nuclear 146.7, HEP* 333.7, Total 3,924.1
- **USA** Oil 944.6, Gas 570.1, Coal 575.4, Nuclear 185.9, HEP* 60.6, Total 2,336.6
- **China** Oil 327.3, Gas 42.3, Coal 1,081.9, Nuclear 11.8, HEP* 90.8, Total 1,554.0
- **Russia** Oil 130.0, Gas 364.6, Coal 111.6, Nuclear 33.9, HEP* 39.6, Total 679.6
- **Japan** Oil 244.2, Gas 73.0, Coal 121.3, Nuclear 66.3, HEP* 19.8, Total 524.6
- **India** Oil 115.7, Gas 33.0, Coal 212.9, Nuclear 4.0, HEP* 21.7, Total 387.3
- **Germany** Oil 121.5, Gas 77.3, Coal 82.1, Nuclear 36.9, HEP* 6.3, Total 324.0
- **Canada** Oil 100.1, Gas 82.3, Coal 32.5, Nuclear 20.8, HEP* 81.7, Total 317.5
- **France** Oil 93.1, Gas 40.5, Coal 13.3, Nuclear 102.4, HEP* 12.8, Total 262.1
- **UK** Oil 82.9, Gas 85.1, Coal 39.1, Nuclear 18.5, HEP* 1.7, Total 227.3

**Energy consumption 2005 World total**
Oil 3,836.8 Gas 2,474.7 Coal 2,929.8 Nuclear 627.2 HEP* 668.7 Total 10,537.1
* Hydroelectric power

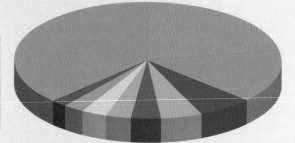

**See also**
Pollution fact file: page 70

Oil well pump at work

## Top coal producers

| | Country | 2005 production (tonnes oil equivalent) |
|---|---|---|
| 1 | China | 1,107,700,000 |
| 2 | USA | 576,200,000 |
| 3 | Australia | 202,400,000 |
| 4 | India | 199,600,000 |
| 5 | South Africa | 138,900,000 |
| | *UK* | *14,600,000* |
| | World total | 2,887,200,000 |

## Top oil producers

| | Country | 2005 production (tonnes) |
|---|---|---|
| 1 | Saudi Arabia | 526,200,000 |
| 2 | Russia | 470,000,000 |
| 3 | USA | 310,200,000 |
| 4 | Iran | 200,400,000 |
| 5 | Mexico | 187,100,000 |
| | *UK* | *84,700,000* |
| | World total | 3,895,000,000 |

## Top natural gas producers

| | Country | 2005 production (tonnes oil equivalent) |
|---|---|---|
| 1 | Russia | 530,200,000 |
| 2 | USA | 488,600,000 |
| 3 | Canada | 164,500,000 |
| 4 | UK | 86,300,000 |
| 5 | Iran | 77,000,000 |
| | World total | 2,422,400,000 |

## Nuclear power

Countries that consume the most energy produced by nuclear power.

| | Country | 2005 production (tonnes oil equivalent) |
|---|---|---|
| 1 | Russia | 538,200,000 |
| 2 | USA | 473,100,000 |
| 3 | Canada | 166,900,000 |
| 4 | UK | 86,300,000 |
| 5 | Iran | 79,200,000 |
| | World total | 2,486,700,000 |

## Hydroelectricity

Countries that consume the most energy produced by hydroelectric power.

| | Country | 2005 production (tonnes oil equivalent) |
|---|---|---|
| 1 | China | 90.8 |
| 2 | Canada | 81.7 |
| 3 | Brazil | 77.0 |
| 4 | USA | 60.6 |
| 5 | Russia | 39.6 |
| | *UK* | *1.7* |
| | World total | 668.7 |

Wind farm in California, USA

## Wind energy

Windmills were used in Persia (now Iran) in the 7th century, and in Europe since the 12th century, but they were first used for making electricity in the late 19th century. Today, California, USA, is the world's leading area for wind-generated electricity. Tehachapi Wind Resource, California, produces as much wind energy as the rest of the USA combined.

## How much power?

All electrical appliances use energy. The amount depends on their size and purpose: an electric heater might use ten times as much energy as a single light bulb.

The energy an appliance uses is measured in watts. These are named in honour of Scottish engineer James Watt (1736–1819), who first worked out how to measure energy.

Air conditioner 2500–3000 watts
Central heating pump 800 watts
Coffee percolator 500–750 watts
Computer 400 watts
Cooker 10,000 watts
Deep freeze 1000–2000 watts
Dishwasher 2000–2500 watts
Electric blanket 50–150 watts
Electric kettles 2200–3000 watts
Electric razor 6 watts
Fan 50–100 watts
Fluorescent light 60 watts
Food mixer 450 watts
Hair dryer 1000–1500 watts
Iron 1000–1500 watts
Light bulb 100 watts
Microwave oven 1500 watts
Photocopier 1500 watts
Printer 350 watts
Radiator (oil filled) 1000–2000 watts
Radio, CD player, etc 40–200 watts
Refrigerator 1000 watts
Sewing machine 100 watts
Toaster 750–1500 watts
Tumble dryer 2400 watts
TV (colour) 250 watts
Vacuum cleaner 800–1400 watts
Washing machine 3000–4000 watts

## The world's energy sources

A century ago, few homes had electricity and cars were a rare sight. Today, much of the world's energy is turned into electricity for homes, to power equipment in factories, and to fuel our cars, buses, aircraft and other transport. These are some of the main sources of this energy.

**Oil**
The first oil wells were drilled less than 150 years ago but oil, and petroleum which comes from it, has become the most important energy source. Almost 40 per cent of the world's energy supply comes from oil. Most oil is found in the Middle East and has to be taken by tankers or pipelines to places where it is used around the world.

**Coal**
Coal is the world's second most important source of energy. It makes up about 27 per cent of the total. Coal is a fossil fuel and is made from plants that lived and died 300 million years ago. The world's coal reserves will last about another 192 years. This is nearly three times as long as gas (67 years) and almost five times as long as oil (41 years).

**Natural gas**
The third main source of power comes from gas that occurs naturally beneath the Earth's surface. It accounts for 23 per cent of the world total. The gas is mainly methane, with some ethane, propane and other gases. It is collected and taken to where it is needed by pipelines.

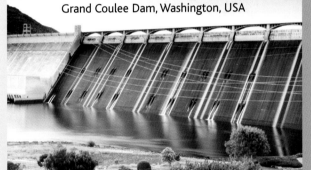
Grand Coulee Dam, Washington, USA

**Nuclear power**
The fourth most important power source (7% of the world total) is nuclear power. A nuclear reaction releases huge amounts of heat which in turn heats water or other liquid and drives a turbine to produce electricity. The first nuclear power station to produce electricity for public use was Calder Hall, UK, which opened in 1956.

**Hydropower**
Flowing water has been used as a power source since the Middle Ages. Modern hydropower uses water flowing through turbines in dams to produce electricity.

**Solar energy**
The Sun's warmth can be stored to produce energy. Mirrors and glass were used to collect heat in ancient times, but the first houses to use solar heating were not built until 1955. Solar energy is becoming more popular and the technology is getting better all the time. The world's largest solar energy generating plants are in the Mohave Desert, California, USA. They are designed to use the Sun's rays to heat oil which drives a generator. It creates enough electricity for a small town.

**Tidal energy**
Using waves and marine currents to release energy is expensive and as yet small-scale. The first and largest tidal power station on the Rance river, St Malo, France, was completed in 1967. It can produce enough energy every year to supply power to 120,000 households.

# Buildings & Structures

## Walking tall

The Grand Canyon's Skywalk, Arizona, opened in 2007. The walkway juts 20 m (70 ft) out of the rock and has a glass floor so visitors can look down onto the Colorado river 1,220 m (4,000 ft) below.

# GREAT BUILDINGS

# Great religious buildings

The world's major religions, including Christianity, Islam, Judaism, Buddhism, Hinduism and Sikhism, have inspired many of the world's greatest buildings. Some are shrines to the religion's founders. Others are places of pilgrimage. Several are among the world's largest structures. These are the tallest churches.

**1 The Chicago Methodist Temple*** Chicago, USA, built 1924, 173 m (568 ft)
**2 Ulm Cathedral** Ulm, Germany, built 1890, 161 m (528 ft)
**3 Notre Dame de la Paix** Yamoussoukro, Côte d'Ivoire, built 1989, 158 m (519 ft)
**4 Cologne Cathedral** Cologne, Germany, built 1880, 156 m (513 ft)
**5 Rouen Cathedral** Rouen, France, built 1876, 148 m (485 ft)
* Built on top of a 25-storey, 100 m (328 ft) building

## Sagrada Familia

Spanish architect Antonio Gaudí's Sagrada Familia Cathedral in Barcelona, Spain, was begun in 1883, but it is still not finished. Its tallest spires are planned to be 170 m (558 ft).

Sagrada Familia Cathedral, Barcelona

## Largest churches
Salt Lake Temple, Utah, USA (1893) has a floor area of 23,506 sq m (253,015 sq ft). St Peter's in the Vatican (1612), the centre of the Roman Catholic Church, is 218.7 m (717.5 ft) long and covers an area of 23,000 sq m (247,572 sq ft). It was the largest Christian cathedral in the world until 1989, when it was overtaken by the 30,000 sq m (322,917 sq ft) basilica in Yamoussoukro, Côte d'Ivoire.

## Tallest mosques
The Great Hassan II Mosque, Casablanca, Morocco (1993) is the tallest mosque at 210 m (689 ft). The Saddam Mosque, Baghdad, Iraq was designed to be the largest in the Middle East, with a record-breaking 280 m (919 ft) minaret, but it has not been completed.

## Largest mosque
The Masjid al Haram is the holy mosque of Makkah (formerly Mecca), the birthplace of the prophet Muhammad. Millions of Muslim pilgrims visit the mosque every year. The mosque covers 82,000 sq m (882,640 sq ft) and the surrounding yards cover another 985,000 sq m (10,602,442 sq ft). Together they can accommodate up to 1.2 million worshippers.

## Largest Buddhist temple
The largest Buddhist temple in the world is Borobudur (many Buddhas), near Yogyakarta, Java, Indonesia. It was built between AD 750 and 842. The temple covers 60,000 sq m (645,834 sq ft) and contains 56,634 cu m (2 million cu ft) of stone.

## Largest Hindu temple
Angkor Wat, Cambodia, built between 879 and 1191, is the largest religious structure in the world. The complex of buildings inside its walls and moat covers 83,110 sq m (894,588 sq ft).

## Largest synagogue
The world's largest synagogue is Temple Emanu-El, New York City, USA. It opened in 1929 and occupies an area of 3,523 sq m (37,921 sq ft).

## Lighthouses
### Tallest in the world
The biggest lighthouse ever built was the Pharos of Alexandria, which stood 124 m (407 ft) tall. It was one of the Seven Wonders of the world. The world's tallest lighthouse today is in Yamashita Park, Yokohama, Japan, and is 106 m (348 ft) tall.

### Tallest in the UK
The Bishop Rock lighthouse off the Scilly Isles, built in 1858, is 49 m (161 ft) tall and has a helipad on top. The equally tall Eddystone lighthouse, off Plymouth, was originally made of wood. The one there now is the fifth on the site, and was opened in 1882.

### Tallest in the US
The Cape Hatteras lighthouse in North Carolina was built in 1870. It is the tallest in the USA at 59.7 m (196 ft). The lighthouse was being eroded by the sea so between 1999 and 2000 the entire 2,540-tonne building was moved 884 m (2,900 ft) inland, very slowly, on tracks.

**See also**
Holy places: page 162

Millennium Dome, London, UK

# Biggest domes and roofs

In 1434, the Duomo Cathedral in Florence, Italy, had the largest dome in the world. It was 45.5 m (149.3 ft) across and was still the world's largest dome 400 years later.

The diameter of the Millennium Dome is almost eight times greater, thanks to modern building techniques and materials. Some of the domes in the list below are supported by struts and cables, others are free-standing. Some can even be opened.

**The Millennium Dome**, London, UK, was completed in 1999. It measures 358 m (1,175 ft) in diameter. The span is supported by steel masts that project through the dome.

**Wembley Stadium**, London, UK, was completed in 2007. It has the largest single-span roof in the world (supported only at the sides). It measures 315 m (1,033 ft) in diameter.

**The Georgia Superdome**, Atlanta, Georgia, USA was completed in 1992 with a diameter of 256 m (840 ft). It has the world's largest cable-supported fabric roof.

**The Fantasy Entertainment Complex**, Kyosho, Japan, was completed in 2002. It has a diameter of 216 m (710 ft).

**The Houston Astrodome**, Houston, Texas, USA, was completed in 1966. It measures 216 m (710 ft) in diameter.

**The Louisiana Superdome**, New Orleans, Louisiana, USA, was completed in 1975. It measures 207 m (680 ft) in diameter.

**SkyDome**, Toronto, Canada, was completed in 1989 with a diameter of 205 m (674 ft). It has the world's largest retractable roof.

**The Multi-Purpose Arena**, Nagoya, Japan, was completed in 1997. It measures 187 m (614 ft) in diameter.

**Tacoma Dome**, Tacoma, Washington, USA, was completed in 1983 with a diameter of 162 m (532 ft).

**The Superior Dome**, Marquette, Michigan, USA, was completed in 1991 and has a diameter of 160 m (523 ft).

# Obelisks and columns

Obelisks are stone columns made in ancient Egypt almost 4,000 years ago. Some were taken as trophies by invading armies and are now in cities such as Istanbul, Rome, London, Paris and New York. More recently, people have built memorials based on the design of obelisks.

● A column commemorating the battle of San Jacinto (1836) near Houston, Texas, USA, is the world's tallest monument at 174 m (570 ft). It was completed in 1939.

● The Washington Monument, Washington DC, USA, was completed in 1884. It is 169 m (555 ft) tall, made of 36,491 stone blocks on an iron frame and weighs 82,421 tonnes. It was the world's tallest structure for five years until it was overtaken by the Eiffel Tower in 1889.

● The Wellington Monument in Dublin, Ireland is a stone obelisk made to celebrate the victories of the Duke of Wellington. It was completed in 1861 and is Europe's tallest obelisk at 63 m (206 ft).

● The Monument in London commemorates the Great Fire of London in 1666. It was built in 1667 and is 62 m (202 ft) tall.

● Nelson's Column in Trafalgar Square, London, was completed in 1842 to celebrate Britain's great naval commander. The column is 44 m (145 ft) high and has a 5 m (17 ft) statue of Nelson on top.

● The tallest Egyptian obelisk is in the Piazza San Giovanni in Laterano, Rome, Italy. It measures 32 m (106 ft). The tallest still in Egypt is in Karnak and is 30 m (97 ft) tall. The ancient Egyptian obelisk in New York is 22 m (73 ft) and the London obelisk, Cleopatra's Needle, is 21 m (69 ft).

# Modern pyramids

The ancient Egyptian pyramids are the best known, but this style of building has also been used in modern times.

**"Mad Jack" Fuller's tomb, Brightling, East Sussex.** Jack Fuller, an eccentric landowner and Member of Parliament, had his own 8 m (25 ft) pyramid tomb built in 1811. It is said that his body is inside, wearing a top hat!

**Louvre Museum Pyramid, Paris, France** The architect I. M. Pei designed the 22 m (71 ft) glass pyramid which was built in 1989 as the main entrance to the Louvre Museum, Paris, France.

**Christa McAuliffe Planetarium, Concord, New Hampshire, USA** Christa McAuliffe was killed in the *Challenger* space shuttle disaster. The pyramid-shaped planetarium named after her opened in 1990.

**Luxor Hotel and Casino, Las Vegas, Nevada, USA** This was opened in 1993. It is 107 m (350 ft)-tall and at its entrance is a sphinx that shoots laser beams from its eyes.

**Rainforest Pyramid, Galveston, Texas, USA** This 38 m (125 ft)-tall pyramid, finished in 1993, houses one of the world's largest indoor rainforests.

# Transport & Travel

## Giant of the skies

In just over 100 years, aircraft have developed from rickety biplanes to the Airbus A380, the largest jet airliner ever built. Almost as long as a football pitch, its two passenger decks can carry up to 840 people.

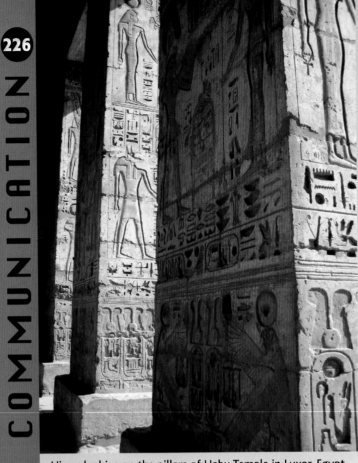

Hieroglyphics on the pillars of Habu Temple in Luxor, Egypt

# Hieroglyphics

The simplest of all writing systems use pictures. These are called pictograms and look like the things they describe – just like many road signs and computer icons today.

Writing or carving pictograms is very slow and a lot of work, so people began to use simpler versions of images, such as hieroglyphics. Ancient Egyptian hieroglyphics were used on obelisks, wall paintings, tombs and papyri (documents on a type of paper made from reeds). They are symbols that represent an object, a sound or an idea. They are not a code: you cannot simply convert an Egyptian hieroglyph into a letter and read it as we read words in a book. People stopped using hieroglyphics in the 1st century AD. From then on, no one could understand them until 1822 when French scholar Jean François Champollion worked out how to translate the text of the Rosetta Stone in the British Museum.

# Morse code

By using Morse code you can send a signal in a series of dots and dashes. The signal can be sent by sound or by flashing lights. There are five parts to the code: a dot, a dash, a short gap or pause (between letters), a medium gap (between words) and a long gap (between sentences).

Morse was created by and named after American artist and inventor Samuel Finley Breese Morse (1791–1872). He sent the first Morse code message from Washington DC, to Baltimore, Maryland, on 24 May 1844. It read "What hath God wrought!" An international version of Morse code became widely used to send telegrams by wire. Once people could send messages by radio transmissions they still used Morse code in situations such as warfare, when clear voice signals were not always possible.

# Keeping in touch

From cave paintings onwards, there have always been ways of conveying information and ideas to other people. Pictographs are pictures or symbols that represent words. Egyptian hieroglyphics are pictographs. They eventually developed into alphabets so that languages could be written down.

People have also used signs and flags to communicate with each other and found ways of turning language into codes to send messages quickly. Until inventions such as Morse code, the fastest anyone could send information from place to place was at the speed of a horse. Now electronic messages can be sent around the world instantaneously via e-mail.

| | | |
|---|---|---|
| A ·— | N —· | 0 ————— |
| B —··· | O ——— | 1 ·———— |
| C —·—· | P ·——· | 2 ··——— |
| D —·· | Q ——·— | 3 ···—— |
| E · | R ·—· | 4 ····— |
| F ··—· | S ··· | 5 ····· |
| G ——· | T — | 6 —···· |
| H ···· | U ··— | 7 ——··· |
| I ·· | V ···— | 8 ———·· |
| J ·——— | W ·—— | 9 ————· |
| K —·— | X —··— | |
| L ·—·· | Y —·—— | |
| M —— | Z ——·· | |

# Semaphore

In 1791 French inventor Claude Chappe (1763–1805) and his brothers developed a way of signalling called semaphore. They used two wooden arms which could both be set to seven positions. This made a total of 196 combinations, each representing a letter or other symbol. The signalling device was mounted on a high building. It could be seen from a distance by an operator viewing it through a telescope from the next semaphore station. From this, a system of signalling using human arms and flags was developed and used at sea to send information from ship to ship. This system was kept up to the 1960s, even after radio was commonly used to send messages at sea.

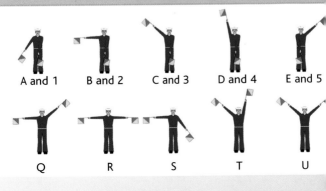

A and 1    B and 2    C and 3    D and 4    E and 5

Q    R    S    T    U

## Sign language

Everyone makes hand gestures to show certain feelings: you might rub your stomach to show you are hungry, raise your fist as a threat or hold your thumb up to show approval.

Sign languages for the deaf were first used in 17th-century Europe. In the 18th century, schools were set up where national systems of sign language developed. Signers use the different finger positions, a variety of hand movements – upward, downward and so on – and make the signs against certain parts of the body such as the neck, arm and wrist. Both hands are used in the British system, but only one is used in American Sign Language.

Deaf children learning sign language with their teacher

## Post firsts

**First air letter** England to France, by balloon, 1785
**First mail carried by rail** UK, 1830
**First postage stamps in regular use** Penny Blacks, UK, 1840
**First Christmas cards** invented by Henry Cole, UK, 1843
**First US stamps** 1847
**First perforated stamps** Penny Reds, UK, 1847

**First letter boxes in UK** (St Helier, Jersey), 1852
**London postal districts first used** 1858
**First postcard sent** USA, 1861
**First picture postcard** Switzerland, 1872
**First commemorative stamps** Germany, 1887
**First Christmas stamp** Canada, 1898
**First airmail service** India, 1911

**First transatlantic airmail service** 1939
**First postcodes** Germany, 1942
**First zip** (Zone Improvement Plan) codes, USA, 1963
**First self-adhesive stamps** Sierra Leone, 1964
*Harry Potter and the Goblet of Fire* stamps issued in Australia in 2005

A Morse key for sending messages

Penny Black stamp

### Most valuable stamp

The world's most valuable single stamp is a Swedish Treskilling Yellow. It was issued in 1855 and used in 1857 to mail a letter. The stamp was printed with the wrong colour ink (yellow instead of green), so it is unique. It was sold for £1.4 million ($2.3 million) at an auction in Switzerland in 1996, making it the world's most valuable object by weight. The stamp is now part of a private stamp collection in Denmark.

F and 6   G and 7   H and 8   I and 9   J and alphabetic   K and 0   L   M   N   O   P

V   W   X   Y   Z   break   error   numerals   The Semaphore alphabet

## Most valuable comics

Copies of American comic books with the first appearances of superheroes Superman and Batman are the most valued by collectors. In perfect condition, an *Action Comics* No. 1, with the first Superman story, could be worth up to $3,328,000 (£1,694,000). *Detective Comics* No. 27, the first to feature Batman, is valued at up to $2,560,000 (£1,303,200).

## All about comics

Captain America

### Comic strips

A comic strip is a story told in a series of pictures published in a newspaper. The New York *Daily Graphic* was the first newspaper to feature a comic strip. It started on 11 September 1875 with *Professor Tigwissel's Burglar Alarm*. The first regular strip was The Yellow Kid, which began in a supplement of the New York World on 5 May 1895. A syndicated comic strip is one that appears in more than one newspaper. Some appear in hundreds of papers all over the world.

### Comics

In the UK, weekly collections of cartoon strips and jokes began to appear in the 1880s and 1890s. Comics such as *Dandy* (1937) and *Beano* (1938) are still published today. From the 1890s in the USA, series of cartoon strips began to appear in newspapers and were syndicated nationwide. *Katzehjammer Kids*, which was first published in 1897, still appears in many newspapers and magazines.

### Comic books

The first American comic book was called *Funnies on Parade* and came out in 1933. The first to be published regularly was *Famous Funnies* in 1934. Many comic books were about the adventures of a single superhero, such as Batman or Superman, who used special powers to fight crime and defeat evil villains.

## Top newspaper-reading countries

**1 Norway** 626*
**2 Japan** 634*
**3 Finland** 518*
**4 Sweden** 481*
*daily copies per 1,000 people

**See also**

Book firsts and records: page 229

## Newspaper fact file

### First newspapers

From 59 BC onwards Roman emperor Julius Caesar had handwritten reports on news posted in public places in Rome. China had newspapers from about AD 713. The first European printed newspapers appeared in Germany in 1609.

The first daily newspaper, *Einkommende Zeitungen*, also started in Germany, in 1650. Britain's first daily paper was the *Perfect Diurnall*, published in London in 1660. America's first successful newspaper was the *Boston News-Letter*, which appeared in 1704.

### Smallest

Newspaper publishers sometimes produce miniature editions for publicity purposes. The smallest regular publication was the *Daily Banner*, published in 1876 in Oregon, USA. It measured just 9.5 x 7.6 cm (3.75 x 3 in).

### Largest

The edition of the Belgian newspaper *Het Volk* published on 14 June 1993 had pages measuring 142 x 99.5 cm (55.9 x 39.2 in), which is more than six times the area of an ordinary broadsheet (large page size) newspaper.

# First appearances

Some comic strip and comic book characters are older than you might think. Below is a list of some famous comic characters' first appearances.

**Rupert Bear** appeared as a strip in the *Daily Express* (UK) on 8 November 1920

**Tintin** *Le Vingtième Siècle* (Belgium) on 10 January 1929

**Popeye** appeared as a strip in *Thimble Theatre* (USA) on 17 January 1929

**Dick Tracy** appeared as a strip in the *Chicago Tribune* (USA) on 4 October 1931

**Flash Gordon** appeared as a syndicated strip (USA) on 7 January 1934

**Desperate Dan** *Dandy* (UK) on 4 December 1937

**Superman** *Action Comics* No. 1 (USA) in June 1938

**Batman** *Detective Comics* No. 27 (USA) in May 1939

**Captain Marvel** *Whiz Comics* No. 1 (USA) in Februrary 1940

**The Green Lantern** *All American Comics* No. 16 (USA) in July 1940

**The Flash** *Flash Comics* No. 1 (USA) in January 1940

**Robin** (Batman's assistant) *Detective Comics* No. 38 (USA) in April 1940

**Wonder Woman** *All-Star Comics* No. 8 (USA) in December 1941

**Captain America** *Captain America Comics* No. 1 (USA) in March 1941

**Dan Dare** *Eagle* (UK) on 14 April 1950

**Peanuts** appeared as a syndicated strip (USA) on 2 October 1950

**Dennis the Menace** (USA) appeared as a syndicated strip (USA) on 12 March 1951

**Dennis the Menace** (UK) *Beano* (UK) on 17 March 1951

**Astérix the Gaul** *Pilote* (France) on 29 October 1959

**Supergirl** *Action Comics* No. 252 (USA) in May 1959

**Spiderman** *Amazing Fantasy* No. 15 (USA) in August 1962

**The Incredible Hulk**\* *Hulk* (USA) in March 1962

**X-Men** *The X-Men* (USA) in September 1963

**Daredevil** *Daredevil* (USA) in June 1964

\* The Hulk had grey skin in March 1962, but became The Incredible Hulk, with green skin, in the May issue two months later.

# Magazine fact file

**First-ever popular magazine**
*Mercure Galant*, a gossip magazine, was first published in Paris in March 1672.

**First women's magazine**
*The Ladies' Mercury* was first published in London on 27 June 1693.

**First American magazine**
*The American Magazine*, published in Philadelphia, probably began on 13 February 1741.

**First children's magazine**
The *Lilliputian Magazine* appeared in the UK in June 1751 and ran for just over a year. The first in the USA was the *Children's Magazine*, published in January 1789.

**First fashion magazine**
The Paris magazine *Le Cabinet des Modes* was first published in 1785.

**Longest-running US magazine**
*Scientific American* was launched on 28 August 1845 and is the longest continuously published magazine in the USA. At first, it was a four-page newspaper and included features on science and technology as well as topics such as religion and poetry. Later it began to focus on science and is now the world's most popular scientific journal.

**First photograph in a magazine**
Each copy of the June 1846 issue of the *Art Union* (UK) contained a photograph by Henry Fox Talbot, one of the inventors of photography.

# Heaviest

The Sunday edition of the *New York Times* for 14 September 1987 contained 1,612 pages and weighed 5.4 kg (12 lb). At one time 127 hectares (314 acres) of forest containing almost 63,000 trees had to be chopped down to make one edition of the paper. Nowadays, much of the paper used for newspapers is recycled.

## Top selling

The *Yomiuri Shimbun* (Japan) sells more than 14.2 million copies a day. *Bild-Zeitung* (Germany) is the highest-circulation newspaper outside Japan, selling more than 4.2 million copies a day. *The Sun* (UK) sells 3.4 million copies, more than any other English-language newspaper in the world. The USA's biggest-selling newspaper is *USA Today*, which sells 2.6 million a day.

## Most mistakes

*The Times* (UK) of 22 August 1978 contained 97 misprints in one story about the Pope. He was called "the Pop" throughout the article.

The Faces of Tutankh

WHITAKER'S WORLD OF FACTS

# Education & the Arts

## King Tut tours

For the first time since the 1970s the treasures of Pharaoh Tutankhamun have been allowed to leave Egypt. So far over 2.5 million people have seen the Tutankhamun and the Golden Age of the Pharaohs exhibition, which brings together more than 130 ancient Egyptian artefacts.

# Students in further education

The figures give the percentage of school leavers enrolled in further education. These countries have the highest number of students, but information is not available for all countries.

| Country | % | Country | % | Country | % | Country | % |
|---|---|---|---|---|---|---|---|
| South Korea | 89 | Slovenia | 70 | Bermuda | 62 | France | 56 |
| Finland | 87 | Lithuania | 69 | Iceland | 62 | Libya | 56 |
| Sweden | 82 | Russia | 68 | Argentina | 61 | Portugal | 56 |
| USA | 82 | Denmark | 67 | Belarus | 61 | Ireland | 55 |
| Norway | 80 | Spain | 66 | UK | 60 | Japan | 54 |
| Australia | 72 | Ukraine | 66 | Poland | 59 | Hungary | 52 |
| Greece | 72 | Estonia | 64 | Netherlands | 58 | | |
| New Zealand | 72 | Belgium | 63 | Canada | 57 | | |
| Latvia | 71 | Italy | 63 | Israel | 57 | | |

## USA grade system

American children have 12 years of schooling. They start at five and the first year at school is called kindergarten. The grade system begins in the second year with first grade (six year olds) and continues to twelfth grade (18 year olds). In high schools, years have names instead of numbers: ninth grade is known as the freshman year, tenth as the sophomore year, eleventh as the junior year and twelfth as the senior year.

Harvard University, USA

# Education timeline

## 1100s

**3000 BC** The Sumerians pioneer the idea of teaching. Education available only to those who could afford to pay a teacher for each lesson

**590 BC** The city of Athens becomes the first to offer public education to all men for a small fee. Free education available to the sons of war veterans

**597** King's School in Canterbury opens – the first school in the UK

**859** The world's first university still in existence is founded in Fez, Morocco

**1064** The first European university is founded in Parma, Italy

**1160** Oxford University becomes the first university in England

**1538** The first university of the New World opens in Santo Domingo (now the Dominican Republic)

**1635** The first publicly funded high school in the USA opens in Boston

**1636** Harvard University becomes the first university in the USA

**1760** The first school for deaf children opens in Paris. Pupils are taught an early version of sign language

**1781** The first nursery school is opened in Scotland for parents who have to go to work

## Countries with the most...

### Primary school pupils
The country with the most primary school pupils is India, where there are 125,568,597 children in primary school. In China there are 120,998,605 primary school children.

### Secondary school pupils
China has the most secondary pupils – 98,762,802 – although not all children go on from primary to secondary school. In India there are 81,050,129 secondary school children.

### University students
China recently overtook the USA for the number of students at university, 19,417,004 compared with the USA's 16,900,471. There are 11,295,041 at university in India and 8,622,097 in Russia.

### Pupils per teacher at primary school
Primary school children in some African nations are taught in classes of more than 50: there are 72 pupils per teacher in Ethiopia and up to 83 in Congo. At the other end of the scale, there are only 10 per class in Denmark, Hungary and Norway.

### Pupils per teacher at secondary school
In secondary schools in Eritrea there are as many as 55 pupils for each teacher. The average class size in Malawi is 51. Schools in Azerbaijan, Belarus, Georgia, Greece, Montserrat, Norway and Portugal have only nine pupils, Lebanon eight and Andorra and Bermuda only seven.

### See also
Largest countries: page 116

Children at a Chinese boarding school doing their morning exercises

## Schooling around the world

### Time spent at school
● School children in China spend more time at school than children in any other country. They have 251 schooldays a year – 59 days more than British children, and 71 more than American children.

● In the United Kingdom, the United States, France, Canada, Germany, Belgium, the Netherlands, Australia and New Zealand children have 10, 11 or 12 years of education. In most African countries and parts of South America children spend just five or six years at school. Only two African countries, Gabon and Tunisia, have ten years of compulsory schooling.

● In Italy and China, children can legally finish school at the age of 14. In Myanmar, Angola and Pakistan, children are allowed to finish at the age of nine, after only four or five years at school. In several European countries, including Croatia, Denmark, Sweden and Switzerland, parents don't have to send their children to school until they are seven years old – two years later than in many other countries.

### Largest school
The largest school in the world is the City Montessori school in Lucknow, northern India; it has more than 31,000 pupils.

## 1900s

**1783** Poland becomes the first country to ban corporal punishment in schools

**1784** The first school for blind children is started in Paris

**1841** Oberlin College becomes the first university in the USA to award degrees to women

**1871** A school in New York introduces the first distance-learning courses for young people who live too far away from schools to travel to them

**1878** London University becomes the first UK university to award degrees to women

**1987** Corporal punishment is banned in all UK state schools

**1999** Corporal punishment is banned in all independent schools in the UK

**2007** UK confirms intention to raise school leaving age to 18 years old

## Most remote school
The world's most remote school is Kiwirrkurra Remote Community School in Australia. It is a 25-hour road journey from the nearest major town. The 100 pupils and seven teachers at another school in the region, Oombulgurri Remote Community School, can only get to school by light aircraft or by barge. The aircraft takes just 35 minutes, but the barge can take up to 12 hours.

# Music & Performance

## Elvis lives

Elvis week in August 2007 marked the 30th anniversary of the rock and roll legend's death. Events took place in Memphis, USA, including an overnight candlelit vigil outside Elvis's Graceland mansion and a tribute artist contest, featuring Elvis impersonators from around the world.

# A quick history of circus

Open air circuses with acrobats, chariot races, bareback riders and comedy acts were popular in ancient Rome. In the 18th century fixed buildings were used, and in the early 19th century travelling circuses appeared in Europe and America. Troupes moved from place to place, setting up a large tent, or "big top". The most famous American circus proprietor was Phineas T. Barnum (1810–91).

His shows were spectacular, with trick riding, juggling, trapeze acts, tightrope walking, strong men, and wild-cat tamers. They also featured "human oddities", or freak shows, in which Siamese twins, giants or bearded ladies were often paraded before the curious crowd. Since the 20th century, all-human Chinese and Russian circus companies have toured the world, as well as alternative circus troupes such as Circus Oz, Ra Ra Zoo and Archaos, whose acts have included juggling with chainsaws and jumping over blazing motorbikes.

**See also**
Tom Thumb: page 95

Canadian circus troupe Cirque du Soleil (French for "Circus of the Sun")

## Famous playwrights and their famous plays

**Aeschylus** (Greek, c. 525–546 BC) – *The Oresteia*
**J.M. Barrie** (Scottish, 1860–1937) – *Peter Pan*
**Samuel Beckett** (Irish, 1906–89) – *Waiting for Godot*
**Anton Chekhov** (Russian, 1860–1904) – *The Cherry Orchard*
**Noël Coward** (English, 1899–1973) – *Private Lives*
**Euripides** (Greek, c. 484–406 BC) – *The Trojan Women*
**Federico García Lorca** (Spanish, 1898–1936) – *Blood Wedding*
**Oliver Goldsmith** (English 1728–74) – *She Stoops to Conquer*
**David Hare** (English, 1947– ) – *Plenty*
**Henrik Ibsen** (Norwegian, 1828–1906) – *Hedda Gabler*
**Ben Jonson** (English, 1572–1637) – *The Alchemist*
**Christopher Marlowe** (English, 1564–93) – *Doctor Faustus*
**Arthur Miller** (American, 1915–2005) – *The Crucible*
**Molière** (French, 1622–73) – *Tartuffe*
**John Osborne** (English, 1929–94) – *Look Back in Anger*
**Harold Pinter** (English, 1930– ) – *The Birthday Party*
**Peter Shaffer** (English, 1926– ) – *Amadeus*
**William Shakespeare** (English, 1564–1616) – *Hamlet*
**George Bernard Shaw** (Irish, 1856–1950) – *Pygmalion*
**Richard Brinsley Sheridan** (English, 1751–1816) – *The Rivals*
**Neil Simon** (American, 1927– ) – *Plaza Suite*
**Sophocles** (Greek, c. 496–405 BC) – *Antigone*
**Tom Stoppard** (Czech, 1937– ) – *Rosencrantz and Guildenstern are Dead*
**J.M. Synge** (Irish, 1871–1909) – *The Playboy of the Western World*
**John Webster** (English, 1580–1625) – *The Duchess of Malfi*
**Oscar Wilde** (Irish, 1854–1900) – *The Importance of Being Earnest*
**Tennessee Williams** (American, 1911–83) – *A Streetcar Named Desire*

## Theatre records

**First actor**
Thespis was the first performer ever recorded. He was an actor in Greece in 534 BC. At this time, Greek actors used masks, and Thespis was the first to use stage make-up.

**World's oldest theatres**
The oldest indoor theatre in the world is the Teatro Olimpico, Vicenza, Italy, which opened on 3 March 1585. London's oldest theatre is the Theatre Royal, Drury Lane, which opened on 7 May 1663. It burnt down in 1672 and was rebuilt by Sir Christopher Wren. In 1800 it became the world's first theatre to have safety curtains. The oldest surviving theatre in the USA is the Walnut Street Theatre in Philadelphia, Pennsylvania.

**World's biggest theatres**
The National People's Congress Building Theatre, Beijing, China was built in 1959 and can hold audiences of 10,000. The Perth Entertainment Centre, Australia (1976) has up to 8,500 seats, the Chaplin (originally Blanquetta), Havana, Cuba (1949) has 6,500 and Radio City Music Hall, New York, USA, has 6,200. The 3,483-seater Hammersmith Odeon is the largest theatre in Britain, but the Royal Albert Hall in London can hold up to 7,000, depending on the event and how the seating is organized.

The Teatro Olimpico in Vicenza, Italy

### Worst disasters at a theatre

Fires, in which people were burned or trampled to death, have caused the worst disasters at theatres. The worst ever was at Canton (now Guangzhou), China, in 1845 when 1,670 died. Europe's worst was at the Ring Theatre, Vienna, Austria, in 1881, which killed at least 620 people. The worst in the USA was at the Iroquois Theatre, Chicago, in 1903, which left 602 dead. These are the worst single-building (rather than city or forest) fires in history.

## Longest-running shows

*The Golden Horseshoe Revue* (Disneyland, California, 1955–86) 47,250 performances

*The Mousetrap* (London, 1952– ) *22,643 performances

*The Fantasticks* (New York, 1960–2002) 17,162 performances

*La Cantatrice Chauve* (*The Bald Soprano*) (Paris, 1957– ) *15,952 performances

*Shear Madness* (Boston, 1980– ) *11,439 performances

*The Drunkard* (Los Angeles, 1933–59) 9,477 performances

*The Mousetrap* (Toronto, 1977–2004) over 9,000 performances

*Cats* (London, 1981–2002) 8,949 performances

*Les Misérables* (London, 1985– ) *8,852 performances

*The Phantom of the Opera* (London, 1986– ) *8,517 performances

*Perfect Crime* (New York, 1987– ) *8,113 performances

*Tubes* (New York, 1991– ) *8,006 performances

*The Phantom of the Opera* (New York, 1988– ) *7,989 performances

*Cats* (New York, 1982–2000) 7,485 performances

*Starlight Express* (London, 1984–2002) 7,406 performances

*Shear Madness* (Washington, 1987– ) *7,300 performances

* Still running in 2007

## Short runs

A play is expensive to stage, so everyone involved hopes that it will run for long enough to earn back the money spent on it. Shows that run for years earn back their initial investment many times over, but some fail on their first night, or even earlier!

● On 18 December 1816 the one and only performance of J.R. Ronden's *The Play Without an A* took place at the Paris Théâtre des Variétés. It was written with words without the letter "a", which made it very hard to perform and understand. The audience rioted and did not allow the play to finish.

● In 1888, at London's Shaftesbury Theatre, *The Lady of Lyons* failed to make its first night when the safety curtain jammed.

● The *Intimate Revue* opened and closed at the Duchess Theatre, London, on 11 March 1930. It was a disaster from start to finish. The scenery changes took so long that seven scenes were abandoned to allow the long-suffering audience to go home before midnight.

● *Little Johnny Jones*, a musical starring Donny Osmond, opened and closed at the Alvin Theater, New York, on 21 March 1982.

● *Carrie* closed in New York on 17 May 1988 after struggling through five performances. It is said to have cost the Royal Shakespeare Company, who performed it, $7 million.

### Longest play

Neil Oram's *The Warp* was first performed at the ICA (Institute of Contemporary Art) in London from 18–20 January 1979. It lasted 18 hours and 5 minutes.

### Oberammergau

Oberammergau is a town in Bavaria, Germany, where a Passion play (a play dealing with the crucifixion of Christ) is performed. The first play was put on in 1634 after an outbreak of plague in the town. The people vowed to repeat the play every ten years from then on. More than 2,000 people take part in the play, nearly all of them from Oberammergau, and the performance lasts six hours.

Scene from the Singapore production of *Les Misérables*

www.theatremuseum.org.uk    search

John Travolta in
*Saturday Night
Fever*, 1977

# Highest-earning dance films

The most successful dance film of all time is *Saturday Night Fever*. It starred John Travolta as a talented disco dancer and has earned nearly $300 million around the world. Below are some of the other highest-earning dance films in the world.

1 *Saturday Night Fever* (1977)  $285.4 million
2 *The Full Monty* (1997)  $257.9 m.
3 *Dirty Dancing* (1987)  $214.0 m.
4 *Shall We Dance* (2004)  $170.1 m.
5 *Save the Last Dance* (2001)  $131.7 m.
6 *Staying Alive* (1983)  $127.6 m.
7 *Coyote Ugly* (2000)  $113.9 m.
8 *Billy Elliot* (2000)  $109.3 m.
9 *Flashdance* (1983)  $94.9 m.
10 *Footloose* (1984)  $80.0 m.

Girl breakdancing

## Breakdancing

Breakdancing began in New York in the late 1970s and early 1980s. Some of its movements came from martial arts such as kung fu and from gymnastics. It became a feature of hip-hop culture.

## Dance spectaculars

American choreographer Busby Berkeley (1895–1976) staged the most spectacular dance films ever made. He used his knowledge of organizing military parades during World War I to create dance numbers with casts of hundreds.

They were often photographed from cranes high above them, on huge sets and sometimes with giant mirrors so that they formed geometrical patterns apparently vanishing into infinity. His films included *42nd Street* (1933) and *Gold Diggers of 1933* (1933), which was hit by an earthquake during filming in Los Angeles. The quake cut all power and nearly collapsed the set.

## Popular dances

**Barn dances**
These developed from traditional Scottish dancing. They were popular in the USA in the 1890s when they were held to celebrate the building of a barn on a farm. Barn dances are still held today in country areas.

**Belly dance**
The popular name of a style of dance that originated in the Middle East, especially Egypt. It was originally danced only by women, and men were not permitted to watch. An Essex woman named Eileen Foucher set a belly dance record. She danced for 106 hours, from 30 July to 3 August 1984.

**The Charleston**
The Charleston was named after the city in South Carolina, USA and was one of the most popular dances of the 1920s.

**The conga**
People dance the conga in a line, each dancer holding on to the person in front. The conga began in Latin American carnivals and spread to the USA in the 1930s. The Miami Super Conga was held on 13 March 1988. The conga line was made up of 119,986 people – only 14 short of 120,000.

**The hula**
The hip-swaying hula is danced by Polynesian islanders who settled in Hawaii. It was banned by Christian missionaries for a while, but became popular again in the late 19th century.

**The limbo**
This competitive dance comes from Trinidad. Dancers lean back to pass under a bar, which is placed lower and lower. The winner is the dancer who passes under the lowest bar. On 2 March 1991 Dennis Walston, known as King Limbo (USA) limboed under a bar 15.25 cm (6 in) high.

**Lindy Hop**
The Lindy Hop was a version of the Charleston and another dance called the Breakaway. It was named after US aviator Charles Lindbergh (nicknamed Lindy). In 1927 he became the first person to fly solo across the Atlantic.

**Morris dancing**
This is a traditional English folk dance. Dancers wear special costumes with bells, and hold sticks, handkerchiefs and swords.

**The polka**
The polka was originally a Czech peasant dance which developed in Bohemia in the 1830s. It became popular in Paris in the 1840s and eventually spread worldwide.

# Dance marathons

Dance marathons began in New York in 1923, when Alma Cummings won a contest by dancing for 27 hours with six different partners. Marathons were popular during the Depression years of the 1930s, when unemployed people danced non-stop for many days to win money.

**See also**
Film winners:
pages 268–69

The last couple standing won. Dancers were allowed only very short breaks and partners pinched and kicked each other to stay awake or tied themselves together to prevent one from falling down. Dance marathons were banned in many places because they were so dangerous for people's health.

Mike Ritof and Edith Boudreaux danced from 29 August 1930 to 1 April 1931 at the Merry Garden Ballroom, Chicago, USA, to win a prize of $2,000. They danced for a total of 5,154 hours 28 minutes 30 seconds (215 days) with only short rest breaks.

## Dance dummy

In 1921 Sidney E. Feist of Brooklyn, New York, USA, patented a female dummy to help men practise their ballroom dancing steps. The dummy partner had a telescopic leg with a rotating wooden ball at the end so that she could be wheeled around the floor.

### The twist
The twist started when Hank Ballard recorded the song of this name in 1959. It became popular when Chubby Checker performed his cover version on US television on 22 October 1961. A woman called Ra Denny holds the twist record. She twisted for 100 hours at Christchurch, New Zealand, in March 1962.

### The waltz
The waltz began in Austria in the late 18th century. Its name comes from a German word meaning to revolve. Many people were shocked by the dance when it first came to England in 1812 because it involved men and women dancing close to each other.

## Flamenco dancing

Flamenco is popular in Andalusia, Spain, and comes from Moorish and gypsy dancing. It is lively and exciting; the dancers usually play castanets and are accompanied by guitars, clapping and drumming.

www.streetswing.com/histmain.htm    search

# BALLET

## Best-known ballets

| Ballet | Composer | Choreographer | First performed |
|---|---|---|---|
| La Bayadère | Minkus | Petipa | 1877 |
| Cinderella | Prokofiev | Ashton | 1948 |
| Coppélia | Delibes | Saint-Léon | 1870 |
| The Firebird | Stravinsky | Fokine | 1910 |
| Giselle | Adam | Perrot/Coralli | 1841 |
| The Nutcracker | Tchaikovsky | Ivanov | 1892 |
| Romeo and Juliet | Prokofiev | Lavrovsky | 1940 |
| The Sleeping Beauty | Tchaikovsky | Petipa | 1890 |
| Swan Lake | Tchaikovsky | Petipa | 1895 |
| La Sylphide | Schneitzhoeffer | F. Taglioni | 1832 |
| Les Sylphides | Chopin | Fokine | 1909 |

## Best-known ballet companies

**Alvin Ailey American Dance Theater** (New York, USA), founded 1958
**American Ballet Theater** (New York, USA), founded 1940
**Australian Ballet** (Melbourne, Australia), founded 1962
**Ballet Rambert** (London, UK), founded 1926
**Ballets Russes**\* (Moscow, Russia), founded 1909
**Bolshoi Ballet** (Moscow, Russia), founded 1776
**Dance Theater of Harlem** (New York, USA), founded 1961
**English National Ballet** (London, UK), founded 1950
**Kirov/Marlinsky Ballet** (St Petersburg, Russia), founded 1935
**Martha Graham Dance Company** (New York, USA), founded 1927
**Merce Cunningham Dance Company** (New York, USA), founded 1953
**National Ballet of Canada** (Toronto, Canada), founded 1951
**New York City Ballet** (New York, USA), founded 1948
**Paris Opéra Company** (Paris, France), founded 1669
**Royal Ballet** (London, UK), founded 1936
**Royal Danish Ballet** (Copenhagen, Denmark), founded 1748

\* not in existence today

## Ballet terms

**arabesque**
Position in which the dancer stands on one leg, with arms extended, the body bent forwards and the other leg stretched back

**ballerina**
A female ballet dancer

**barre**
The bar dancers hold on to while they practise, to help them balance

**choreographer**
The person who works out the steps and movements in a ballet

**corps de ballet**
Chorus of dancers (not those dancing solo)

**entrechat**
Rapid crossing and uncrossing of the feet during a jump

**fouetté**
A turn in which one leg is whipped round

**glissade**
A gliding movement

**jeté**
A jump from one foot to the other

**pas**
A dance step

**pas de deux**
A dance for two (usually the principal male and female dancers in the company)

**pas seule**
A solo dance

**pirouette**
A complete turn on one leg

**plié**
A knee-bending movement

**pointes**
On the tips of the toes. Dancers wear special point shoes with blocks in the toes to help them stand on their toes

**positions**
A range of five positions that are the basis of ballet dancing

**prima ballerina**
The leading ballerina in a company

**tutu**
The stiff skirt worn by ballerinas performing classical ballet

*Sleeping Beauty* by the Royal Ballet

### See also
Famous last words: page 304

Darcey Bussell dancing with Igor Zelensky

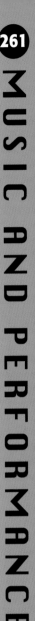

# Famous ballet dancers

**Carlos Acosta** (Cuban, 1973– ) Trained in Cuba and became a principal dancer with the Royal Ballet in London. He has also staged his own show.

**Mikhail Baryshnikov** (Russian, 1948– ) One of the greatest male dancers. He began with the Kirov in Russia but later joined the American Ballet Theatre.

**Matthew Bourne** (British, 1960– ) Began as a dancer and became a famous choreographer and director. He is best known for his production of *Swan Lake*, in which all the swans are played by male dancers.

**Darcey Bussell** (British, 1969– ) Became a principal dancer with the Royal Ballet at the age of 20. She is one of their most popular soloists, and in 1995 she was awarded an OBE for her work in dance. She retired in 2007.

**Michael Clark** (British, 1962– ) Danced with the Royal Ballet and Merce Cunningham companies before becoming a choreographer and starting his own company. He is best known for his very original shows and for using music such as punk in his work.

**Sir Anton Dolin** (British, 1904–83) Originally danced with Diaghilev's Ballets Russes. He founded the London Festival Ballet (now English National Ballet).

**Sir Anthony Dowell** (British, 1943– ) He was principal dancer with the Royal Ballet for many years and was Director of the Royal Ballet for 15 years from 1986.

**Dame Margot Fonteyn** (British, 1919–91) Royal Ballet prima ballerina, she is most famous for her long-term partnership with Rudolf Nureyev.

**Dame Beryl Grey** (British, 1927– ) Prima ballerina at the Sadler's Wells Ballet, London and the first English ballerina to perform with the Bolshoi.

**Sylvie Guillem** (French, 1965– ) Principal guest artist with the Royal Ballet, she is a versatile and athletic dancer, famous for her extraordinarily high leg extensions.

**Dame Alicia Markova** (British, 1910–2004) She danced with Anton Dolin and they are most famous for their *Giselle*. Dolin and Markova formed a ballet company.

**Rudolf Nureyev** (Russian, 1938–93) Former Kirov star who defected to the West and became the most popular male dancer of his generation.

**Anna Pavlova** (Russian, 1881–1931) Became the most famous ballerina of her generation through her world tours.

**Dame Marie Rambert** (Polish/British, 1888–1982) Dancer and teacher whose dance company promoted many new works.

## Vaslav Nijinsky

(Russian, 1890–1950) One of most famous of all male dancers. He was a leading dancer with the Ballets Russes and best known for his performance in Stravinsky's *Rite of Spring*.

**Maria Taglioni** (Swedish/Italian, 1804–84) One of the first ballet stars, famous for her role in *La Sylphide*.

# Ballet firsts and records

### First ballet
In the late 16th century, performances that included dancing, music and acting were given at the French court of Henri II and Catherine de Médici. The *Ballet Comique de La Reine* (1581) was the first recorded.

### First professional ballerina
On 21 January 1681 Mademoiselle de La Fontaine appeared in Jean Baptiste Lully's *The Triumph of Love* at the Paris Opéra.

### First ballet in the USA
On 7 February 1827 Francisquy Hutin performed a ballet in the play *The Deserter* at the Bowery Theatre, New York. The women in the audience were so shocked by it that they fled from the theatre.

### Most curtain calls for a ballet performance
In October 1964 Margot Fonteyn and Rudolf Nureyev received 89 curtain calls after their performance in *Swan Lake* at the Staatsoper, in Vienna, Austria.

### Most pirouettes
Delia Gray (15) performed 166 consecutive turns at The Playhouse, Harlow, Essex, UK, on 2 June 1991.

## First tutu and first on points
Ballerina Maria Taglioni (1804–84) wore a muslin dress known as a tutu when she danced in *La Sylphide* at the Paris Opéra on 12 March 1832. The dress allowed more freedom of movement so became popular in classical ballet. In the same ballet she danced on points without support – the first time any dancer had done so.

www.ballet.co.uk    search

# Film, TV & Radio

## World-wide web

The third *Spider-Man* film was released in 2007 and has one of the largest production budgets of all time. The film franchise has made over $2.5 billion worldwide, putting each instalment among the top 20 highest-earning films ever made.

# The American Film Institute's top films

The American Film Institute has listed greatest films in a number of categories, based on the views of a panel of 1,500 film experts.

## AFI's greatest films

1 *Citizen Kane* (1941)
2 *Casablanca* (1942)
3 *The Godfather* (1972)
4 *Gone with the Wind* (1939)
5 *Lawrence of Arabia* (1962)
6 *The Wizard of Oz* (1939)
7 *The Graduate* (1967)
8 *On the Waterfront* (1954)
9 *Schindler's List* (1993)
10 *Singin' in the Rain* (1952)

### Funniest films
1 *Some Like It Hot* (1959)
2 *Tootsie* (1982)
3 *Dr Strangelove, or: How I Learned to Stop Worrying and Love the Bomb* (1964)
4 *Annie Hall* (1977)
5 *Duck Soup* (1933)
6 *Blazing Saddles* (1974)
7 *M*A*S*H* (1970)
8 *It Happened One Night* (1934)
9 *The Graduate* (1967)
10 *Airplane!* (1980)

### Love stories
1 *Casablanca* (1942)
2 *Gone With the Wind* (1939)
3 *West Side Story* (1961)
4 *Roman Holiday* (1953)
5 *An Affair to Remember* (1957)
6 *The Way We Were* (1973)
7 *Doctor Zhivago* (1965)
8 *It's a Wonderful Life* (1946)
9 *Love Story* (1970)
10 *City Lights* (1931)

### Thrillers
1 *Psycho* (1960)
2 *Jaws* (1975)
3 *The Exorcist* (1973)
4 *North by Northwest* (1959)
5 *The Silence of the Lambs* (1991)
6 *Alien* (1979)
7 *The Birds* (1963)
8 *The French Connection* (1971)
9 *Rosemary's Baby* (1968)
10 *Raiders of the Lost Ark* (1981)

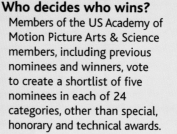

Orson Welles in *Citizen Kane*

# The Oscars®

**What is an Oscar?**
The Academy Awards or "Oscars" have been presented since 1929. The award is a gold-plated statuette made of tin, copper and antimony. It is 34.3 cm (13.5 in) high and weighs 3.8 kg (8.4 lb). Winning an Oscar is important because it encourages more people to see the film and helps the individual winners' careers.

**Why is it called an Oscar?**
According to legend, Academy librarian Margaret Herrick named it when she declared that the statuette looked like her Uncle Oscar!

**Who decides who wins?**
Members of the US Academy of Motion Picture Arts & Science members, including previous nominees and winners, vote to create a shortlist of five nominees in each of 24 categories, other than special, honorary and technical awards.

**Who can win an Oscar?**
The main categories are Best Picture, Best Director, Best Actor Best Actress, Best Supporting Actor and Best Supporting Actress. There are other awards eg screenplay, cinematography, soundtrack, documentary, animated feature, foreign film.

# Oscar® winners

These are the Best Picture, Best Actor and Best Actress winners for the last 25 years. The date given is the date of release. Oscars are awarded the following year.

| Year | Best Picture | Best Actor | Best Actress |
|---|---|---|---|
| 2006 | *The Departed* | Forest Whitaker | Helen Mirren |
| 2005 | *Crash* | Philip Seymour Hoffman | Reese Witherspoon |
| 2004 | *Million Dollar Baby* | Jamie Foxx | Hilary Swank |
| 2003 | *The Lord of the Rings: The Return of the King* | Sean Penn | Charlize Theron |
| 2002 | *Chicago* | Adrien Brody | Nicole Kidman |
| 2001 | *A Beautiful Mind* | Denzel Washington | Halle Berry |
| 2000 | *Gladiator* | Russell Crowe | Julia Roberts |
| 1999 | *American Beauty* | Kevin Spacey | Hilary Swank |
| 1998 | *Shakespeare in Love* | Roberto Benigni | Gwyneth Paltrow |
| 1997 | *Titanic* | Jack Nicholson | Helen Hunt |
| 1996 | *The English Patient* | Geoffrey Rush | Frances McDormand |
| 1995 | *Braveheart* | Nicholas Cage | Susan Sarandon |
| 1994 | *Forrest Gump* | Tom Hanks | Jessica Lange |
| 1993 | *Schindler's List* | Tom Hanks | Holly Hunter |
| 1992 | *Unforgiven* | Al Pacino | Emma Thompson |
| 1991 | *The Silence of the Lambs* | Anthony Hopkins | Jodie Foster |
| 1990 | *Dances With Wolves* | Jeremy Irons | Kathy Bates |
| 1989 | *Driving Miss Daisy* | Daniel Day-Lewis | Jessica Tandy |
| 1988 | *Rain Man* | Dustin Hoffman | Jodie Foster |
| 1987 | *The Last Emperor* | Michael Douglas | Cher |
| 1986 | *Platoon* | Paul Newman | Marlee Martin |
| 1985 | *Out of Africa* | William Hurt | Geraldine Page |
| 1984 | *Amadeus* | F. Murray Abraham | Sally Field |
| 1983 | *Terms of Endearment* | Robert Duvall | Shirley MacLaine |
| 1982 | *Gandhi* | Ben Kingsley | Meryl Streep |

## Highest paid actress

Julia Roberts earned a record $25 million for *Mona Lisa Smile* (2003). These are the highest-paid actresses per film in 2006.

| | Pay per film $US million |
|---|---|
| Nicole Kidman | 16–17 |
| Drew Barrymore | 15 |
| Cameron Diaz | 15 |
| Reese Witherspoon | 15 |
| Renee Zellweger | 15 |
| Halle Berry | 14 |
| Angelina Jolie | 10 |
| Charlize Theron | 10 |
| Kirsten Dunst | 8–10 |
| Jennifer Aniston | 8 |

Reese Witherspoon, Best Actress in 2006

## Top ten film songs

| | Song | Film |
|---|---|---|
| 1 | Over the Rainbow | *The Wizard of Oz* (1939) |
| 2 | As Time Goes By | *Casablanca* (1942) |
| 3 | Singin' in the Rain | *Singin' in the Rain* (1952) |
| 4 | Moon River | *Breakfast at Tiffany's* (1961) |
| 5 | White Christmas | *Holiday Inn* (1942) |
| 6 | Mrs Robinson | *The Graduate* (1967) |
| 7 | When You Wish Upon a Star | *Pinocchio* (1940) |
| 8 | The Way We Were | *The Way We Were* (1973) |
| 9 | Stayin' Alive | *Saturday Night Fever* (1977) |
| 10 | The Sound of Music | *The Sound Of Music* (1965) |

**See also**
Awards: page 155

## Most wins
These three films have each won 11 Oscars, including Best Picture: *Ben-Hur* (1959), *Titanic* (1997) and *The Lord of the Rings: The Return of the King* (2003).

## A no-win situation
*The Turning Point* (1977) and *The Color Purple* (1985) had 11 nominations each but neither of them won a single Oscar. *Gangs of New York* (2002) received 10 nominations, also without winning anything.

## Long and short
*Gone with the Wind* (1939) was the longest film (238 minutes) and the first colour film to win Best Picture. *Marty* (1955) was the shortest Best Picture winner at 91 minutes.

## Black and white
*Marty* was also one of the last black and white films to win Best Picture. *The Apartment* (1960) and *Schindler's List* (1993) are the only black and white films to have won since.

Marlene Dietrich

# Top 10 screen legends

This is the Top 10 of the American Film Institute's list of the greatest American screen legends.

| Actor | Actress |
|---|---|
| 1 Humphrey Bogart | Katharine Hepburn |
| 2 Cary Grant | Bette Davis |
| 3 James Stewart | Audrey Hepburn |
| 4 Marlon Brando | Ingrid Bergman |
| 5 Fred Astaire | Greta Garbo |
| 6 Henry Fonda | Marilyn Monroe |
| 7 Clark Gable | Elizabeth Taylor |
| 8 James Cagney | Judy Garland |
| 9 Spencer Tracy | Marlene Dietrich |
| 10 Charlie Chaplin | Joan Crawford |

# Actors who have played Superman

**Kirk Alyn (1910–99)**
*The Adventures of Superman* (1948) and *Atom Man vs Superman* (1950), both made as cinema serials
**George Reeves (1914–59)**
*Superman and the Mole Men* (1951) and the *Superman* TV series (1953–57)
**Christopher Reeve (1952–2004)**
*Superman* (1978), *Superman II* (1980), *Superman III* (1983) and *Superman IV: The Quest for Peace* (1987)
**Brandon Routh (1979– )**
*Superman Returns* (2006)

**Dean Cain (1966– )**
*Lois & Clark: The New Adventures of Superman* (TV series, 1993–97)
**Tom Welling (1977– )**
*Smallville: Superman the Early Years* TV series (2001– ) about Superman as a teenager

...and Supergirl
**Helen Slater (1963– )**
*Supergirl* (1984)

# Stars of the most $100 million-plus films

These are the stars who have appeared (or supplied voices) in the greatest number of films that have made more than $100 million at the US box office. Tom Cruise and Tom Hanks share the lead, both having appeared in 15 of the top-earning films.

Tom Cruise

| Star | $100 m. + films |
|---|---|
| Tom Cruise | 15 |
| Tom Hanks | 15 |
| Eddie Murphy | 12 |
| Harrison Ford | 11 |
| Mel Gibson | 11 |
| Samuel L. Jackson | 11 |
| Jim Carrey | 10 |
| Morgan Freeman | 10 |
| James Earl Jones | 10 |

## Top stars

Since the 1920s, cinemas across the USA have nominated the top stars of the year according to the number of people who pay to watch their films. These are the top stars of 2006.

1 Johnny Depp
2 Leonardo DiCaprio
3 Will Smith
4 Denzel Washington
5 Tom Hanks
6 George Clooney
7 Will Ferrell
8 Dakota Fanning
9 Adam Sandler
10 Sacha Baron Cohen

# Movie monsters

Ever since cinema began, film-makers have played on everyone's fear of monsters. These are some of the most popular monster films.

**Aliens**
Hundreds of films have been made about alien monsters attacking Earth. The most successful of these was *Independence Day* (1996).

**Dinosaurs**
One of the first cartoons was *Gertie* (1914). It featured a drawing of a brontosaurus that comes to life. Dinosaur films *Jurassic Park* (1993) and its two sequels, *The Lost World: Jurassic Park* (1997) and *Jurassic Park III* (2001), are among the biggest blockbusters of all time.

**Egyptian mummies**
*The Mummy* (1932) featured an Egyptian mummy that comes to life and attacks people. *The Mummy* was remade in 1999 and its sequel, the comedy-adventure *The Mummy Returns* (2001), has made more than $433 million.

**Frankenstein's monster**
Frankenstein is the name of the creator of the monster, not the monster itself. The original story was written in 1816 by English writer Mary Shelley. It was first made into a silent film in 1910 by the inventor Thomas Edison and has been remade many times since. *Mary Shelley's Frankenstein* (1994) is the highest-earning of all the versions.

# Stage names

Actors and actresses choose stage names for a variety of reasons. Their real names may be the same as or similar to those of other people, or they may be difficult to spell or pronounce.

Here are some famous performers who decided to change their names.

| Film name | Real name |
|---|---|
| Woody Allen | Allan Stewart Konigsberg |
| Jennifer Aniston | Jennifer Linn Anastassakis |
| Mel Brooks | Melvin Kaminsky |
| Nicolas Cage | Nicholas Kim Coppola |
| Michael Caine | Maurice Joseph Micklewhite |
| Jackie Chan | Chan Kong-sang |
| Tom Cruise | Thomas Cruise Mapother IV |
| Kirk Douglas | Issur Danielovitch Demsky |
| Whoopi Goldberg | Caryn Elaine Johnson |
| Cary Grant | Archibald Alexander Leach |
| Richard E. Grant | Richard Grant Esterhuysen |
| Goldie Hawn | Goldie Jean Studlendegehawn |
| Hulk Hogan | Terry Gene Bollea |
| Angelina Jolie | Angelina Jolie Voight |
| Ben Kingsley | Krishna Bhanji |
| Queen Latifah | Dana Elaine Owens |
| Jet Li | Li Lian Jie |
| Marilyn Monroe | Norma Jean Baker |
| Demi Moore | Demetria Gene Guynes |
| Natalie Portman | Natalie Hershlag |
| Winona Ryder | Winona Horowitz |
| Susan Sarandon | Susan Abigail Tomalin |
| Christian Slater | Christian Michael Leonard Hawkins |
| Sigourney Weaver | Susan Weaver |

Poster for the original horror-adventure film *King Kong* (1933); the film has been remade twice, most recently in 2005

**Funny monsters**
Some of the most successful cartoon monsters are those in *Monsters, Inc.* (2001). The monsters are led by Sulley, whose secret is that the monsters are scared of children!

**Killer creatures**
Giant ape King Kong is one of the most famous animal monsters and the star of the film *King Kong* (1933, 1976 and 2005).

Giant spiders have featured in films such as *Arachnophobia* (1990) and *Eight Legged Freaks* (2002). Harry Potter also meets an army of huge spiders in *Harry Potter and the Chamber of Secrets* (2002). Other famous killer creatures include sharks (*Jaws*, 1977), alligators (*Lake Placid*, 1999) and snakes (*Anaconda*, 1997 and *Snakes on a Plane*, 2006).

**Vampires**
Irish writer Bram Stoker's vampire novel *Dracula* was first published in 1897. Since then it has been made into countless films. The version starring Bela Lugosi (1931) is one of the most famous. *Bram Stoker's Dracula* (1992) and *Van Helsing* (2004) have been the most successful at the box office.

**Zombies**
Zombies are the "undead" – bodies that come out of their graves and terrorize the living. They have been the subject of many films, including *Night of the Living Dead* (1968) and the comedy *Shaun of the Dead* (2004).

This was billed as the first "Rom-Com-Zom" (Romantic Comedy Zombie film).

### See also
Mythical creatures: pages 170–71

www.afi.com       search

# Video and DVD fact file

● The terms video recording and videotape were first used in the early 1950s, but only among TV professionals.

● The abbreviation VCR (video cassette recorder) was first used in the UK and USA in 1971.

● The first domestic video cassette recorders were sold in 1974, but both machines and tapes were very expensive and few people bought them.

● The VHS (video home system) was launched in 1976 in the US and 1978 in Europe.

● By 1980 about 7,687,000 homes had video recorders; by 1996 the global figure was put at 400,976,000.

● DVD (digital video disc or digital versatile disc) players and discs were launched in Japan and the USA in 1997.

● Worldwide, sales of DVDs overtook video sales in 2002.

● By 2003 almost one in three UK households had a DVD player; the figure is predicted to rise to 83 per cent by 2007.

● In 2006 High Definition DVD players and discs went on sale. These next-generation formats are able to store much more high-quality data.

## TV-owning countries

| Country | TVs per 1,000 people in 2006 | Country | TVs per 1,000 people in 2006 |
|---|---|---|---|
| Norway | 1,552 | Latvia | 859 |
| Bermuda | 1,070 | Japan | 843 |
| UK | 1,101 | Netherlands | 761 |
| Denmark | 975 | Australia | 724 |
| Romania | 893 | Canada | 706 |
| USA | 882 | Ireland | 694 |

A 1950s US magazine advertisement for TVs

## First countries to have television*

The BBC's first broadcasts used Baird's mechanical television system. In this, spinning disks were used to scan images.

This was later dropped in favour of US inventor Philo Taylor Farnsworth's electronic system. Electronic television did not rely on moving parts, was more reliable and gave a better picture.

| Country | Year |
|---|---|
| UK | 1936 |
| USA | 1939 |
| USSR | 1939 |
| France | 1948 |
| Brazil | 1950 |

\* High-definition regular public broadcasting service

## TV viewing

● In the average US home, the TV is switched on for 7 hours 40 minutes a day.

● US children aged 2 to 17 watch an average of 19 hours 40 minutes' TV every week. That is 1,023 hours a year compared with 900 hours a year in school.

● In the UK children aged 8 to 15 spend an average of 2 hours 13 minutes a day watching TV and adults over 16 spend an average of 2 hours 23 minutes.

## TV milestones     1930s                                              1940s

**1922**
18 October, BBC (British Broadcasting Company) founded

**1929**
First transmissions of Scottish inventor John Logie Baird's experimental mechanical television system and, in the USA, Philo T. Farnsworth's electronic TV system

**1936**
22 November, BBC opens the world's first regular high-definition television service, from Alexandra Palace, London

**1937**
21 June, Wimbledon Tennis Championships first broadcast

**1938**
30 April, television coverage of the FA Cup Final
31 May, first BBC TV panel game, *Spelling Bee*

**1939**
1 September, BBC television service is suspended throughout World War II
30 April, Franklin D. Roosevelt is the first president to appear on TV, opening the World's Fair in New York

10 June, the first king and queen on TV in the USA are King George VI and Queen Elizabeth, seen visiting the World's Fair

**1941**
1 July, the first ever TV commercial, for a Bulova clock, is broadcast by WNBT New York, during a game between the Brooklyn Dodgers and the Philadelphia Phillies

**1946**
1 June, first TV licences are issued in the UK (cost £2)
7 June, BBC television broadcasts resume

7 July, first British children's TV programme, *For the Children*, is broadcast

**1947**
21 February, America's first regular daytime serial, or soap opera, *A Woman to Remember*, begins its run

**1948**
29 July, London Olympic Games is televised

**1951**
24 December, in the USA *Amahl and The Night Visitors* becomes the world's first commercial colour broadcast

# Radio milestones

**1896**
2 June, Italian inventor Guglielmo Marconi applies for first British "wireless" patent

**1906**
24 December, first radio programme (music and speech) broadcast by Professor Reginald Fessenden from the US coast and received by ships. The first radios were crystal sets, operated by adjusting metal wires known as cat's whiskers

**1920**
15 June, Marconi broadcasts a concert by opera singer Dame Nellie Melba

**1922**
18 October, BBC (British Broadcasting Company) founded. The first BBC broadcast was made on 14 November – the six o'clock news read by Arthur Burrows

**1923**
26 April, first daily weather forecast by the BBC

**1926**
24 January, launch of *The Week's Good Cause*, the BBC's longest-running programme

**1933**
28 August, first BBC woman announcer, Sheila Borrett

**1939–45**
During World War II the BBC provides information and stirring speeches from Winston Churchill and other wartime leaders

**1951**
1 January, launch of *The Archers*, longest-running BBC radio serial

**1964**
Pirate radio stations broadcast from ships to UK, encouraging the BBC to launch a pop music station (Radio 1, 30 September 1967)

**1970**
24 February, National Public Radio launched in the USA

**1993**
First Internet radio broadcasts

**1995**
First experimental DAB (digital audio broadcasting) in UK. DAB gives listeners better quality reception, easy tuning and text information

**2002**
BBC launches five new DAB channels

**2004**
Sales of DAB digital radios top 1 million

**2005**
BBC radio begins to make programmes available as podcasts that can be downloaded to computers, MP3 and DAB players

## Why soap opera?

Radio (and later TV) serials about everyday life in the USA have been sponsored by soap manufacturers since the 1930s. They advertised their products during the shows. The name of these serials has been shortened to soaps since 1943.

www.bbc.co.uk   search

Portable radio from the 1950s

LW  MW  UKW

## 2000s

**1953**
2 June, the coronation of Queen Elizabeth II is watched live by about 20 million people in the UK and 200 million worldwide
21 November, current affairs programme Panorama is launched; goes on to become the longest-running programme on British TV

**1954**
1 January, the *Tournament of Roses* parade at Pasadena, California, USA, becomes the first programme ever broadcast coast-to-coast

11 January, first TV weather forecast in the UK
9 April, Britain's first TV soap opera, *The Grove Family*

**1955**
22 September, first TV advert in the UK, for Gibbs SR toothpaste

**1957**
13 May, first schools programmes broadcast in UK
25 December, the Queen's first TV Christmas message broadcast

**1958**
16 October, *Blue Peter* starts, and becomes the longest-running children's programme

**1969**
21 July, first live broadcasts from the Moon (*Apollo XI*)
15 November, BBC1 and ITV start broadcasting in colour

**1981**
1 August, MTV launched; The Buggles' *Video Killed the Radio Star* the first music video to be broadcast

**1989**
5 February, Sky begins satellite broadcasting in the UK

**1997**
9 November, BBC1 begins broadcasting 24 hours a day, seven days a week (previously, TV closed down at night)

**2000**
18 July, UK launch of *Big Brother* starts a fashion for reality TV

**2006**
High Definition television (HDTV) becomes available in the UK and other countries

**2007**
US announces that all TV broadcasts will be digital only from 2009

# Oldest sporting events

Doggett's Coat and Badge Race is the world's oldest continuous sporting event. It is a rowing contest held on the River Thames in England and has been held every year since 1715. The Newmarket Town Plate horse race is even older, but the race was discontinued for a while.

| Event | First held | Event | First held |
|---|---|---|---|
| Newmarket Town Plate horse race | 1665 | Football League championship (England) | 1888 |
| Doggett's Coat and Badge Race (rowing) | 1715 | Stanley Cup ice hockey competition | 1893 |
| Real Tennis Championship | 1740 | US Open golf championship | 1895 |
| St Leger horse race | 1776 | Davis Cup tennis tournament | 1900 |
| Epsom Derby horse race | 1780 | Baseball World Series | 1903 |
| County Cricket Championship | 1827 | Tour de France cycle race | 1903 |
| Oxford and Cambridge Boat Race | 1829 | Ryder Cup golf tournament | 1927 |
| Grand National steeplechase | 1836 | FIFA Soccer World Cup | 1930 |
| Henley Regatta | 1839 | Formula One World Championship | 1950 |
| British Open golf championship | 1860 | Super Bowl (US football championship) | 1967 |
| Melbourne Cup horse race | 1861 | Cricket World Cup | 1975 |
| America's Cup yachting series | 1870 | Athletics World Cup | 1977 |
| Football Association Challenge Cup | 1872 | World Athletics Championships | 1983 |
| Kentucky Derby horse race | 1875 | Breeders' Cup horse race series | 1984 |
| Test Match cricket | 1877 | Rugby Union World Cup | 1987 |
| Wimbledon Lawn Tennis Championships | 1877 | | |

# Top sporting events

These are the leading events in the world's most popular sports, in addition to the Olympic Games.

**American football** Super Bowl

**Athletics** IAAF (International Association of Athletics Federations)

**Grand Prix Auto racing (US)** Indianapolis 500

**Baseball** World Series

**Basketball** NBA (National Basketball Association) Final

**Cycling** Tour de France

**Golf** British Open, US Open, Ryder Cup (every two years)

**Horse racing** Epsom Derby, Grand National, Breeders' Cup, Kentucky Derby

**Ice hockey** Stanley Cup

**Motor racing** World Formula One Championship

**Rallying** Paris-Dakar Rally

**Rugby League** Challenge Cup, Super League

**Rugby Union** Six Nations Tournament, World Cup (every four years)

**Soccer** UEFA Champions League, FIFA World Cup (every four years)

**Tennis** Wimbledon Championships, US Open

Grand National steeplechase (19th century)

**See also**

Major rock events: page 255

# Sports timeline

Experts argue about the exact origins of many sports. The dates here are generally agreed to be when these sports were first played or contested on an organized basis.

| | | | | | |
|---|---|---|---|---|---|
| Athletics | 3800 BC | Soccer | 1848 | Basketball | 1891 |
| Horse racing | AD 1540 | Tenpin bowling | 1850 | Rugby League | 1895 |
| Boxing | 1681 | Show jumping | 1864 | Darts | 1896 |
| Rowing | 1715 | Cycling | 1867 | Motor cycling | 1896 |
| Ice skating | 1742 | Badminton | 1873 | Speedway | 1902 |
| Cricket | 1744 | Lawn tennis | 1873 | | |
| Golf | 1744 | American football | 1874 | | |
| Swimming | 1791 | Hockey (field) | 1875 | | |
| Baseball | 1839 | Hockey (ice) | 1887 | | |
| Rugby Union | 1839 | Motor racing | 1887 | | |

Bare-knuckle boxing match (1820)

## Biggest soccer crowd

The biggest-ever crowd for a soccer match was at the 1950 World Cup Final. The match between Brazil and Uruguay at the Maracanã Stadium (now called the Journalista Mário Filho Stadium) in Brazil was watched by 199,854 people. The biggest crowd for a soccer match in Britain was at Hampden Park, Glasgow, on 17 April 1937. Scotland was playing England and 149,547 people paid to watch and another 10,000 may have got in without paying!

The Journalista Mário Filho Stadium in Rio de Janeiro, Brazil, was built for the 1950 World Cup and held almost 200,000 people.

## Biggest crowds

In the past, more than 100,000 people at a time crammed into American football's Rose Bowl, the old Wembley Stadium and other venues across Europe to watch sport. Today, there are laws which limit the number of people allowed in a sports stadium. Outdoor events such as the New York City Marathon and the Tour de France now draw the biggest crowds. They are held over open roads and people don't have to pay to watch them.

● About 2.5 million people watch the New York Marathon – the biggest crowd for a single day at a sporting event. As many as 15 million people turn out to see the Tour de France during its three weeks.

● The record crowd for a golf tournament was set at the US Open, Flushing Meadows, 2005, which was attended by 659,538 people.

● In horse racing, more than 60,000 watch the Grand National and about 120,000 go to the Epsom Derby every year.

● Cricket attracts big crowds. Nearly a million people watched the 1936–37 series between Australia and England over its three months. More than 400,000 people watched the India v Pakistan Test match in Calcutta in 1998–99.

● Some of the biggest crowds at US sporting events are for Indy car races. About 270,000 fans attend the Indianapolis 500 every year and as many as 332,000 attended the 2006 Canadian Grand Prix in Montreal.

### Strange sport

A world championship in mobile phone throwing has been held in Finland every year since 2000. Competitors take part in individual or team events. There is also an under-12 category. The current world record stands at 94.97 m (311 ft 7 in) for men and 53.52 m (175 ft 7 in) for women.

## Sport on TV

TV audiences for many sporting events were larger 30 years ago than they are today. Fewer people had televisions, but there were not as many channels and no video recorders, so more people watched events live.

| UK event | Audience* |
|---|---|
| World Cup Final, England v West Germany, 1966 | 32,500,000 |
| World Cup, Brazil v England, 1970 | 32,500,000 |
| FA Cup Final replay, Chelsea v Leeds United, 1970 | 32,000,000 |
| World Heavyweight boxing match, Muhammad Ali v Joe Frazier, 1970 | 27,000,000 |

| USA event | Audience* |
|---|---|
| Super Bowl XXXVIII, New England Patriots v Carolina Panthers, 2004 | 143,600,000 |
| Super Bowl XL, Pittsburgh Steelers v Seattle Seahawks, 2006 | 141,400,000 |
| Super Bowl XLI, Indianapolis Colts v Chicago Bears, 2007 | 140,000,000 |
| Super Bowl XXXVII, Tampa Bay Buccaneers v Oakland Raiders, 2003 | 138,900,000 |
| Super Bowl XXX, Dallas Cowboys v Pittsburgh Steelers, 1996 | 138,488,000 |
| Super Bowl XXVIII, Dallas Cowboys v Buffalo Bills, 1994 | 134,800,000 |
| Super Bowl XXVII, Dallas Cowboys v Buffalo Bills, 1993 | 133,400,000 |
| Super Bowl XXXII, Denver Broncos v Green Bay Packers, 1998 | 133,400,000 |

* Number of people who watched at least part of broadcast

# THE OLYMPICS

## Summer Olympics

The modern Olympic Games have been held every four years since 1896, except during World Wars I and II. Over this time the numbers of competitors, events and nations taking part have all increased dramatically.

Winter Paralympic events for athletes with disabilities have been held since 1976. The Summer Paralympics began in 1960 and were first held in conjunction with the regular Summer Olympics in 1988.

| Year/City/country | Competitors | No. of nations | Events | Most golds | Most medals |
|---|---|---|---|---|---|
| 1896 Athens, Greece | 245 | 14 | 43 | USA 11 | Greece 47 |
| 1900 Paris, France | 1,225 | 26 | 95 | France 26 | France 95 |
| 1904 St Louis, USA | 687 | 13 | 91 | USA 79 | USA 245 |
| 1906 Athens, Greece | 884 | 20 | 76 | France 15 | France 40 |
| 1908 London, UK | 2,035 | 22 | 110 | UK 54 | UK 138 |
| 1912 Stockholm, Sweden | 2,547 | 28 | 102 | USA 25 | Sweden 64 |
| 1920 Antwerp, Belgium | 2,669 | 29 | 154 | USA 41 | USA 95 |
| 1924 Paris, France | 3,092 | 44 | 126 | USA 45 | USA 99 |
| 1928 Amsterdam, Netherlands | 3,014 | 46 | 109 | USA 22 | USA 56 |
| 1932 Los Angeles, USA | 1,408 | 37 | 117 | USA 41 | USA 103 |
| 1936 Berlin, Germany | 4,066 | 49 | 129 | Germany 33 | Germany 89 |
| 1948 London, UK | 4,099 | 59 | 136 | USA 38 | USA 84 |
| 1952 Helsinki, Finland | 4,925 | 69 | 149 | USA 40 | USA 76 |
| 1956* Melbourne, Australia | 3,342 | 72 | 145 | USSR 37 | USSR 98 |
| 1960 Rome, Italy | 5,348 | 83 | 150 | USSR 43 | USSR 103 |
| 1964 Tokyo, Japan | 5,140 | 93 | 163 | USA 36 | USA 90 |
| 1968 Mexico City, Mexico | 5,531 | 112 | 172 | USA 45 | USA 107 |
| 1972 Munich, West Germany | 7,123 | 121 | 195 | USSR 50 | USSR 99 |
| 1976 Montreal, Canada | 6,028 | 92 | 198 | USSR 49 | USSR 125 |
| 1980 Moscow, USSR | 5,217 | 80 | 203 | USSR 80 | USSR 195 |
| 1984 Los Angeles, USA | 6,797 | 140 | 221 | USA 83 | USA 174 |
| 1988 Seoul, South Korea | 8,465 | 159 | 237 | USSR 55 | USSR 132 |
| 1992 Barcelona, Spain | 9,367 | 169 | 257 | EUN† 45 | EUN 112 |
| 1996 Atlanta, USA | 10,744 | 197 | 271 | USA 44 | USA 101 |
| 2000 Sydney, Australia | 10,651 | 199 | 300 | USA 39 | USA 97 |
| 2004 Athens, Greece | 11,099 | 202 | 301 | USA 35 | USA 103 |

\* The equestrian events in 1956 were held in Stockholm, Sweden, from 10–17 June, because of quarantine restrictions in Australia at the time.

† The Unified Team (EUN) was made up of the former Soviet republics of Russia, Ukraine, Kazakhstan and Uzbekistan.

## The big five

Only five sports have been contested at every Summer Olympics since the first Modern Olympics in 1896. These are cycling, fencing, gymnastics, swimming and track and field. Rowing would have been on this list, but the events in 1896 were cancelled due to bad weather.

## Out of the Olympics

Various sports have been dropped from the Olympic Games over the years. These include croquet, underwater swimming, duelling pistol shooting, stone-throwing, lacrosse, archery with live birds, tug-of-war, club-swinging and rope climbing.

## The Olympic flag

The five-ring Olympic flag was first raised at the 1920 Antwerp Olympics. The rings on the flag represent the five major regions of the world: the Americas, Europe, Asia, Africa and Australasia. At least one of the colours on the flag (blue, yellow, black, green and red) can be found on the flags of every nation in the world.

## One and only

Softball is the only sport that women contest at the Olympics but men do not. The sport has been played at three Olympics (1996, 2000, 2004) and the USA has won gold each time.

# Olympic firsts     1800s                                                          1900s

**1896** First modern Olympics. Doves released to symbolize peace

**1896** First American gold medal winner, James Connolly (triple jump)

**1896** First British gold medal winner, Launceston Elliot (weightlifting)

**1900** First women competitors. First woman to win a gold medal, Charlotte Cooper from Great Britain for tennis

**1908** First parade of athletes with national flags

**1908** First athlete to win ten gold medals (in four Olympics, 1900, 1904, 1906 and 1908), Ray Ewry (USA)

**1912** Electronic timing and photo-finish equipment first used

**1920** Olympic oath, "We swear that we will take part in the Olympic Games in a spirit of chivalry, for the honour of our country and for the glory of sport", first taken, by Belgian fencer Victor Boin

**1920** Olympic flag first raised

**1924** First Olympics with more than 100 women competitors (there were 136 women and 2,956 men)

**1924** First live radio transmissions of events

**1928** First Olympic flame, large results display board first used

## Olympic history

The ancient Olympic Games were dedicated to the Olympian gods and held at Olympia, on the border between Greece and Macedonia. They began in 776 BC and were held every four years. There were fewer events than now, and only Greeks could take part. The 293rd and last Olympiad was held in AD 392. After this, they were banned by the Emperor Theodosius. The games were revived in 1896 when the first modern Olympic Games were held in Athens.

# Top medal winners

These athletes have won the most medals in the history of the Summer Olympics from 1896–2004.

| Athlete | Sport | Years | Gold | Silver | Bronze | Total |
|---|---|---|---|---|---|---|
| Larissa Latynina (USSR) | Gymnastics | 1956–64 | 9 | 5 | 4 | 18 |
| Nikolai Andrianov (USSR) | Gymnastics | 1972–80 | 7 | 5 | 3 | 15 |
| Boris Shakhlin (USSR) | Gymnastics | 1956–64 | 7 | 4 | 2 | 13 |
| Edoardo Mangiarotti (Italy) | Fencing | 1936–60 | 6 | 5 | 2 | 13 |
| Takashi Ono (Japan) | Gymnastics | 1952–64 | 5 | 4 | 4 | 13 |
| Paavo Nurmi (Finland) | Athletics | 1920–28 | 9 | 3 | 0 | 12 |
| Sawao Kato (Japan) | Gymnastics | 1968–76 | 8 | 3 | 1 | 12 |
| Alexei Nemov (Russia) | Gymnastics | 1996–2000 | 4 | 2 | 6 | 12 |

Athlete Ray Ewry (USA) won only ten medals but they were all gold! He still holds the record for the most individual gold medals. Ewry won his medals between 1900 and 1908 in the standing jump events: high jump, long jump and triple jump. Amazingly, Ewry had suffered polio as a child, but overcame his illness to become one of the greatest athletes ever.

The opening ceremony of the 2004 Olympics was watched by 72,000 spectators in the Olympic Stadium in Athens, Greece.

## 2000s

**1928** First women competitors in track and field events

**1932** First Olympic logo, three-tier victory stand, national anthem played and flag raised for winner

**1936** Introduction of Olympic torch relay (from Olympia, Greece, to Berlin, Germany)

**1936** Games televised for the first time

**1956** Athletes enter closing ceremony together to symbolize unity

**1956** First games in the southern hemisphere (Melbourne, Australia)

**1960** First Summer Paralympics, held in Rome, Italy

**1960** Worldwide TV coverage for the first time

**1984** Professionals allowed to compete for the first time

**2004** Women competed in freestyle wrestling for the first time. Ukraine, Japan and China all won gold medals

**2004** First Olympics broadcast over the Internet

www.olympic.org/uk     search

Yankees All-Star Alex Rodriguez

Major League baseball started in the USA when the National League was formed in 1876. The rival American League was started in 1901, and in 1903 the World Series, a best-of-nine game event, was held between the winners of each league's championship. In the first series the Boston Red Sox beat the Pittsburgh Pirates 5–3. The World Series has been a best-of-seven games series since 1905, except in 1919–21 when it went back to a nine-game series.

**Most wins** American League: New York Yankees – 26 between 1923 and 2000; National League: St Louis Cardinals – 10 between 1926 and 2006
**Most consecutive wins** New York Yankees – 5 (1949–53)

## Baseball

Baseball is one of the most popular sports in the USA and is also played in Japan, Mexico, Cuba and a number of South American countries. It is played by two teams of nine players each.

Medieval manuscripts show ball games with bats, and a game called "base-ball" appears in a picture published in London in 1744. The game of rounders was first described in 1828, and this or a similar game was known among British settlers in America. The first rules were drawn up in 1845 by Alexander Joy Cartwright Jr and the first match under these rules played on 19 June 1846.

## Golf majors

Tiger Woods

The four big competitions in golf are known as the majors. They are the US Masters, British Open, US Open and US PGA Championship, and are played in that order every year.

The Masters, founded in 1934, is the only one of the four played on the same course each year, at Augusta National in Georgia, USA. The oldest of the majors is the British Open, which was first held in 1860. It is also the only one played outside the USA. The US Open was first played in 1895 and the US PGA in 1916.

**Players with most professional major wins**

**Jack Nicklaus (USA)** 18:
3 British Open; 4 US Open;
5 US PGA; 6 Masters
**Tiger Woods (USA)** 12:
3 British Open; 2 US Open;
3 US PGA; 4 Masters
**Walter Hagen (USA)** 11:
4 British Open; 2 US Open;
5 US PGA

**Ben Hogan (USA)** 9:
1 British Open; 4 US Open; 2 US PGA;
2 Masters
**Gary Player (S Africa)** 9:
3 British Open; 1 US Open; 2 US PGA;
3 Masters
**Tom Watson (USA)** 8:
5 British Open; 1 US Open; 2 US Masters

## Tiger Woods

At just 21 years, three months and 14 days, Tiger Woods was the youngest-ever Masters champion. In 2001 Tiger won his second US Masters and became the first player to hold all four professional major championships at the same time.

# Basketball

Basketball is hugely popular in the USA and is now played in other parts of the world, as well as at the Olympics. The game is played by two teams of five players each, usually on an indoor court.

Players score points by shooting the ball through the basket. The National Basketball Association (NBA) in the USA was formed in 1949. It contains 30 teams divided into two conferences, Eastern and Western. At the end of the season the two conference winners meet in a best-of-seven series for the NBA Championship.

## Record breakers

Outstanding player Kareem Abdul-Jabbar (Milwaukee Bucks and Los Angeles Lakers) scored a record 38,387 points during his career.

**Teams with most wins**
Boston Celtics: 16
Minneapolis/Los Angeles Lakers: 14
Chicago Bulls: 6

Corliss Williamson (Sacramento Kings) drives for the basket

# Rugby

The game of rugby probably started in 1823 at Rugby School in England, when William Webb Ellis picked up a football and ran with it. The first rules were drawn up in 1848 and the Rugby Football Union (RFU) was formed by Edwin Ash in 1871.

Today's game of Rugby Union is played between two teams of 15 players. The two biggest events are the International Championship and the World Cup. The International Championship began in 1884 and was originally played by four teams: England, Ireland, Scotland and Wales. France joined in 1910 and Italy in 2000, making it a six-nation tournament. The Rugby World Cup was launched in 1987 and has been held every four years since then. In 2003, 20 teams took part and nearly two million people attended the 48 matches.

## Rugby League

Rugby League dates from 29 August 1895, when 21 major clubs in the north of England formed a league outside the RFU. They were protesting against the RFU's refusal to pay players who had to take time off work. To make Rugby League less like Rugby Union they changed various rules, including reducing the team size from 15 to 13. Rugby League is now played in Australia, New Zealand, France, Russia and some Pacific nations, as well as in Britain. One of the major events in Rugby League is the Challenge Cup, open to British, French and Russian teams. There is also a Rugby League World Cup, first played in 1954. The last was in 2000 and the next will be in Australia in 2008.

# Test cricket

Cricket is a bat and ball game played between two teams of 11 players. The aim is to score more runs than the opposing team. Among the major competitions are the Test matches, which are normally played over five days.

They are called Test matches because they were started as a test of the relative skills of the two sides. Test matches are played between teams representing their countries. There are currently ten countries that play Test cricket.

# Australian Rules football

This is a tough, fast-moving game, in which players can kick, bounce, catch or punch the ball. It has been played in Australia since the Melbourne Football Club was formed in 1858. The season-long series of matches ends in the Grand Final at the Melbourne Cricket Ground.

There are 18 players in an Australian Rules team. This is more than any other team sport. The game is played on one of the biggest pitches. The oval-shaped area measures 135–185 x 110–155 m (443–607 x 361–508 ft). A professional soccer pitch measures 90–120 x 45–90 m (295–394 x 148–295 ft) wide.

## The Ashes

Cricket's most famous trophy is the Ashes. England and Australia were the first two Test teams. When England lost to Australia at home in 1882, the *Sporting Times* joked that English cricket was dead and that its body would be cremated and the ashes taken to Australia. When the England team next visited Australia, it was presented with a tiny urn containing the burnt bails from the wicket used in the Third Test. Since then, whichever team wins an England-Australia Test series is said to have won the Ashes. The trophy is kept at Lord's Cricket Ground in London.

www.cricinfo.com          search

**FOOTBALL**

# The World Cup

The first soccer World Cup was played in 1930 in Uruguay. Thirteen teams took part and the hosts beat Argentina 4–2 in the final in Montevideo.

The Italian team that won the 2006 World Cup

They won the Jules Rimet trophy, named after the president of FIFA (Fédération Internationale de Football Association) when the competition began. Brazil were allowed to keep the trophy after winning it for the third time in 1970 and it was replaced by the FIFA World Cup trophy. The World Cup final takes place every four years.

| Winning country | Year | Winning country | Year |
|---|---|---|---|
| Uruguay | 1930 | Brazil | 1970 |
| Italy | 1934 | West Germany | 1974 |
| Italy | 1938 | Argentina | 1978 |
| Not held | 1942 | Italy | 1982 |
| Not held | 1946 | Argentina | 1986 |
| Uruguay | 1950 | West Germany | 1990 |
| West Germany | 1954 | Brazil | 1994 |
| Brazil | 1958 | France | 1998 |
| Brazil | 1962 | Brazil | 2002 |
| England | 1966 | Italy | 2006 |

## World Cup facts

● The first World Cup goal was scored by Lucien Laurent of France. The goal came 19 minutes into the first World Cup game on 13 July 1930.

● The first player to score four goals in a World Cup match was Ireland's Paddy Moore in a qualifying match against Belgium in 1934. It was the Republic's first ever World Cup match.

## Most World Cup wins

| | |
|---|---|
| Brazil | 5 |
| Italy | 4 |
| West Germany | 3 |
| Uruguay | 2 |
| Argentina | 2 |

## International caps

On 10 May 1886 the English Football Association decided: "That all players taking part for England in future international matches be presented with a white silk cap with red rose embroidered on the front. These to be termed International Caps."

This tradition has spread throughout world football. The number of caps show how many times players have represented their countries. The following footballers are the most-capped players in their countries.

| Player | Country | Years | Caps |
|---|---|---|---|
| Mohamed Al-Deayea | Saudi Arabia | 1990–2006 | 181 |
| Claudio Suárez | Mexico | 1992–2006 | 178 |
| Cobi Jones | USA | 1992–2004 | 164 |
| Lothar Matthäus | Germany | 1980–2000 | 150 |
| Cafu | Brazil | 1990–2006 | 142 |
| Luis Figo | Portugal | 1991–2006 | 127 |
| Lilian Thuram | France | 1994–2006 | 126 |
| Paolo Maldini | Italy | 1988–2002 | 126 |
| Andoni Zubizarreta | Spain | 1985-1998 | 126 |
| Peter Shilton | England | 1970–1990 | 125 |
| Pat Jennings | Northern Ireland | 1964–1986 | 119 |
| Roberto Fabián Ayala | Argentina | 1994–2006 | 107 |
| Steve Staunton | Republic of Ireland | 1989–2002 | 102 |
| Kenny Dalglish | Scotland | 1972–1987 | 102 |
| Neville Southall | Wales | 1982–1998 | 92 |

## Soccer timeline  1800s

**500 BC** Football (tsu chu, meaning to kick a ball) played in China

**1314** First reference to football in England when Edward II prohibited the game because "too many people were bustling over footballs on London streets"

**1848** The first rules of football drawn up at Cambridge University

**1852** First inter-school football match, Westminster v Harrow

**1855** Sheffield football club, the oldest still in existence, formed

**1862** Notts County, the oldest current League club, formed

**1863** Football Association (FA) formed

**1870** First international match, England v Scotland, played at Kennington Oval

**1871** FA Cup launched

**1872** Corner kick introduced

**1873** Scottish FA formed; Scottish Cup started

**1874** Shin pads first worn

**1875** The crossbar replaced a tape across the top of the goals

**1876** Welsh FA formed

**1878** Irish (now Northern Ireland) FA formed

**1878** Referee's whistle first used

**1885** Professional football legalized

**1888** Football League formed

**1889** The term "soccer" first used; May be an abbreviation of association football – the FA was formed to standardize the rules of the game

**1890** Scottish League formed

**1891** Goal nets first used

**1891** Linesmen (now assistant referees) replace umpires

**1891** Penalty kick adopted by the FA

## American Football records

The first international American football game took place at Cambridge, Massachusetts, on 14 May 1874, between Harvard University and McGill University of Montreal, Canada.

The first Rose Bowl college football game was at Pasadena, California, on 1 January 1902 between the Universities of Michigan and Stanford. It has been held annually since 1916.

The New England Patriots (wearing blue and white) have won three Super Bowls this century.

## American football

American football, or Gridiron, is the number one sport in the USA. The National Football League (NFL) is split into two conferences, the American Football Conference (AFC) and National Football Conference (NFC). Each conference is split into four divisions – North, South, East and West – and each division has four teams.

Each team plays 16 matches and the top teams go through to play-offs. The two conference winners then meet in a final – the Super Bowl – currently played in early February. The winning team receives the Vince Lombardi Trophy.

| No. | Year | Winners | No. | Year | Winners | No. | Year | Winners | No. | Year | Winners |
|---|---|---|---|---|---|---|---|---|---|---|---|
| I | 1967 | Green Bay Packers | XII | 1978 | Dallas Cowboys | XXII | 1988 | Washington Redskins | XXXI | 1997 | Green Bay Packers |
| II | 1968 | Green Bay Packers | XIII | 1979 | Pittsburgh Steelers | XXIII | 1989 | San Francisco 49ers | XXXII | 1998 | Denver Broncos |
| III | 1969 | New York Jets | XIV | 1980 | Pittsburgh Steelers | XXIV | 1990 | San Francisco 49ers | XXXIII | 1999 | Denver Broncos |
| IV | 1970 | Kansas City Chiefs | XV | 1981 | Oakland Raiders | XXV | 1991 | New York Giants | XXXIV | 2000 | St Louis Rams |
| V | 1971 | Baltimore Colts | XVI | 1982 | San Francisco 49ers | XXVI | 1992 | Washington Redskins | XXXV | 2001 | Baltimore Ravens |
| VI | 1972 | Dallas Cowboys | XVII | 1983 | Washington Redskins | XXVII | 1993 | Dallas Cowboys | XXXVI | 2002 | New England Patriots |
| VII | 1973 | Miami Dolphins | XVIII | 1984 | Los Angeles Raiders | XXVIII | 1994 | Dallas Cowboys | XXXVII | 2003 | Tampa Bay Buccaneers |
| VIII | 1974 | Miami Dolphins | XIX | 1985 | San Francisco 49ers | XXIX | 1995 | San Francisco 49ers | XXXVIII | 2004 | New England Patriots |
| IX | 1975 | Pittsburgh Steelers | XX | 1986 | Chicago Bears | XXX | 1996 | Dallas Cowboys | XXXIX | 2005 | New England Patriots |
| X | 1976 | Pittsburgh Steelers | XXI | 1987 | New York Giants | | | | XL | 2006 | Pittsburgh Steelers |
| XI | 1977 | Oakland Raiders | | | | | | | XLI | 2007 | Indianapolis Colts |

## 1900s

**1904** FIFA formed in Paris; first international match outside Britain – Belgium v France played near Brussels
**1907** Professional Footballers' Association (PFA) formed (as the Football Players and Trainers Union)
**1921** FA of Ireland (Republic of Ireland) formed
**1923** First Wembley Cup Final (Bolton v West Ham)

**1928** Players' numbers introduced
**1930** First World Cup in Uruguay
**1932** Substitutes formally agreed by FIFA
**1950** England's first World Cup (lost 1–0 to USA)
**1954** Union of European Football Associations (UEFA) formed
**1955** European Cup started
**1960** Football League Cup started
**1965** Football League agrees use of substitutes

**1968** Red cards introduced (at the Mexico Olympic Games)
**1975** Scottish Premier Division (now Premier League) formed
**1981** Football League changed the number of points for a win from two to three
**1982** Professional foul rule introduced

## 2000s

**1992** FA Premier League formed
**1993** Champions' League replaces the European Cup
**2004** Greece are surprise winners of the European Championship
**2007** David Beckham moves to Los Angeles Galaxy for $150 million over 5 years

http://www.fifa.com  search

# Badminton

Badminton probably came from an old children's game called "battledore and shuttlecock". The battledore is a small wooden bat which the player uses to hit the shuttlecock. The game was popular in India and other Asian countries, and the aim was to keep the shuttlecock in the air as long as possible. British army officers played the game in India in the 1860s and they added a net to hit the shuttlecock over. They called the game "poona".

When the officers returned to England they continued enjoying poona. The game was renamed badminton at a garden party at the home of the Duke of Beaufort in 1873. His home was called Badminton House. By 1877 the first official rules of the game were drawn up and in 1893 the first governing body, The Badminton Association of England, was set up. The Badminton Club of New York began in 1878, although the game did not become popular until the 1930s.

### Badminton's greatest player

Rudy Hartono from Indonesia won the world's oldest badminton tournament, the All-England Championships, a record eight times between 1968 and 1976. He was also the 1980 world champion at the age of 32, and unbeaten in six Thomas Cup ties.

# Pelota

Pelota is the name given to a variety of sports that are played by hitting a ball with the hand, a racquet, or a basket attached to the hand. Pelota and its variations were first played during the 13th century in the Basque region of Spain. There are variations of the game depending upon the equipment used.

- Played with the hand it is called *pelota mano*, or just pelota.
- Played with a racquet, it is called *frontenis*.
- Played with a hand basket, it is called *jai-alai*.

The game is similar to squash – players hit the ball against the end wall of a three-sided court, if possible, out of reach of their opponent. Pelota is popular in Spain, Mexico, South America, Cuba, Italy and many US states, including Florida.

## New rules for table tennis

Traditionally, the winner of a table tennis game was the first player to score 21 points, but in 2001 the International Table Tennis Federation (ITTF) announced changes in the rules. These included a new scoring system in which the first player to score 11 points wins the game. In national and international tournaments all matches are played to either the best-of-5 games or the best-of-7.

Pelota player in action

# Lawn tennis timeline    1800s                                                2000s

**1877** First Wimbledon Championship
**1881** First US Championship
**1891** First French Championship – until 1925 for French nationals
**1896** Tennis played at the first Modern Olympics in Athens
**1900** Davis Cup began after Dwight F. Davis donated a trophy
**1905** First Australian Open
**1913** International Lawn Tennis Federation founded in Paris with 12 member countries

**1922** Seeding (method of ranking players) first used, at the US National Championships
**1923** Women's tennis became international with the launch of the Wightman Cup (named after US team captain Hazel Wightman)
**1938** Donald Budge (USA) became the first player to complete the Grand Slam

**1950** Louise Brough (USA) became the first woman to complete the Grand Slam
**1963** The Federation Cup, the women's equivalent of the Davis Cup, began
**1968** Tennis tournaments were opened to professional players, effectively ending the amateur game
**1971** The tie-break was introduced by the British LTA as an experiment

**1972** Davis Cup changed from being run on a challenge basis to a knockout tournament involving all competing nations
**1973** Introduction of official world rankings by the ATP and LTA
**1988** Tennis revived as an Olympic sport after 64 years
**2004** World ranking points first allocated to competitors in the Olympic Games

## Tennis scoring

No one knows exactly how the tennis scoring system came about, but it may have started in France in medieval times. People think the system may be based on the movement of the hand of a clock at one end of the court: on winning a point, the hand would be moved 15 minutes, or a quarter round the clock. Next comes 30, half the clock, and so on. As a player had to win four points to win the game, the first round the clock face won. The score 40 may be used instead of 45 because in French quarante (40) is easier to say than quarante-cinq (45). When both sides reach 40 the score is deuce. This comes from the French quarante à deux, or 40 to both, or simply from deux, two, as players must gain two points to win. "Love", the zero score, may come from the French word l'oeuf, meaning egg, as the symbol for zero is egg-shaped.

## Serena and Venus Williams

Serena Williams (born 1981) has won 8 Grand Slam singles titles, which is three more than her older sister Venus (born 1980). Both players have been ranked World No. 1 and have each earned more than $16 million in prize money.

Serena Williams

## Lawn tennis Grand Slam events

The Grand Slam consists of the Australian, French, Wimbledon and US Championships. A player is said to have completed the Grand Slam if he or she holds all four titles simultaneously, although not necessarily in the same year. These events were originally for amateur players but are now open to all, including professionals.

### Wimbledon Championships

First held in 1877, Wimbledon is the world's most famous tennis championship. From 1877 to 1921 it was a challenge event with the defending champion qualifying for the next year's final. Women first took part in 1884. Since 1968 Wimbledon has been an open event. This means it is open to all players, including professionals.

### US Open

This was first held in 1881. Until 1911, the US tournament operated as a challenge system, with the defending champion automatically going through to the following year's final. Women first competed in 1887. Two championships were held in 1968 and 1969, one for amateurs and an open championship. It became completely open in 1970.

### French Open

The French Open was first held in 1891 and until 1925 it was only for French nationals. It became the French Open in 1968 and has been played at the Stade Roland Garros (named after a famous French aviator) since 1928. Women have competed since 1897.

### Australian Open

This competition was first held in 1905 as the Australasian Tennis Championship. Women first competed in 1922. The competition became the Australian Championship in 1927, and since 1969 has been the Australian Open. It is played at Melbourne every January.

### Most titles in Grand Slams

Australian Roy Emerson won 28 Grand Slam titles between 1961 and 1967. He is the only male player to win singles and doubles titles at all four Grand Slam events. Margaret Court (née Smith), also from Australia, won a record 62 Grand Slam titles, between 1960 and 1973.

## Squash champions

### Jahangir Khan

Jahangir Khan is the greatest male squash player of all time. He has won six World Open titles, three World Amateur titles, four World Masters and ten consecutive British Open titles. Khan was born in Karachi in 1963. His father Roshan was a British champion, as were Roshan's cousins Hashan and Azam. At one point in his career, Jahangir competed for an amazing five years and eight months without defeat, playing more than 800 matches. He was voted Pakistan's Sportsman of the Millennium and elected President of the World Squash Federation in 2002.

### Heather McKay

Heather McKay (born Blundell) dominated ladies' squash during the 1960s and 1970s. She was born in New South Wales, Australia in 1942, the eighth of 11 children. Between 1962 and 1977 she won 16 consecutive British Open titles and remained undefeated for 17 years before her retirement. She lost just two games in her career. In 1999 Heather McKay became a founder member of the WISPA Hall of Fame, and was awarded the Australian Sports Medal in 2000.

COMBAT, STRENGTH AND TARGET SPORTS

## Boxing weights

Boxing matches are held between two contestants of similar weight. The weight classes were first used in the 19th century and more were added during the 20th century.

| Weight class | Max kg (lb) |
| --- | --- |
| Strawweight/Mini flyweight | 48 (106) |
| Junior flyweight/ Light flyweight | 49 (108) |
| Flyweight | 51 (112) |
| Junior bantam/ Super flyweight | 52 (115) |
| Bantamweight | 54 (119) |
| Junior featherweight/ Super bantamweight | 55 (121) |
| Featherweight | 57 (126) |
| Junior lightweight/ Super featherweight | 59 (130) |
| Lightweight | 61 (134) |
| Junior welterweight/ Super lightweight | 65 (143) |
| Welterweight | 67 (148) |
| Junior middleweight/ Super welterweight | 70 (154) |
| Middleweight | 73 (161) |
| Super middleweight | 76 (168) |
| Light heavyweight | 79 (174) |
| Cruiserweight | 91 (201) |
| Heavyweight | >91 (201) |

Muhammad Ali defeating Sonny Liston, 1965

## Boxing's greatest champions

● "Sugar" Ray Robinson was one of the best boxers in any weight division. His first world title was at welterweight in 1946. Moving up a division, he beat Jake La Motta in 1951 to capture the middleweight title. He even had a crack at the light heavyweight title, but failed after a 14th-round knockout. Robinson was born in Detroit in 1920 and turned professional in 1940. He went on to have 201 fights and won 174 of them, 109 with knockouts.

● "Sugar" Ray Leonard was born in Wilmington, Carolina in 1956. He began boxing at 14 and in 1976 won the Olympic light welterweight title. He turned professional in 1977. Two years later he won the first of many world titles when he beat Wilfred Benitez to become welterweight champion. Leonard went on to become the first man to win world titles at five different weights, all within ten years. He held welterweight, light middleweight, middleweight, light heavyweight and super middleweight titles.

● Oscar de la Hoya from Los Angeles first became famous at the 1992 Barcelona Olympics – he won the USA's only boxing gold that year. La Hoya turned professional after the Olympics. He went on to become only the third man to capture world titles at five different weights, from junior lightweight to junior middleweight. His greatest win was beating his idol Julio Cesar Chavez in four rounds at Caesar's Palace, Las Vegas, in 1996.

## Muhammad Ali

Muhammad Ali was born Cassius Clay in Louisville, Kentucky in 1942. He burst on to the boxing scene at the 1960 Rome Olympics where he took the light heavyweight gold medal. In 1964, aged 22, he won his first world heavyweight title by beating Sonny Liston. He beat George Foreman ten years later to become only the second man to regain his title. In 1978, at the age of 36, he beat Leon Spinks to become the first man to win the title a third time. He lost his last world title fight to Larry Holmes in 1980.

www.wwe.com    search

# Snooker and pool

Snooker was first played by British army officers in India and later became popular in Britain, while pool began in America. One of pool's top events is the Mosconi Cup, named after the great American pool player and 14 times world champion Willie Mosconi. It is now an annual contest in the UK and pitches the best pool players from Europe against those from the USA.

### Pool champion
Earl Strickland from Greensboro, North Carolina has won three world titles (1990, 1991, 2002). He has also been the US Open champion five times. Nicknamed "The Pearl", he has appeared in nine Mosconi Cups, winning 31 matches out of 45, and he has captained the team twice.

### Snooker champions
The greatest players of the modern game still playing are Steve Davis and Stephen Hendry. Between them they have won the Embassy World Professional Snooker title 13 times, and both have won all the other major trophies in the game. Davis won six world titles between 1981 and 1989. Scottish-born Hendry has won a record seven, including five consecutive titles between 1992 and 1996.

## Hossein Rezazadeh

Hossein Rezazadeh (Iran) holds the men's weightlifting record. He lifted 472.5 kg (1,041.7 lb) at the Sydney Olympics in September 2000. This is heavier than a cow!

# Wrestling

The World Wrestling Federation was started in the 1960s as the WorldWide Wrestling Federation (WWWF) by Vince McMahon. In the early 1980s Vince's son, Vince McMahon Jr, renamed it WWF.

The sport changed and became widely popular. Characters such as Hulk Hogan became household names, attracting huge crowds to live matches and millions of followers via TV. The WWF is now known as WWE®, World Wrestling Entertainment, Inc. The two biggest events in the WWE calendar are Wrestle Mania, which decides the world champions, and the Royal Rumble. The first WWF Wrestle Mania was at Madison Square Garden on 31 March 1985.

## Top wrestlers

● Texan Shawn Michaels is one of the most popular of all wrestlers. He weighs in at about 116 kg (255.7 lb). Michaels has won the WWE title, WWE World Heavyweight title, the WWE World Tag Team title and twice won the Royal Rumble, among many other top honours and titles.

● The Rock (real name Dwayne Johnson) is 1.94 m (6.36 ft) tall and weighs 118 kg (260.11 lb). He has been the WWE Champion, the WWE World Tag Team Champion and was the winner of Royal Rumble 2000. He took to the sport after a brief professional football career, and has also appeared in several films, including *The Mummy Returns* (2001), *The Scorpion King* (2002) and *Be Cool* (2005).

● Triple H, or "The Game", made his WWE debut in 1995 as Hunter Hearst Helmsley. He weighs around 118 kg (260.11 lb). He has been WWE Champion, WWE World Heavyweight Champion, WWE World Tag Team Champion, King of the Ring and Royal Rumble. He is the only man to win the Grand Slam, King of the Ring and Royal Rumble.

## Hulk Hogan

Hulk Hogan's real name is Terry Bollea. He is 2.03 m (6.66 ft) tall and weighs a massive 122 kg (269 lb). His first ring name was Sterling Golden and then he became Terry Boulder before settling with Hulk Hogan. He played the wrestling villain Thunderlips in *Rocky III* in 1982, and has appeared in other films, including *Spy Hard* (1996) and *Muppets from Space* (1999).

# Weightlifting records

In an Olympic weightlifting competition contestants perform two types of lifts, the snatch, and the clean and jerk. They have three attempts at each. The score is the total of the best of each type of lift.

In the snatch the contestant lifts the bar from the floor directly above the head and holds it for two seconds. In the clean and jerk the contestant first takes the bar from the floor to the shoulders and then above the head.

A new women's world record was set at the 2004 Athens Olympics when Gonghong Tang of China successfully lifted 305 kg (672.4 lb).

Iranian weightlifter Hossein Rezazadeh

# Olympic water sports

## Sailing

The first Modern Olympics in 1896 should have included sailing, but the races could not be held because of bad weather. Sailing was included for the first time four years later in Paris and has been a full Olympic sport since 1908. Boardsailing made its debut in 1988. Men and women have competed together in sailing events over the years, but in 1988 women had events of their own. Until the 2000 Olympics, sailing was known as yachting.

**Top gold-medal winning nations (1900–2004)**
Great Britain 24
Norway 17
USA 17

## Rowing

Rowing was to have been part of the 1896 Olympics, but the events were cancelled. It was first included in Paris four years later, and has appeared at every Olympics since. Women first competed in 1976.

**The top gold-medal winning nations (1900–2004)**
East Germany 33
USA 30
Germany/West Germany 27
Great Britain 22

## Canoeing

Canoeing was first included as a demonstration sport in 1924, and did not become a full Olympic sport until 1936. Women took part for the first time in 1948.

**Top gold-medal winning nations (1936–2004)**
USSR/Unified Team 30
Germany/West Germany 28
East Germany 14
Hungary 17
Sweden 15

Michael Phelps swimming in the 2004 Olympic Games

## Mark Spitz

When swimmer Mark Spitz took part in the 1968 Mexico Olympics he was already a record holder – he set a total 26 world records during his career. He predicted he would win six gold medals at the Olympics, but he won just two, both in relay events.

But in 1972, in Munich, Spitz became the first and only person to win seven gold medals at one Summer Olympics. He also set new world records with all his medals.

**Mark Spitz's gold medals at the 1972 Olympics**

| Event | Time (min:sec) |
|---|---|
| 200 m butterfly | 2:00.70 |
| 4 x 100 m freestyle | 3:26.42 |
| 200 m freestyle | 1:52.78 |
| 100 m butterfly | 0:54.27 |
| 4 x 200 m freestyle | 7:35.78 |
| 100 m freestyle | 0:51.22 |
| 4 x 100 m medley | 3:48.16 |

Start of the men's coxless fours rowing final at the 2004 Olympic Games. Great Britain is the 3rd boat from the top.

### Rowing knights

British rower Steve Redgrave won gold medals at five consecutive Olympic Games (1984–2000), while Matthew Pinsent won gold medals at four consecutive Games – in coxless pairs (with Steve Redgrave) in 1992 and 1996 and coxless fours in 2000 and 2004. Pinsent and Redgrave were knighted for their rowing achievements.

## Olympic swimming

These are the top medal-winning Olympic swimmers. Totals include medals won in relays.

| Swimmer | Gold | Silver | Bronze | Total |
|---|---|---|---|---|
| **Men** | | | | |
| Mark Spitz (USA) | 9 | 1 | 1 | 11 |
| Matt Biondi (USA) | 7 | 2 | 1 | 10 |
| Aleksandr Popov (Russia) | 4 | 5 | 0 | 9 |
| Zoltán Halmay (Hungary) | 3 | 5 | 1 | 9 |
| **Women** | | | | |
| Jenny Thompson (USA) | 8 | 1 | 1 | 10 |
| Dara Torres (USA) | 4 | 1 | 4 | 9 |
| Dawn Fraser (Australia) | 4 | 4 | 0 | 8 |
| Kornelia Ender (GDR) | 4 | 4 | 0 | 8 |
| Shirley Babashoff (USA) | 2 | 6 | 0 | 8 |

www.fina.org  search

## Olympic Tarzans

Johnny Weissmuller won the 100 metres freestyle at the 1924 Paris Olympics. He went on to win a total of five golds and one bronze medal during his Olympic career. While training for the 1932 Olympics, he was offered a $500-a-week contract to advertise swimwear. A Hollywood executive saw the adverts and offered Weissmuller the role of Tarzan. In 1932 he made his debut in the film *Tarzan the Ape Man*. He played the character in 11 more films over the next 16 years. He was the first of four Olympic medallists to play the film role. The others were Buster Crabbe (freestyle swimmer), Herman Brix (shot put) and Glenn Morris (decathlon).

## The America's Cup

The America's Cup is the top sailing trophy and one of the best known trophies in the sporting world. It began in 1851 when the English Royal Yacht Squadron organized a 10-km (6-mile) regatta of 17 boats around the Isle of Wight. The 31-m American schooner *America* entered and won the trophy, then called the One Hundred Guinea Cup.

# Swimming strokes

**Breaststroke**
The breaststroke was the first stroke used in competitive and recreational swimming. It is also the stroke that most people learn when they first take up swimming. The first reference to the breaststroke was in a French book in 1696. The sidestroke, with a scissor leg action, developed from breaststroke. Top swimmers can swim the breaststroke at 1.37 m (4.5 ft) a second.

**Backstroke**
The backstroke is the only stroke in which the swimmers start in the water, rather than diving in. The stroke, in which swimmers lie on their backs and use their arms in a windmill style, was first made popular in the USA by Harry Hebner in 1912. An earlier form of the backstroke was first seen at the 1900 Olympics. For this fast stroke, top speed is about 1.52 m (5 ft) a second.

**Butterfly**
In this stroke, both arms enter and leave the water at the same time, while the legs perform a dolphin kick. It was developed in the 1930s and evolved from the breaststroke. Swimming coach David Armbruster developed the arm movement of the stroke at the University of Iowa in 1934 and the following year one of his swimmers, Jack Sieg, developed the foot and leg movements. The two combined produced the butterfly. The stroke was not officially approved until 1953 and became an Olympic event in 1956. Maximum speed is 1.67 m (5.5 ft) a second.

**Front crawl/freestyle**
In 1844 two native Americans competing in a swimming regatta in London introduced their new revolutionary overarm stroke. Flying Gull beat Tobacco to take the winner's medal. The stroke was later developed by Englishman John Trudgen, and then by Australian Richard Cavill, who realized the importance of kicking the feet at the same time as moving the arms. Front crawl is the fastest swimming stroke and has a maximum speed of 1.71 m (5.6 ft) a second.

Competitors in the America's Cup, 2003

After *America*'s win, the trophy was re-named the America's Cup and given to the New York Yacht Club. There it remained unless won by a challenger. Over the next 132 years the New York Yacht Club successfully defended the trophy against 25 challengers, until in 1983 it was won by Australia. In 2003 the trophy returned to Europe when Russell Coutts in *Alinghi* won for Switzerland – a landlocked country! The latest Cup was held at Valencia, Spain, in 2007.

# Tour de France

The oldest and best-known of the world's great cycling tours is the Tour de France. The others are the Vuelta – Tour of Spain, and Giro – Tour of Italy.

● The Tour de France was first staged in 1903 when the course was made up of six stages over 2,428 km (1,508.7 miles). Now the race is 5,000 km (3,106.9 miles) or more and the course takes in more than 20 stages, often going into neighbouring countries.

● The famous yellow jersey (*maillot jaune*) is worn by the current overall time leader in a race. It was first worn in 1919.

● The longest race was in 1926 when Lucien Buysse of Belgium won after 5,745 km (3,569.8 miles).

● Around 15 million people every year line the streets to watch the Tour de France over its three weeks.

● The first US winner of the Tour de France was Greg LeMond who won it in 1986, and again in 1989 and 1990. He was also the first English-speaking winner of the race.

● Eddie Merckx has won more of the big three tours than any other man. He has won the Tour de France five times, the Giro five times and the Vuelta once.

## Lance Armstrong

Lance Armstrong (USA) has won the Tour de France a record seven times, two more than Jacques Anquetil (France), Eddie Merckx (Belgium), Bernard Hinault (France) and Miguel Indurain (Spain).

# Olympic cycling

Cycling was included in the first Modern Olympics in 1896. Léon Flameng (France) won the first cycling gold in the 100 km race. Only two men competed – Flameng and Georgios Kolettis of Greece – and they had to race around a 333.3 m (1,093.5 ft) track 300 times! During the race, Kolettis's bicycle needed repairing, so Flameng waited for him while the repairs were carried out. Cycling has been included in every Olympics since then. Below are the current Olympic events (BMX racing will be introduced in 2008).

## Men
### Track
Sprint (1,000 metres)
Time trial (1,000 metres)
Individual pursuit (4,000 metres)
Team pursuit (4,000 metres)
Points race (40 kilometres)
Madison (60 kilometres)
Keirin (2,000 metres)
### Road
Road race (individual)
Time trial (individual)
### Mountain bike
Cross-country

## Women
### Track
Sprint (1,000 metres)
Time trial (500 metres)
Individual pursuit (3,000 metres)
Points race (25 kilometres)
### Road
Road race (individual)
Time trial (individual)
### Mountain bike
Cross-country

Lance Armstrong

# Mountain biking

Mountain biking, or off-road biking, was started in 1974 by a group of Californian enthusiasts, who modified their bikes. By 1977, there was so much interest in the sport that manufacturers started to produce mountain bikes, and in 1983 the National Off-Road Bicycle Association (NORBA) was formed.

There are two types of mountain bike competitions – downhill riding and cross-country – and the first world championships were held in 1990. Cross-country mountain biking was first held at the Olympics in 1996. Competitors ride over a hilly, sometimes mountainous, natural course. Men race 40 to 50 km (24.85 to 30.07 miles), and women 30 to 40 km (18.64 to 24.85 miles).

The top male and female riders are both French. Nicolas Vouilloz won seven men's downhill world titles between 1995 and 2002. Anne-Caroline Chausson (France) has won 16 World Championship titles. She won the downhill event every year from 1996 to 2003 and again in 2005.

Olympic women's mountain bike race

# Formula One

The Formula One World Championship normally lasts from March until October. In 2007 there were 17 races. Since 2003 the points system has been:

winner – 10 points
2nd – 8 points
3rd – 6 points
4th – 5 points
5th – 4 points
6th – 3 points
7th – 2 points
8th – 1 point.

The driver with the most points at the end of the season is the champion. There is also a manufacturers' championship.

Michael Schumacher in a Ferrari at the US Grand Prix

## World champion

German Michael Schumacher is the world's most successful Formula One driver. He has won a record seven world titles (1994, 1995, 2000, 2001, 2002, 2003, 2004) and also has the most race wins in a season – 13 in 2004.

# Motor cycle racing

Grand Prix bikes come in engine sizes 125 cc, 250 cc and Moto GP (which replaced the old 500 cc event). Grand Prix bikes are made in small numbers just for racing. Superbikes are made in larger quantities and can be used on the road.

## Top manufacturers

● An Aprilia machine first won at 250 cc in 1987, and the make is now dominant in both the 125 and 250 cc classes. They enjoyed their first Superbike success in 2000.

● Honda are the most successful manufacturer in motor cycle racing. They have won 48 Grand Prix world titles and have had 607 race wins. They are now also making a name for themselves in Superbike racing.

● Kawasaki bikes won their first world title (125 cc) in 1969. They have now won nine world titles in three classes as well as producing the 1993 Superbike world champion.

● The Yamaha company started in 1887 as musical instrument manufacturers and made their first motor cycle in 1955. They entered a bike in the 1961 French Grand Prix, but did not compete regularly until 1964, when they won the world 250 cc title.

● Suzuki began life as clothing makers before starting to make motor cycles. They won their first Grand Prix in 1962 and in the same year won the first ever 50 cc title.

● Ducati have been in Grand Prix racing since the 1950s. They are now by far the most successful manufacturer in Superbike history.

## One and only

One of the great Indy 500 drivers was A.J. Foyt, the first of only three men to win the race four times. He won in 1961, 1964, 1967 and 1977. He drove a record 18,966 km (11,785 miles) in 34 Indy 500 races. Foyt started racing in 1953. He is the only man to win the Indy 500, the Daytona 500 and the Le Mans 24 Hour races.

## Young winners

● In 2005 Fernando Alonso (Spain) became the youngest-ever winner of the Formula One World Driver's Championship aged 24 years, 2 months.

● In 1952 Troy Ruttman (USA) won the Indianapolis 500 (at that time part of the Formula One World Championship) aged 22 years, 3 months. Bruce McLaren (New Zealand) was the same age when he won the US Grand Prix in 1959.

● Other young Formula One World Champions are Emerson Fittipaldi (Brazil), aged 25 years, 9 months, in 1972; Michael Schumacher (Germany), who won in 1994 at the age of 25 years, 10 months.

## Indianapolis 500

The biggest event in American motor racing is the Indianapolis 500, which is not just a race but a day-long carnival. The auto race is part of the Memorial Day celebrations at the end of May and crowds of 250,000 flock to the Indianapolis raceway from all over the USA.

The course, which opened in 1909, is known as The Brickyard because the original circuit was made out of thousands of bricks. The first Indy 500 was held in 1911 and was won by Ray Harroun in his Marmon Wasp. Contestants race over 200 laps of the 4 km (2.48 miles) oval circuit.

www.formula1.com   search

# Winter Olympics

The Winter Games (officially the International Winter Sports Week, but later recognized as the first Winter Olympics) was first held in 1924. It included five events: Nordic skiing, figure skating, speed skating, bobsledding and ice hockey.

Winter Olympics were held in the same years as the Summer Olympics until 1992, but since 1994 they have taken place every four years between the Summer Games.

- Alpine skiing
- Biathlon (cross-country skiing and rifle-shooting)
- Bobsleigh
- Cross-country skiing
- Curling
- Figure skating
- Freestyle skiing
- Ice hockey
- Luge
- Nordic combined
- Short-track speed skating
- Skeleton (similar to the luge but competitors travel on their stomachs, head first)
- Ski-jumping
- Snowboarding
- Speed skating

## Snowboarding

Snowboards were invented in the 1970s, and the sport started to become popular in the 1980s. In 1998 snowboarding was included in the Winter Olympics for the first time, with Halfpipe and Parallel giant slalom events. Snowboard cross was added in 2006.

## Top medal winners at the Winter Olympics (1924–2006)

| Athlete – Men | Sport | Gold | Silver | Bronze | Total |
|---|---|---|---|---|---|
| Bjorn Dählie (Norway) | Cross-country | 8 | 4 | 0 | 12 |
| Sixten Jernberg (Sweden) | Cross-country | 4 | 3 | 2 | 9 |
| Ole Einar Bjoerndalen (Norway) | Biathlon | 5 | 3 | 1 | 9 |
| Ricco Gross (Germany) | Biathlon | 4 | 3 | 1 | 8 |
| Kjetil André Aamodt (Norway) | Alpine skiing | 4 | 2 | 2 | 8 |
| Sven Fischer (Germany) | Biathlon | 4 | 2 | 2 | 8 |

| Athlete – Women | Sport | Gold | Silver | Bronze | Total |
|---|---|---|---|---|---|
| Raisa Smetanina (USSR/Unified Team) | Cross-country | 4 | 5 | 1 | 10 |
| Stefania Belmondo (Italy) | Cross-country | 2 | 3 | 5 | 10 |
| Lyubov Egorova (Unified Team/Russia) | Cross-country | 6 | 3 | 0 | 9 |
| Uschi Disl (Germany) | Biathlon | 2 | 4 | 3 | 9 |
| Claudia Pechstein (Germany) | Speed skating | 5 | 2 | 2 | 9 |

## Top medal-winning nations at the Winter Olympics (1924–2006)

| Country | Gold | Silver | Bronze | Total |
|---|---|---|---|---|
| USSR/Unified Team/ Russia | 122 | 89 | 86 | 297 |
| Norway | 96 | 102 | 84 | 282 |
| USA | 78 | 81 | 59 | 218 |
| Germany/ West Germany | 76 | 78 | 57 | 211 |
| Austria | 50 | 64 | 71 | 185 |

www.vancouver2010.org    search

# Winter Olympic facts and figures    1900s

**1924 Chamonix, France**
There were 294 competitors from 16 nations. Norway won the most medals (17) and tied with Finland for gold medals (4).

**1928 St Moritz, Switzerland**
Twenty-five nations and 495 competitors took part. Norway won the most medals (15) and the most golds (6).

**1932 Lake Placid, USA**
A total of 306 competitors from 17 nations competed. USA won the most medals (12) and the most golds (6).

**1936 Garmisch-Partenkirchen, Germany**
There were 755 competitors from 28 nations. Norway won most medals (15) and most gold medals (7).

**1948 St Moritz, Switzerland**
A total of 28 nations and 713 competitors took part. Norway, Sweden and Switzerland tied for top medal position (10). Norway and Sweden tied for most golds (4).

**1952 Oslo, Norway**
A total of 732 competitors from 30 nations took part. Norway held both top medal (16) and top gold (7) position.

**1956 Cortina D'Ampezzo, Italy**
Thirty-two nations and 818 competitors took part. USSR were top medal winners (16) with the most gold wins (7).

**1960 Squaw Valley, USA**
Thirty nations took part with 665 athletes. USSR again won the most medals (21) and most golds (7).

**1964 Innsbruck, Austria**
Thirty-six nations and 1,186 athletes took part. USSR won most medals (25) and most golds (11) for the third time.

**1968 Grenoble, France**
A total of 1,293 athletes competed from 37 nations. Norway won most medals (14) and most gold medals (6).

Competitors in the Men's Snowboard Cross final at the Turin 2006 Winter Olympics

## The Stanley Cup

Every player on the winning team takes the Stanley Cup home for 24 hours to show off to family and friends. New York Islander Clark Gillies used it in 1980 to feed his dog, and in 1996 Colorado Avalanche defenceman Sylvain Lefebvre baptized his daughter in it.

## Ice hockey

Ice hockey probably developed from a game called bandy that was played on ice-covered pitches. The modern game is played over three 20-minute periods between two teams. Each team has six players on the ice at any one time. The object is to move the puck (a hard rubber disc) across the ice with a stick (maximum length 160 cm [63 in]) and put it into the opponent's goal.

The National Hockey League (NHL) was formed in 1917. Today the NHL is made up of 30 teams split into two conferences. The Eastern Conference has 15 teams divided into three divisions: Atlantic, North-East and South-East. The Western Conference is also divided into three divisions: Central, North-West and Pacific. At the end of season the leading teams in each conference play each other. The winner of each plays for the Stanley Cup.

### NHL's top goalscorers

| Player | Goals |
| --- | --- |
| Wayne Gretzky | 894 |
| Gordie Howe | 801 |
| Brett Hull | 741 |
| Marcel Dionne | 731 |
| Phil Esposito | 717 |
| Mike Gartner | 708 |

### Top teams Stanley Cup wins

| | |
| --- | --- |
| Montreal Canadiens | 24 |
| Toronto Maple Leafs | 13 |
| Detroit Red Wings | 10 |
| Boston Bruins | 5 |
| Edmonton Oilers | 5 |

## Ice skating

### Famous skaters

● Ulrich Salchow, born in Sweden in 1877, was the greatest men's figure skater of all time. He won the first Olympic skating title at the 1908 London Olympics and between 1901 and 1911 he was the world champion on ten occasions.

● Norway's Sonja Henie won Olympic golds in 1928, 1932 and 1936. She also won ten world titles. She won nearly 1,500 cups and medals during her career. After leaving the sport in 1936 she became a film star and appeared in 11 films.

### Fastest speed skaters

● Shani Davis (USA) set a new men's world record at Salt Lake City on 20 November 2005 when he covered 1,000 m in 1 minute 7.03 seconds, representing a speed of 53.71 km/h (33.4 mph).

● Cindy Classen of Canada set a women's world record of 1 minute 13.46 seconds for the 1000 m at Calgary on 24 March 2006. The next day, she lowered the record further to 1 minute 13.11 seconds.

## Young star

The first athlete aged under 14 to win a Winter Olympic gold was Kim Yoon-mi of South Korea. She was in the winning 3,000 m speed skating relay team at Lillehammer, Norway in 1994.

## Ski-jumping

In 2005 the world ski-jumping record was broken three times within 75 minutes! At the final meeting of the 2004–05 Ski Jumping World Cup Bjørn Einar Romøren (Norway) set a new mark at 234.5 m (769.3 ft). Then Matti Hautamaeki (Finland) put the record up to 235.5 m (772.6 ft) before Romøren re-took the record with a leap of 239 m (784.1 ft).

## 2000s

**1972 Sapporo, Japan**
There were 1,232 competitors from 35 nations. USSR were top of the overall medal table (16) and won most gold medals (8).

**1976 Innsbruck, Austria**
Thirty-seven nations and 1,128 athletes took part. USSR won most medals (27) and most gold medals (13).

**1980 Lake Placid, USA**
There were 1,067 competitors from 37 nations. USSR won most medals overall (22) and most golds (10).

**1984 Sarajevo, Yugoslavia**
A total of 1,278 competitors from 49 nations took part. USSR won most medals (25) but East Germany topped the gold medal table (9).

**1988 Calgary, Canada**
Fifty-seven nations fielded 1,423 athletes. USSR won most medals (29) and most golds (11).

**1992 Albertville, France**
Sixty-three nations with 1,801 competitors took part. Germany won most medals (26) and most gold medals (10).

**1994 Lillehammer, Norway**
1,739 athletes from 67 nations took part. Norway won most medals altogether (26) but Russia won most golds (11).

**1998 Nagano, Japan**
There were 72 nations taking part and 2,302 athletes. Germany won most medals (29) and most gold medals (12).

**2002 Salt Lake City, USA**
Seventy-eight nations fielded 2,399 athletes. Germany again won most medals (35) and most golds (12).

**2006 Turin, Italy**
A record 2,663 athletes from 82 nations took part. Germany were the top medal winners for the third time in a row (29) and also won most gold medals (11).

### See also

The Olympics: pages 282–83

# Greyhound racing

Dog racing has been popular since ancient times, when dogs were used for hunting. Modern greyhound racing takes place on an oval-shaped track over distances from 210 m (689 ft) to 1,097 m (3,599 ft). An electric "hare" goes round the track, and the dogs are released from traps to chase it.

In the UK most greyhound races are run with six dogs, but in the USA they are run with eight. There is a draw before the race to decide which trap each dog starts from. Each dog wears a coloured jacket which matches its starting trap.

# Harness racing

In harness racing the horses pull the drivers who sit in a two-wheeled cart called a sulky. There are two forms of harness racing – pacing and trotting.

The difference between pacing and trotting is in the way the horse moves. A pacing horse moves its right front and back legs together, then its left front and back legs. A trotter moves its left front leg and right back leg at the same time, followed by its right front leg and left back leg.

## Main races

The leading race for trotters is the Hambletonian. This race was first held at Syracuse, New York, in 1926 and is now run every year at The Meadowlands, East Rutherford, New Jersey. It is named after a trotter called Hambletonian. The leading race for pacers is The Little Brown Jug, named after a 19th-century horse. It has been held at Delaware, Ohio, every year since 1946.

Hambletonian harness race

### Top drivers

Herve Filion, born in Quebec, Canada, is the most famous driver in harness-racing history and set many records in his 35-year career. In 1968 he became the first driver to win 400 races in a season. He went on to achieve 400 or more wins per season in 14 other years. He was forced to retire in 1995 but made a comeback in 2002. He achieved his goal of reaching 15,000 wins before finally retiring the following year with a total of 15,086 wins.

John Campbell, from Ontario, Canada, is the top money-winning jockey in the sport. He started driving in 1972 at the age of 17 and was the first man to pass the $100 million and $200 million milestones in career earnings. He won the Hambletonian six times.

### Top horse

Moni Maker was the first horse to pass the $5 million mark. Remarkably, she achieved this during a four-year career between 1997–2000. She won 60 of her 91 trotting races and won the Horse of the Year Award in 1998 and 1999. In 2003, the Italian-bred horse Varenne surpassed Moni Maker's career winning record.

## Rodeo

Professional rodeo developed from the early days of ranching, when bull riding and calf roping were common activities. The first known rodeo with prize money was held at Deer Trail, Colorado, in 1869. The All-Round Cowboy World Champion is decided each year – the champion is the cowboy who wins the most money over a series of events. Top cowboys win more than $250,000 a year.

# Record horse jumps

● The highest officially recognized horse jump is 2.47 m (8.1 ft). The jump was made by Captain Alberto Larraguibel Morales (Chile) on Huasó on 5 February 1949 at Santiago, Chile. Richard "Dick" Donnelly (USA) claimed to have cleared 2.51 m (8.3 ft) on a horse named Heatherbloom in Richmond, Virginia, USA, in 1902, but this is an unofficial record.

● The world record height jumped by a horse in a puissance competition (in which horses jump a limited number of obstacles) was set on 9 June 1991. German rider Franke Sloothaak on Optibeurs Leonardo cleared 2.4 m (7.9 ft) in Chaudfontaine, Switzerland.

● The longest horse jump over water is 8.4 m (27.5 ft). The jump was made by André Ferreira (South Africa) on 25 April 1975 in Johannesburg, South Africa, on a horse named Something.

# The Breeders' Cup

The Breeders' Cup Limited was started in 1982 to encourage thoroughbred racing throughout the USA. The first Breeders' Cup day was held on 10 November 1984 at Hollywood Park, Inglewood, California. It is now one of the most important race days anywhere and entries come from all around the world.

There are eight races on Breeders' Cup Day, which is held at a different course each year in October or November. The total prize money for the 2006 Breeders' Cup was $20 million. The top race is the Breeders' Cup Classic. It runs over one mile two furlongs and has total prizemoney of $5 million with the winner receiving more than $2.7 million.

Winner of the Breeders' Cup Classic 2002

## Most successful jockey

Laffit Pincay Jr was the first man to win more than 9,500 races. He won the Breeders' Cup seven times, and the Kentucky Derby once. He retired in 2003 having won more than $225 m. In December 2006, Russell Baze (Canada) passed Pincay's world record of 9,530 wins.

# Top horse races

## England

● The Epsom Derby was first held in 1780 and is now run over one-and-a-half miles at Epsom Downs each June. The first winner was a horse named Diomed. Jockey Lester Piggott won the Derby a record nine times.

● The Grand National is the world's best-known steeplechase, a horse race over a course with obstacles to be jumped. It was first run as the Grand Liverpool Steeplechase in 1839. The race now takes place every spring over four-and-a-half miles at Aintree in England and the winning horse has to clear 30 challenging fences. The famous horse Red Rum won the race a record three times between 1972–76.

## France

● The Prix de L'Arc de Triomphe was first run in 1920. It takes place on the first Sunday in October every year and covers 2,400 m over the Longchamps race course, Paris. Alleged, ridden by Lester Piggott, won the race in 1977 and 1978 and was the last horse to win two years in a row.

## Australia

● The most important horse race in Australia is the Melbourne Cup which dates from 1861. It is run on the first Tuesday in November at the Flemington Park race track in Victoria. Trainer Bart Cummings won the race a record 11 times between 1965 and 1999.

## United States

● The Kentucky Derby was first held in 1875. It is run over one mile two furlongs at Churchill Downs, Kentucky, on the first Saturday in May and is the most famous of all US horse races. Eddie Arcaro and Bill Hartack have been the most successful jockeys with five wins each.

## Breeders' Cup records

| | |
|---|---|
| Most wins (jockey) | 15 (Jerry Bailey) |
| Most prize money (jockey) | $23,033,360 (Pat Day) |
| Most wins (trainer) | 18 (D. Wayne Lukas) |
| Most prize money (trainer) | $19,645,520 (D. Wayne Lukas) |
| Most used track | Churchill Downs, Kentucky, used in 1988, 1991, 1994, 1998, 2000, 2006 |

## Breeders' Cup firsts

The 2003 Breeders' Cup produced two firsts. Julie Krone, who rode Halfbridled to victory in the Juvenile Fillies race, was the first woman to ride a winner at the event. One race ended in a dead heat – the first in Breeders' Cup history.

http://www.bhs.org.uk          search

# Last
## Lists

### Crocodile hunter

After years of daring encounters with crocodiles, snakes and other deadly creatures, the popular Australian naturalist and wildlife TV presenter Steve Irwin was tragically killed by a stingray in September 2006.

# Unusual deaths

**Aeschylus**

Aeschylus was a famous Greek dramatist who died in 456 BC. A prediction that he would be killed by a blow from heaven came true when an eagle carrying a tortoise dropped it on his head.

**King Alexander of Greece**

He died after being bitten by his pet monkey in 1920.

**Francis Bacon**

This Elizabethan philosopher caught a chill while trying to deep-freeze a chicken by stuffing it with snow. He died in 1626.

**Hilaire Belloc**

Although born in France, Hilaire Belloc was an English writer and member of parliament. He died in 1953 after a burning coal fell out of his fire and set him ablaze.

**Madéleine-Sophie Blanchard**

Madame Blanchard was the widow of pioneer balloonist Jean-Pierre Blanchard. She was killed in Paris in 1819, when fireworks set fire to her balloon.

**Jerome Cardan**

Cardan was an Italian physician, mathematician and astrologer. He starved himself to death in 1576 to make sure that his own prediction of his death would come true.

**Lord Carnarvon**

Carnarvon was an amateur Egyptologist who financed the excavation of Tutankhamun's tomb in 1922. Several months after opening the tomb, Carnarvon died suddenly from a mosquito bite. This began the legend of the curse of Tutankhamun.

**Isadora Duncan**

This American dancer was strangled in 1927 by her scarf. It became caught in the wheel of a Bugatti sports car in which she was a passenger.

**Anton Dvorák**

The Czech composer died in 1904 of a chill which he caught while train-spotting.

**Frederick, Prince of Wales**

Frederick was the son of George II and heir to the British throne. He died in 1751 after being hit by a cricket ball.

**Harry Houdini (Erich Weiss)**

Houdini was a famous escapologist who claimed he could withstand being punched in the stomach. He died in 1926 – after being punched in the stomach.

**William Huskisson**

Huskisson was a British member of parliament. He was run down by a train during the opening of the first railway in 1830.

**Jean-Baptiste Lully**

This Italian-French composer died in 1687 after accidentally stabbing his foot with a stick while beating time. The short conductor's baton came into use soon afterwards.

**Thomas Midgley**

Midgley was an American inventor who was strangled in 1944 by a machine he had invented to help him move after contracting polio. He invented three products that have since been found to be environmentally harmful: lead in petrol, CFCs in fridges and aerosols, and the insecticide DDT.

# Forever young

The following are some of the most famous people who died early and so remain forever young in our minds.

| Name/cause/year | Age at death |
|---|---|
| **King Edward V** of England, murdered, 1483 | 12 |
| **Saint Agnes** martyred, c. 304 | 13 |
| **King Edward VI** of England, natural causes, 1553 | 15 |
| **Anne Frank** German diarist, in concentration camp, 1945 | 15 |
| **Lady Jane Grey** Queen of England, executed, 1554 | 16 |
| **Thomas Chatterton** English poet, took poison, 1770 | 17 |
| **Anastasia** Grand Duchess of Russia, assassinated, 1918 | 17 |
| **Ritchie Valens** American rock singer, plane crash, 1959 | 17 |
| **King Tutankhamun** Egyptian pharaoh, c. 1340 BC | 18 |
| **Heliogabalus** Roman Emperor, assassinated, 222 | 18 |
| **Joan of Arc** French heroine, burned at the stake, 1431 | 19 |
| **Catherine Howard** Queen of Henry VIII, beheaded, 1542 | 20 |
| **Billy the Kid (William H. Bonney)** American outlaw, shot, 1881 | 21 |

| Name/cause/year | Age at death |
|---|---|
| **Eddie Cochran** American rock singer, car accident, 1960 | 21 |
| **Pocahontas** Native American Indian princess, smallpox, 1617 | 22 |
| **Buddy Holly** American rock singer, plane crash, 1959 | 22 |
| **Aaliyah (Aaliyah Haughton)** singer, plane crash, 2001 | 22 |
| **River Phoenix** actor, drug overdose, 1993 | 23 |
| **Clyde Barrow** US outlaw, shot by Texas Rangers, 1934 | 24 |
| **James Dean** American film actor, car crash, 1955 | 24 |
| **Lee Harvey Oswald** assassin of John F. Kennedy, murdered, 1963 | 24 |
| **John Keats** English poet, tuberculosis, 1821 | 25 |
| **"Red Baron" Manfred von Richthofen** German flying ace, shot down, 1918 | 25 |
| **Jean Harlow** film actress, illness, 1937 | 26 |
| **Brian Jones** Rolling Stones guitarist, drowned, 1969 | 26 |
| **Jimi Hendrix** rock guitarist, drugs, 1970 | 27 |
| **Kurt Cobain** Nirvana lead singer, shooting suicide, 1994 | 27 |
| **Anne Brontë** British writer, tuberculosis, 1849 | 29 |

# Famous last words

**Julius Caesar, 44 BC**

Roman emperor, who was assassinated by conspirators, including Brutus, a man he thought was his friend. According to legend and Shakespeare, Caesar said: "Et tu Brute?" (You as well, Brutus?)

**Caligula, AD 41**

Roman emperor who was assassinated: "I am still alive!"

**Catherine de Medici, 1589**

Queen of France: "Ah, my God, I am dead!"

**Joseph Henry Green, 1863**

British doctor, after checking his own pulse: "Stopped."

**General John Sedgwick, 1864**

In the American Civil War, Sedgwick was shot by a sniper as he remarked: "They couldn't hit an elephant at this distance."

**Viscount Palmerston, 1865**

British Prime Minister: "Die, my dear doctor? That's the last thing I shall do."

**Billy the Kid (aka William Bonney, Henry McCarty), 1881**

American outlaw, before being shot by Sheriff Pat Garrett: "Who is it?"

**Marie Antoinette, 1893**

French queen, who accidentally trod on her executioner's foot as she went to the guillotine: "Pardonnez-moi, monsieur." (Pardon me, sir.)

**Oscar Wilde, 1900**

Opinions differ about the Irish writer's last words. Some people claim he said: "Either these curtains go/that wallpaper goes, or I do."

**Prince Philippe**
Prince Philippe, heir to the French throne, was killed when his horse tripped over a pig in the streets of Paris in 1131.

**Pliny the Elder**
Roman writer Pliny was choked by the fumes of the erupting volcano Vesuvius in AD 79.

**Sir Thomas Urquhart**
Urquhart was the Scottish author of books with extraordinary titles such as *Logopandecteision*. He died laughing when told of the Restoration of Charles II in 1660.

**William III**
This British king died in 1701, after a fall from his horse when it stumbled over a molehill. His opponents drank a toast to the mole, calling it "The little gentleman in black velvet".

**See also**

Volcanic eruptions: page 46

Joan of Arc, 15th-century French heroine who was burned at the stake aged 19

Poster for Houdini show

**Queen Victoria, 1901**
British queen: "Oh, that peace may come." (a reference to the war at the time in South Africa). "Bertie!" (her husband, Prince Albert).

**Captain Lawrence Oates, 1912**
Oates was a member of Scott's expedition to the South Pole. He was terribly injured from frostbite and went to his death rather than hold up his companions. When he left the tent he said, "I am going outside and may be some time."

**Anna Pavlova, 1931**
Ballerina: "Get my swan costume ready!"

**Lytton Strachey, 1932**
English writer: "If this is dying, then I don't think much of it."

**Douglas Fairbanks Sr, 1939**
American film actor: "I've never felt better."

**Heinrich Himmler, 1945**
Nazi leader, as he committed suicide by taking poison: "I am Heinrich Himmler!"

**H.G. Wells, 1946**
English novelist, author of *The Time Machine*: "I'm all right."

**John F. Kennedy, 1963**
Moments before he was shot, Kennedy replied to "You certainly can't say that the people of Dallas haven't given you a nice welcome, Mr President" with his final words, "No, you certainly can't."

www.findagrave.com     search

# Entertainment lasts

## Shakespeare's last play
Most people agree that *The Tempest*, 1611, is the last play Shakespeare wrote, although some think he may have written a later play that has been lost. Shakespeare died in 1616, and *The Tempest* was first published in 1623.

## Charles Dickens' last story
*The Mystery of Edwin Drood* was Charles Dickens' last novel. It was published in monthly episodes, but ended, unfinished, when Dickens died in 1870.

## Beethoven's last symphony
Ludwig van Beethoven's Ninth Symphony was the last he composed before his death in 1827. He promised the London Philharmonic Society that he would write his Tenth Symphony for them, but died before he could begin work on it.

## The last Beatles concert
The Beatles last played together in public at Candlestick Park, San Francisco, on 29 August 1966. Their last publicly performed song was "Long Tall Sally".

## The last silent film
*The Four Feathers* (1929) was the last silent film released by a major studio. The 1976 film *Silent Movie* does contain one word, "Non!" (French for no), which is spoken by Marcel Marceau, a mime artist.

## The sixth and last Star Wars film
*Star Wars: Episode III – Revenge of the Sith* was released in 2005. It made almost $850 million worldwide, bringing the total for the series, which started in 1977, to $4.3 billion.

# Crime and punishment lasts

### Last executions for witchcraft in America
On 22 September 1692 seven women and one man were hanged for witchcraft at Salem and other places in New England.

### Last beheading in the UK
On 9 April 1747, 80-year-old Simon Fraser, Lord Lovat, was beheaded for treason at Tower Hill, London.

### Last person to be burned at the stake in England
Catherine Murphy belonged to a gang of coiners (coin forgers). She was strangled and then burnt at the stake at Newgate, London, on 18 March 1789.

### Last duel in the UK
The last duel in the UK in which a person was killed was fought by two Frenchmen at Egham in Surrey. Emile (or Emanuel) Barthelemy shot Frédéric Cournet on 19 October 1852. Barthelemy was found not guilty, but two years later he was hanged for murdering another man.

### Last public hanging in the UK
Michael Barrett was hanged outside Newgate Prison, London, on 26 May 1868 for the murder of Sarah Ann Hodgkinson. She was one of several victims who died from a bomb he had planted.

### Last witness to the assassination of Abraham Lincoln
Samuel James Seymour, who died on 13 April 1956, was the last surviving witness to the assassination of the American president. Seymour was only five years old when he saw John Wilkes Booth shoot Abraham Lincoln at Ford's Theatre, Washington DC, on 14 April 1865.

### Last person executed by guillotine
The last person to be executed in public was the murderer Eugene Weidmann who had his head cut off at Versailles, France, on 17 June 1939. The last official use of the guillotine in France was on 10 September 1977, when Hamida Djandoubi was executed for murder at Baumetes Prison, Marseilles.

## Last Aztec emperor
Montezuma II was removed from power by Spanish invaders and killed in June 1520.

Montezuma II, the last Aztec emperor

# Royal lasts

## The last Egyptian pharaoh
Cleopatra VII ruled from 69 BC, when she was 17 years old, until 30 BC, when Egypt became a province of the Roman empire.

## The last Roman emperor
Romulus Augustus was about 14 when he was removed from power in AD 476. The Roman empire split into western and eastern divisions.

## The last British king killed in battle
Richard III was killed at the battle of Bosworth on 22 August 1485.

## The last British king born abroad
George II was born in Hanover, Germany, on 10 November 1683.

## Last men on the Moon
US *Apollo 17* astronauts Eugene A. Cernan and Harrison H. Schmitt spent three days on the Moon, blasting off to return to Earth on 14 December 1972. This was the last day on which any human walked on the surface of the Moon.

## The last king of France
Louis-Philippe (1773–1850) reigned from 1830 until 24 February 1848, when he gave up his throne. Disguised as "Mr Smith", he travelled to England where he lived until his death.

## The last emperor of China
Hsüan T'ung gave up his throne on 12 February 1912 and later took the name Henry Pu-yi. The film *The Last Emperor* (1987) is about his life.

## The last tsar of Russia
Nicholas II was removed from power by the Russian Revolution of 1917, and murdered with his family at Ekaterinburg in July 1918. Their remains were reburied in St Petersburg in July 1998.

## Transport lasts

### The last stagecoach
Horse-drawn stagecoaches carried passengers and mail in Britain from the 17th century until the 19th century, when they were gradually replaced by trains. The Royal Mail between Inverness and Thurso, Scotland, last operated in October 1874.

### The last horse-drawn London bus
The last horse-drawn bus ran in London on 25 October 1911.

### The last Model T Ford
The Model T, first produced in 1908, was one of the most popular cars of all time. The last US-made Model T (number 15,007,033) rolled off the production line on Thursday 26 May 1927.

### The last Routemaster bus
The Routemaster double-decker bus was introduced in London on 8 February 1956 and was a familiar sight in the capital for almost 50 years. The last Routemaster service ran on Friday 9 December 2005, although there are still two heritage routes in operation.

### Last flight of Concorde
Concorde was the world's only supersonic airliner. It was in service for 34 years until it made its last commercial flight, from New York to London, on 24 October 2003.

Pharos of Alexandria

### Last of the Seven Wonders
The last of the Seven Wonders of the world to be built was the 124 m (406.9 ft) Pharos (lighthouse) of Alexandria, Egypt, which was completed in 279 BC. It was partly knocked down by invaders and later destroyed by an earthquake. The only one of the Seven Wonders that survives today is the Great Pyramid at Giza in Egypt.

### Last voyage of the Titanic
The last voyage of the *Titanic* was also its first. It sank on 15 April 1912 after striking an iceberg, killing 1,517 people.

Prow of the wreck of the *Titanic*

**See also**
The Seven Wonders of the ancient world: pages 206–07

**See also**
Shipwrecks: page 218

# Author's acknowledgements

The author would like to thank the following people, organizations and publications for kindly supplying information for this book.

## Whitaker's Almanack 2007

Academy of Motion Picture Arts and Sciences (AMPAS)*
American Film Institute
American Forests
Amnesty International
Association of Leading Visitor Attractions
Alexander Ash
Caroline Ash
Nicholas Ash
Box Office Mojo
BP Statistical Review of World Energy 2006
Richard Braddish
Thomas Brinkhoff
British Broadcasting Corporation (BBC)
The British Council
British Film Institute
British Library
British Museum
British Phonographic Industry (BPI)
Central Intelligence Agency (CIA)
Richard Chapman
Christian Research
Christie's
Computer Industry Almanac
Department for Environment, Food and Rural Affairs (DEFRA)
Earth Impact Database
The Economist
Emporis
Energy Information Administration
Ethnologue
Euromonitor
Food and Agriculture Organization of the United Nations (FAO)
Global Education Digest (UNESCO)
Global Forest Resources Assessment (FAO)
Gold Fields Mineral Services
Nathalie Golden
Russell E. Gough
Monica Grady
Robert Grant

Greyhound Racing Association of America
Home Accident Surveillance System (HASS)
Home Office
Human Development Report (United Nations)
Imperial War Museum
International Centre for Prison Studies
International Federation of Audit Bureaux of Circulations
The International Institute for Strategic Studies, The Military Balance 2006–2007
International Olympic Committee (IOC)
International Telecommunication Union (ITU)
International Union for the Conservation of Nature (IUCN)
Internet Movie Database (IMDb)
Internet World Stats
London Zoo
Dr Benjamin Lucas
Mattel, Inc
Chris Mead
Mike Melvill
National Aeronautics and Space Administration, USA (NASA)
National Basketball Association, USA (NBA)
National Football League, USA (NFL)
National Statistics
Natural History Museum
AC Nielsen
The Nobel Foundation
Organisation for Economic Co-operation and Development (OECD)
Organisation Internationale des Constructeurs d'Automobiles (OICA)
Felicity Page
Parker Brothers
Patent Office
Periodical Publishers Association
Tony Pattison
Population Reference Bureau
Recording Industry Association of America (RIAA)
Dafydd Rees
Louise Reip
Royal Astronomical Society

Royal Observatory, Greenwich
Screen Digest
Screen International
Robert Senior
Sotheby's
Time magazine
Tree Register of the British Isles
United Nations (UN)
United Nations Children's Fund (UNICEF)
United Nations Educational, Scientific and Cultural Organization (UNESCO)
United Nations Environment Programme
United Nations Population Division (UNPD)
US Census Bureau International Data Base
US Geological Survey
US Patent Office
Variety
Lucy T. Verma
Ward's Motor Vehicle Facts & Figures 2006
WebElements
World Association of Girl Guides and Girl Scouts
World Association of Newspapers
World Bank
World Christian Database
World Gazetteer
World Health Organization (WHO)
World of Learning
World Organization of the Scout Movement
World Tourism Organization (WTO)

population data
© by Stefan Helders
www.world-gazetteer.com

* The terms "Academy Award(s)"® and "Oscar(s)"® are registered trademarks and service marks of the Academy of Motion Picture Arts and Sciences. This book is neither endorsed by nor affiliated to the Academy of Motion Picture Arts and Sciences.

**Country names**
The following abbreviations are used for country names on page 285
BUL: Bulgaria
CHN: China
CUB: Cuba
CZE: Czech Republic
DEN: Denmark
ETH: Ethiopia
FRA: France
GBR: Great Britain
GDR: German Democratic Republic (1955–90)
MAR: Morocco (Maroc)
QAT: Qatar
ROM: Romania
RUS: Russian Federation
UKR: Ukraine
USA: United States of America
USSR: Union of Soviet Socialist Republics (1922–91)

# Picture acknowledgements
**L = left, R = right, C = centre, T = top, B = bottom**

Page 8 Alexander Hafemann/iStockphoto; 10 Reuters/Corbis; 11T Jeremy Swinborne/iStockphoto; 12C Jeremy Horner/Corbis; 14TL Eileen Tweedy/The Art Archive; 15B David Taylor/Getty Images; 16C Charles & Josette Lenars/Corbis; 17TR REGIS MADEC/Thaiworldview.com; 18 Denis Scott/Corbis; 19B NASA; 19TC NASA; 20TR NASA; 20BR NASA; 20C NASA; 20CR NASA; 22BL NASA; 22CL NASA; 22CR NASA; 22C NASA; 22TR NASA; 23BL NASA; 23BC NASA; 23BR NASA; 23TL NASA; 24CL Gianni Dagli Orti/Corbis; 24C NASA; 24TR NASA; 24TC NASA; 25CL NASA; 25C NASA; 26CL Roger Ressmeyer/Corbis; 26TR Bettmann/Corbis; 27C NASA; 28R NASA; 29TL NASA; 30CL NASA; 30C NASA; 31TR NASA; 32 Paul Souders/Corbis; 34C Charles & Josette Lenars/Corbis; 35T Timothy Ball/iStockphoto; 36BL Theo Allofs/ZEFA Corbis; 36TL iStockphoto; 37CL Robyn Glover/iStockphoto; 38B Andre Klaassen/iStockphoto; 38T Frank Leung/iStockphoto; 40T Daniel Leclair/Reuters/Corbis; 41C Stewart Westmorland/Corbis; 41BL John Pitcher/iStockphoto; 44TR Shaun Lowe/iStockphoto; 44TC Clint Spencer/iStockphoto; 46B Gary Braasch/Corbis; 47T Koch Valerie/iStockphoto; 48 Tom Brakefield/Corbis; 50TR Peter Fuchs/iStockphoto; 51BL Frans Lanting/Corbis; 51C Jon Rasmussen/iStockphoto; 52CR Richard Nowitz/Corbis; 53TR Brad Thompson/iStockphoto; 54TL Jim Jurica/iStockphoto; 55R iStockphoto; 55BL iStockphoto; 56CL Amos Nachoum/Corbis; 57TR Will Burgees/Reuters/Corbis; 57CL Don Bayley/iStockphoto; 58TR Tim Davis/Corbis; 58BL Anastasiya Maksymenko/iStockphoto; 59B Tim Davis/Corbis; 60TL Thomas Bedenk/iStockphoto; 61CL Dan Guravich/Corbis; 61TR Will Schmitz/iStockphoto; 62B Jeremy Edwards/iStockphoto; 63TR Steve Geer/iStockphoto; 64CR Jose Carlos Pires Pereira/iStockphoto; 65TR Wolfgang Kaehler/Corbis; 66B Nico Smit/iStockphoto; 66TR iStockphoto; 68T Christoph Ermel/iStockphoto; 69BR Jameson Weaton/iStockphoto; 70TR Wayne Lawler; Ecoscene/Corbis; 70B Loic Bernard/iStockphoto; 72B Roger Milley/iStockphoto; 73BC Marcelo Wain/iStockphoto; 73CR Nathan Watkins/iStockphoto; 74 Fridmar Damm/ZEFA/Corbis; 75TR Les Cunliffe/iStockphoto; 76TR Liz Van Steenburgh/iStockphoto; 76CR Liz Van Steenburgh/iStockphoto; 78CR Bettmann/Corbis; 78CL Donall O Cleirigh/iStockphoto; 80L Strauss/Curtis/Corbis; 81T Alexander Kolomietz/iStockphoto; 84TL Hulton-Deutch Collection/Corbis; 84R Carole Gomez/iStockphoto; 85TR Nogues Alain/Corbis Sygma; 86L iStockphoto; 87TL Bettmann/Corbis; 87C Andrey Zyk/iStockphoto; 89TL Bettmann/Corbis; 90 Jens Neith/ZEFA/Corbis; 91TR Carol Munoz/iStockphoto; 92TR Stephen Sweet/iStockphoto; 93C Maria Boytunoa/iStockphoto; 94C Bettmann/Corbis; 95R Bettmann/Corbis; 95BL Corbis; 96TL Maria Bibikova/iStockphoto; 97TR David Pollack/Corbis; 97L Roberta Casaliggi/iStockphoto; 98TL Swim Ink 2, LCC/Corbis; 98CR Kelly Cline/iStockphoto; 99TR Mary Evans Picture Library; 100 2007 Hebrew University/Getty Images; 102CR iStockphoto; 102TR Jose Marafona/iStockphoto; 103R David Lewis/iStockphoto; 104CL Falk Kienas/iStockphoto; 104C Eliza Snow/iStockphoto; 105T Bettmann/Corbis; 106B Karim Hesham/iStockphoto; 107TR Jivko Kazakov/iStockphoto; 107TL Francisco Orellana/iStockphoto; 108TR Jack Tzekov/iStockphoto; 108CL John Woodworth/iStockphoto; 109L Palazzo Baberini. Rome/Dagli Orti/The Art Archive; 109C John Steele/iStockphoto; 110TL Corbis; 110CB Wally McNamee/Corbis; 111TR Natalia Bratslavsky/iStockphoto; 116BR Bob Krist/Corbis; 116T Arne Thaysen/iStockphoto; 117BR Ivan Mateev/iStockphoto; 118B James Rabinowitz/iStockphoto; 119T Yann Arthus-Bertrand/Corbis; 120TL Randy Mayes/iStockphoto; 121B Steven Miric/iStockphoto; 122BL Fabian Guignard/iStockphoto; 122BL Dennis Sabo/iStockphoto; 124TC Mike Morley/iStockphoto; 124BR Emilia Kun/iStockphoto; 125TC Rob Broek/iStockphoto; 126TL iStockphoto; 126B Stephen Hoerold/iStockphoto; 127TR Ekatrina Fribus/iStockphoto; 128TL Klemen Demsar/iStockphoto; 128BR Marisa Allegra/iStockphoto; 129TR Mark Weiss/iStockphoto; 130T John Woodworth/iStockphoto; 131BR Alan Toby/iStockphoto; 132BL Paul Almasy/Corbis; 132TL Andrew Cribb/iStockphoto; 133BL Steven Tilson/iStockphoto; 134BR Torleif Svensson/Corbis; 134TR iStockphoto; 135TR Michel de Nijs/iStockphoto; 136TL iStockphoto; 136CR John Sigler/iStockphoto; 137TR iStockphoto; 138B iStockphoto; 139TR iStockphoto; 140TL Stefan Tordenmalm/iStockphoto; 140B Ondrej Cech/iStockphoto; 141C Andy Green-AGMIT/iStockphoto; 142B Lisa Kyle Young/iStockphoto; 142TR Felix Mockel/iStockphoto; 143C Matthew Scholey/iStockphoto; 144 Franck Robichon/EPA/Corbis; 145TR Sandra O'Claire/iStockphoto; 146TL Frank May/DPA/Corbis; 147CR Bettmann/Corbis; 148TR Gianni Dagli Orti/Corbis; 148BL Nik Wheeler/Corbis; 149LC Dave Wirtzfeld/iStockphoto; 149LC Dave Wirtzfeld/iStockphoto; 149LC Dave Wirtzfeld/iStockphoto; 150 TL Historical Picture Archive/Corbis; 150CR Bettmann/Corbis; 150CL Peter Spiro/iStockphoto; 151B iStockphoto; 152TL Bettmann/Corbis; 153C Jim Sugar/Corbis; 154TL NASA; 155C Shannon Stapleton/Corbis; 155BL The Scotsman/Corbis Sygma; 156T Alison Wright/Corbis; 156BL Nancy Kaszerman/Zuma/Corbis; 157B Edward Parsons/UN/ EPA/Corbis; 158 Steve Raymer/Corbis; 160B Sandro Vannini/Corbis; 161C Richard A. Cooke/Corbis; 162C Bennett Dean, Eye Ubiquitous/ Corbis; 163R Ashwin Kharidehal Abhirama/iStockphoto; 164TR Corbis; 164L Nancy Louie/iStockphoto; 165C Elio Clol/Corbis; 166C Fred de Noyelle/Godong/Corbis; 167TR Robert Young/iStockphoto; 168BL Earl & Nazima Kowall/Corbis; 169TR Reuters/Corbis; 169C Nikhil Gangavane/iStockphoto; 170L iStockphoto; 170TR Pam Wardlaw/iStockphoto; 170C Geoffrey Hammond/iStockphoto; 172C Christine Balderas/iStockphoto; 172L iStockphoto; 173B Sharon Dominick/iStockphoto; 174B Jiri Vatka/iStockphoto; 175L Joza Pojbic/iStockphoto; 176 David Furst/Pool/EPA/Corbis; 177TR Lise Gagne/iStockphoto; 178C Owen Franklen/Corbis; 178T Vladimir Melnik/iStockphoto; 180C The Dmitri Baltermants Collection/Corbis; 181T Fine Art Photography Library/Corbis; 182R Jeff Gynane/iStockphoto; 183L Tim Wright/Corbis; 183T Dan Mason/iStockphoto; 184T Gerald French/Corbis; 184C Dusty Cline/iStockphoto; 185B Reuters/Corbis;

## 320

## ACKNOWLEDGEMENTS

**185T** Achim Prill/iStockphoto; **186** Tom Strattman/Getty Images; **187T** Joel Blitt/iStockphoto; **188CL** Sandro Vannini/Corbis; **188R** Bettmann/Corbis; **190BL** Christie's Images/Corbis; **190LR** Neema Frederic/Corbis Sygma; **192R** Tim Graham/Corbis; **192CB** Sascha Burkard/iStockphoto; **192L** iStockphoto; **193R** Archivo Iconografico, SA/Corbis; **194B** Eliza Snow/iStockphoto; **195CR** Eric Foltz/iStockphoto; **196** David Kadlubowski/Corbis; **198L** Asier Villafranca Valasco/iStockphoto; **198B** Jim Jurica/iStockphoto; **199TC** Andrea Jemolo/Corbis; **199TR** Paul Hardy/Corbis; **200B** Roger Antrobus/Corbis; **201T** Pawel Libea/Corbis; **203T** Paul Cheyne/iStockphoto; **204T** iStockphoto; **205C** Donall O Cleirigh/iStockphoto; **206B** Liu Liqun/Corbis; **208** Handout/Reuters/Corbis; **210B** Tony Arruza/Corbis; **212C** Aston Martin; **213T** Bill Nation/Corbis Sygma; **214C** Tim Wimborne/Reuters/Corbis; **215TL** Thomas Hottner/iStockphoto; **215CR** Robert Churchill/iStockphoto; **216B** Underwood & Underwood/Corbis; **216T** Bettmann/Corbis; **217CR** Bettmann/Corbis; **218TL** Eileen Tweedy/Magdalene College Cambridge/The Art Archive; **219BR** Hulton Deutsch Collection/Corbis; **219R** Reuters/Corbis; **220B** Jaques Langevin/Corbis; **220CL** Allison Marles/iStockphoto; **221T** Duncan Gilbert/iStockphoto; **222** *Harry Potter and the Deathly Hallows* by J.K. Rowling (Bloomsbury Publishing PLC); **223T** Catherine dée Auvil/iStockphoto; **224BL** Alison Wright/Corbis; **224T** Andres Balcazar/iStockphoto; **226C** Ian Poole/iStockphoto; **226TL** Robert Dawson/iStockphoto; **227CR** Valerie Crafter/iStockphoto; **228CR** Seth Joel/Corbis; **228T** iStockphoto; **231TR** The Estate of C.S. Lewis, 1950; **232C** Blue Lantern Studio/Corbis; **234T** Blue Lantern Studio/Corbis; **235CL** Marisa Allegra Williams/iStockphoto; **235BR** Rey Rojo/iStockphoto; **236R** Marvel Characters Inc./Corbis; **238** Frank Trapper/Corbis; **239TR** iStockphoto; **240C** Joseph Sohm; ChromoSohm Inc./Corbis; **241T** Michael S Yamashita/Corbis; **242CR** Gillet Luc/iStockphoto; **242TL** Adrian Beesley/iStockphoto; **243TR** Archivo Iconografico, SA/Corbis; **244C** Laryn Bakker/iStockphoto; **244BR** Matej Michelizza/iStockphoto; **247TL** Gabe Palmer/Corbis; **247CR** iStockphoto; **247BR** Olga Shelego/iStockphoto; **248** GILBERT LIZ/CORIS SYGMA; **250TR** Dave Bartruff/Corbis; **251C** Bettmann/Corbis; **253TR** David Lees/Corbis; **253C** Corbis; **254C** Bettmann/Corbis; **255C** Bettmann/Corbis; **255TR** Henry Dilz/Corbis; **256B** Jonathan Drake/Reuters/Corbis; **256BR** Luke Daniek/iStockphoto; **258TL** Sunset Boulevard/Corbis; **258C** Josef Philipp/iStockphoto; **259R** Irving Berkner/iStockphoto; **260B** Robbie Jack/Corbis; **261TL** Robbie Jack/Corbis; **261R** Diane Diederich; **262** The Kobal Collection/Marvel/Sony Pictures; **264TL** Swim Ink 2, LLC/Corbis; **265CR** Yann Arthus-Bertrand/Corbis; **266TR** Trapper Frank/Corbis Sygma; **267TR** Columbia Pictures/Zuma/Corbis; **267BL** Warner Bros/The Kobal Collection; **268CR** RKO/The Kobal Collection; **269CR** Michael Goulding/Orange County Register/Corbis; **270CR** Disney/The Kobal Collection; **271T** Dreamworks/The Kobal Collection; **272C** Mike Segar/Reuters/Corbis; **272TL** Bettmann/Corbis; **273TR** RKO/The Kobal Collection; **274TL** iStockphoto; **275C** Dan Herrick/iStockphoto; **276** Adrian Bradshaw/EPA/Corbis; **277TR** Tracy Hebden/iStockphoto; **278B** Duomo/Corbis; **279TR** Bettmann/Corbis; **280BR** Historical Picture Archive/Corbis; **280CL** Historical Picture Archive/Corbis; **281T** iStockphoto; **282BR** Karl Weatherly/Corbis; **282C** Karl Mathis/EPA/Corbis; **284TL** Tim de Waele/Isosport/Corbis; **284C** Jorge Delgado/iStockphoto; **285R** Duomo/Corbis; **286TL** Tomasso DeRosa/Corbis; **286BR** Simon Bruty/SI/Newsport/Corbis; **287TR** Jeff Lewis/Icon SMI/Corbis; **288TR** AFP/Getty Images; **289CR** Matt A. Brown/Newsport/Corbis; **290T** Susan Mullane/Newsport/Corbis; **290CR** Jim Sugar/Corbis; **290CL** Jolande Gerritsen/iStockphoto; **291C** Jolande Gerritsen/iStockphoto; **292TR** Bettmann/Corbis; **292BL** Duomo/Corbis; **294BL** Andy Clark/Reuters/Corbis; **294TR** David Gray/Reuters/Corbis; **295BR** Maggie Hallahan/Corbis; **296BL** Pichon P/Corbis Sygma; **296TC** Eric Gaillard/Reuters/Corbis; **297T** Michael Kim/Corbis; **298TR** Olivier Marie/EPA/Corbis; **300BL** Kevin R Morris/Corbis; **300TR** Kelly-Mooney Photography/Corbis; **301CR** Steve Boyle/Newsport/Corbis; **302** Getty Images; **304CR** Gianni Dagli Orti/Corbis; **305TR** Corbis; **306CR** Archivo Iconografico SA/Corbis; **306BC** Ralph White/Corbis; **307TL** Bettmann/Corbis